TRAVEL AND TOURISM
OPTIONAL UNITS
Advanced GNVQ

Also available from Addison Wesley Longman

Foundation GNVQ Leisure and Tourism
Carole Jones & Margaret Radcliffe
0-582-29339-1

Intermediate GNVQ Leisure and Tourism   2nd edition
Verité Baker
0-582-27841-4

Covers all four mandatory units of the Intermediate GNVQ.

Advanced GNVQ Leisure and Tourism   2nd edition
Ray Youell
0-582-27842-2

Covers all eight mandatory units of the Advanced GNVQ.

Advanced GNVQ Leisure and Recreation Optional Units
Julie Gibson, Eric Macintyre, Ian Wood, Katherine Kemp & Stephen Pearson
0-582-29338-3

Covers the seven BTEC optional units comprising the Leisure stream of the Advanced GNVQ.

All the above titles have been written to the latest 1995 specifications.

For further information about these and other titles, or to order a copy, please contact:

Longman Customer Information Centre
PO Box 88
Harlow, Essex
CM19 5SR

Telephone: 01279 623928   Fax: 01279 414130

TRAVEL AND TOURISM OPTIONAL UNITS

Advanced GNVQ

Ray Youell MSc MTS

LONGMAN

Addison Wesley Longman Limited
Edinburgh Gate, Harlow
Essex CM20 2JE, England
and Associated Companies throughout the world

First published 1996

British Library Cataloguing in Publication Data
A catalogue entry for this title is available from the British
Library

ISBN 0-582-29337-5

Set in Palatino 10/12 and Helvetica
Printed in Great Britain by Henry Ling Ltd.,
at the Dorset Press, Dorchester, Dorset

Contents

Preface

This book has been written specifically for individuals taking the Travel and Tourism 'pathway' on the Advanced GNVQ in Leisure and Tourism. The material will also prove useful for students on BTEC National courses in Leisure Studies and Travel and Tourism, which are systematically being replaced by GNVQs.

The Advanced GNVQ in Leisure and Tourism is a new work-related qualification designed to offer a choice of opportunities in employment or higher education. Originally called Level 3 qualifications, in 1993 GNVQs were retitled 'Advanced' in order to emphasise their equivalence to 'A' levels. GNVQs are part of the NVQ (National Vocational Qualification) framework, which provides a national system for work-related qualifications, endorsed by the TUC and CBI. GNVQs offer students a flexible qualification based around mandatory, optional and additional units. The mandatory units form the vocational core of the GNVQ, while the optional units, the subject of this book, offer students the choice of extending their achievement. Additional units give the opportunity for further specialism and provide a focus for progression to higher education.

This book is structured around the seven BTEC Travel and Tourism Optional Units of the Advanced GNVQ in Leisure and Tourism, fully in line with the revised 1995 specifications. A variety of activities and assignments, based on the elements within each unit, give students the opportunity of developing useful evidence for inclusion in their portfolios. Up-to-date, industry case studies, with accompanying discussion questions, allow students to reflect on the application of theory into practice. All these evidence-building opportunities help students gain credit for the achievement of the key skills associated with the Advanced GNVQ in Leisure and Tourism.

Ray Youell
Aberystwyth, May 1996

Acknowledgements

Many organisations and individuals have helped in the compilation of this book. Those who have provided valuable information and illustrations are acknowledged within the text. I am grateful to them all for their co-operation and helpful comments.

Unit titles and performance criteria are reproduced by kind permission of the Business and Technology Education Council.

Many former colleagues in FE have provided helpful advice, in particular Sally Ross and Jennie Harlock from Shrewsbury College, and Andrew Calvert from York College. Thanks are also due to Ian Little, Natasha Peachey and Pauline Rawbone at Addison Wesley Longman for their support throughout the project. Finally, thanks to Sue, Megan and Owen for suffering once again!

Unit 16

TRAVEL AGENCY OPERATIONS

Element 16.1
Examine the requirements for running a travel agency

Element 16.2
Investigate the personnel requirements of a travel agency

Element 16.3
Examine the administrative procedures followed by travel agencies

Element 16.1 Examine the requirements for running a travel agency

---

Performance criteria

1. Explain the factors which influence travel agency location.
2. Describe the services offered by travel agencies.
3. Explain the importance of the design and layout of travel agencies.
4. Explain equipment requirements of travel agencies.
5. Explain licensing and financial requirements of travel agencies.
6. Carry out an investigation of a high street travel agency.

Travel agency location

Travel agencies fall into one of three categories:

1. *Multiples* – companies that operate a chain of retail outlets under a single brand name, e.g. Lunn Poly, Going Places, Thomas Cook, etc.
2. *Independents* – single, owner-managed enterprises generally with only one retail outlet.
3. *Miniples* – companies with a small number of branches in a particular region, e.g. Woodcock Travel in Yorkshire.

Of the three, the multiple agencies have access to the largest capital reserves and can choose the more expensive high street locations for their branches. The Lunn Poly chain, for example, had net assets of £28.5 million in 1995, and increased its number of retail travel agencies to a total of 795 in the UK (see Figure 16.1).

Being able to trade in a high street location gives an agency a number of advantages, including:

- Increased visibility
- Greater opportunities for passing trade
- A successful image
- Business from workers in town

Independent agents, who may not be able to justify the high rent and rates of town centre locations, will nonetheless want to be in a position that is not too far away from the main shopping thoroughfares. Given the particular nature of the products that many independent agents sell, their clients are usually more than willing to travel a little further for their specialist advice. Agents located on the outskirts of towns or in city suburbs may have the advantage of easier parking, when compared with high street agencies – a factor of particular significance if older or disabled clients are important customers.

Fig. 16.1 Lunn Poly operated 795 retail outlets across the UK in 1995

For a travel agency that is setting up for the first time, there are no hard and fast rules about competing with existing agents. Travel agencies operate in a free market and ABTA (the Association of British Travel Agents) does not object to new members joining on the grounds of competition with existing businesses. It must be remembered, however, that anybody opening a new agency close to one that has been successfully trading for some years will find it harder to obtain agency agreements with tour operators, airlines, coach companies and other travel principals, since they will often prefer to continue with a proven enterprise rather than take a risk with a new venture.

Trade sources suggest that, for a new travel agency to have a chance of succeeding, it should not open in an area that offers a ratio of less than one agency to 15,000 population. In other words, if a small market town of 75,000 people is currently served by three travel agencies (1 : 25,000 ratio), the opening of a new agency would merit serious consideration. If the same town supported six travel agencies (1 : 12,500 ratio), a new venture is unlikely to be able to survive. Demographics can sometimes come into play when choosing a suitable location for a new agency. Factors such as the age structure of the population, social class of residents and composition of families in an area, can have a bearing on success. For example, an independent agent specialising in up-market holidays for couples whose children have left home, the so-called 'empty nesters', may be able to select a suitable location for an agency by a careful research of local demographic data. Choosing to locate in an area that has a higher than average proportion of residents in the A, B and C1 social classes will increase the agent's chances of successful trading, all other things being equal.

Activity

Carry out some research to find out the number of travel agencies in, and the total population of, your locality. From the figures you find, calculate the ratio of agencies to population. Is your area supporting too many agencies at present?

Services offered by travel agencies

Travel agencies are the retail arm of the travel and tourism industry. In the same way that a clothes shop sells products to shoppers, so travel agencies retail their 'products' and services to the general public. Indeed, the term 'travel shop' is commonly used to refer to travel agency premises. The one major difference between these two types of retail outlet, however, is that, unlike clothes retailers, travel agencies do not buy in 'stock' in advance, but rather react to the wishes of their customers before contacting tour operators and other travel providers. The fact that opening a travel agency does not involve a heavy initial capital outlay on items of stock is an attractive feature to many people considering starting up their own business in the service sector.

Most people associate high street travel agencies with the sale of one particular product: overseas package holidays (also known as inclusive tours). An analysis of the work of a typical agency, however, shows that it actually offers a far wider range of products and services, including:

- Overseas package tours
- UK short breaks
- 'Flight only' sales
- Theatre bookings
- Car hire
- Ferry bookings
- Activity and special interest holidays
- Cruising holidays
- Rail tickets
- Coach holidays and tickets
- Travel insurance
- Foreign exchange and travellers' cheques
- Visa and passport applications
- Hotel bookings

Some travel agents, especially the independents, also run their own tours at certain times of the year, as a way of generating extra revenue.

Travel agencies act as the intermediary between two parties. They provide a service to their customers, usually referred to as clients, while at the same time acting as agents for the company supplying the travel product. These suppliers are known as the 'principals', and may include tour operators, airlines, hotels, ferry companies, Le Shuttle, car hire firms, holiday centres, British Rail, cruise companies, theatres, coach companies, etc. Travel agents earn commission from the principals whose products they sell. The commission payment is usually expressed as a percentage and varies according to the product being sold and the commission policy of the principal. At present, average commission rates are as follows:

- Package holidays   10%
- Airline tickets   7.5–9%
- Ferry bookings   9%
- Travellers' cheques   1%
- Travel insurance   35–40%
- Coach holidays   10%
- British Rail tickets   7%
- Cruises   9%

These figures should only be taken as a guide, since commission levels can fluctuate in response to competitor activity. Some principals offer incentive commission, where the amount paid increases as the sales volume rises. Override commission is another type of extra payment, often paid when an office has 'sole agency' status with a particular principal; British Rail, for example, often appoints only one ticket agency in a town and will advise other agencies to deal with this 'sole agent' when they want rail products. The override commission allows the sole agency to pay the standard 7 per cent commission to the agent and retain a small 'override' to cover its own costs.

Business travel services

Although arranging travel for leisure purposes accounts for the bulk of the work of most high street travel agencies, some may have a business travel specialist, or even a business travel department, catering exclusively for the needs of corporate clients. There are also some travel agencies, known as business house agencies, that deal solely with business travel services for clients. The needs of business travel clients are quite different to those of leisure travellers, since they often need to travel at short notice and on scheduled rather than charter services. This does mean, however, that the value of their business is usually higher than that of holidaymakers, making the extra effort needed to secure and maintain their custom worth while.

Design and layout of travel agencies

When considering the design and layout of an agency, there are two principal issues to be addressed, namely:

- External appearance
- Internal layout

Each of these factors will be investigated further in the next two sections.

External appearance

From the outside, a travel agency should look inviting to the prospective customer, whether it is in a town centre high street location, a city suburb or a small country town. Certain aspects of the external appearance of a travel agency will be 'fixed' – for example, the size of the overall shop frontage, its position in relation to adjacent shops and any 'street furniture', i.e. lamp posts, fire hydrants, litter bins, etc. Within these constraints, the possibilities for alterations to its external design are limited only by the imagination and the budget of the travel agent, plus any restrictions imposed by local planning authorities or landlords in the case of leased property. A major refurbishment to convert an existing shop into a new travel agency may involve, for example, alterations to the size and style of windows and doors, and the design of fascias.

Two areas where the agency staff and management have some control over the external appearance of the premises are:

1. Fascia
2. Window displays

In an effort to convey a single corporate identity and image, the multiple travel agency chains adopt the same style of fascia outside all their branches. Independent agents have greater freedom to design a fascia board that says something about the agency and its products. Either way, an effective fascia board is a very important advertising tool for the agent, visible from a distance. Some fascias are very simple, giving only the name of the agency. Others will include, along with the name, a telephone number, a logo or perhaps a 'strap line', e.g. 'we go further for you' or 'the one-stop-shop'. For maximum effect, and added security, fascias must be illuminated during the hours of darkness, although there may be planning restrictions in certain locations. There may also be local bylaws or planning regulations concerning overhanging signs and fascias on listed buildings. In all such cases, the advice of the local planning authority should be sought.

Window displays are a good way of changing the external appearance of an agency for a short period of time, thereby giving prominence to a particular product or concentrating on different seasons of the year, e.g. city breaks in the autumn and winter, summer sun holidays at the beginning of the main booking season and winter ski scenes. Changing a window display regularly will also generate more interest from passing customers, who may be tempted inside to ask for brochures and information. All travel principals will supply point-of-sale materials for window and shop displays, often in conjunction with brochure launches. What should be avoided at all costs are hand-drawn or hand-written signs, which give a window display an unprofessional look and do little to enhance the image of the travel agent.

Activity

Carry out some research of the external appearance of the travel agencies in your local area, noting positive features that attract attention and those that detract from the overall external appearance. Suggest ways that the negative features could be improved.

Internal layout

A well-planned internal layout of a travel agency can do a lot to help achieve the agency's principal aim of selling holidays and other travel products profitably. It will offer staff an efficient environment within which to perform their selling skills, give them greater job satisfaction and allow them to maximise sales opportunities. From the customers' point of view, it will encourage them to consult staff, examine brochures and, hopefully, stimulate them to make a purchase.

As we saw with the design of fascias, the multiple travel agency chains will adopt a 'house style' inside their premises as well, with corporate colours, logos and graphics reinforcing the brand identity. Independent agents will have greater freedom in finalising the internal layout of their premises, thereby giving more opportunities for individuality.

Any effective internal design of a travel agency should start with an analysis of its main functions, followed by a consideration of how these can best be met through the positioning of furniture and equipment. No two travel agencies are the same, but they nonetheless have similar requirements in terms of internal layout; they all need to incorporate areas for:

- Displaying brochures and other promotional materials
- Conducting sales interviews
- Storage for files
- Storage of reference materials
- Storage of brochure stocks
- Secure storage for money, travellers' cheques, foreign currency, tickets, etc.
- Staff relaxation
- Manager's office
- Computer software and hardware, including VDUs
- Administrative functions
- Toilets and washing facilities

When considering an effective internal layout for a travel agency, it is helpful to group these functions into zones, as shown in Figure 16.2.

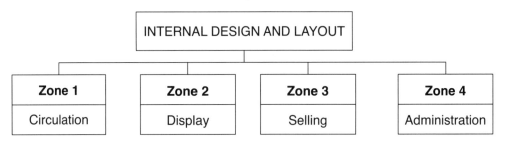

Fig. 16.2 Zoning of functions in a travel agency

Zone 1 is the area concerned with the most important people of all, the customers, and how they circulate around the agency. People like to make their travel purchasing decisions in a relaxed atmosphere, where they are not crowded or overly pestered by staff. The internal design of the agency must reflect these needs with the correct positioning of furniture, fixtures and fittings, which clearly define the circulation routes through the agency. Consideration should also be given to a waiting area for clients when all staff are busy.

Zone 2 is concerned with the display of brochures, timetables, leaflets and other promotional items in the agency. Brochures are crucial to the success of the agency, so time spent on effective display methods will pay dividends. Brochure racks may be fixed to a wall or free-standing, and come in a range of sizes to accommodate different types of brochures. Free-standing racks give greater flexibility, but may not be suitable for large numbers of very heavy brochures. Policies on the racking of brochures will vary between agents, with the multiple agents often directed by their head offices. Some will display large numbers of the same brochure, while others will display a single copy under perspex and instruct customers to ask for a copy from a member of staff. This has the advantage of bringing the customer into contact with a salesperson, but may put some people off, particularly when the agency is very busy. Good use should be made of any available wall space for displaying posters and other point-of-sale materials.

The selling area of the agency (zone 3) is perhaps the most important of all. Staff and customers need a relaxed environment within which the agent has direct access to a VDU, telephone and reference materials, and where the customer can take notes and look at the detail of brochures. Today, many agencies prefer the more informal ambience created by desks and chairs for the selling zone, rather than a high sales counter, which can sometimes create a physical and psychological barrier between the customer and member of staff. Counters do, however, take up less space and may be the only alternative in an agency with a restricted floor area. Agencies that have a quick customer turnover, including some city centre offices selling theatre tickets, sightseeing tours, coach tickets, etc. sometimes opt for counters to reduce the length of stay of customers.

Zone 4 focuses on all the administrative functions of the agency, including the storage of brochure stocks and files, secure storage of valuables, a staff relaxation area, the manager's office, toilets and washing facilities. Sometimes referred to as the 'back office', this zone needs to be away from the customer circulation areas for privacy and security.

Taking all these features and functions into consideration, Figure 16.3 gives a simplified example of the layout of a typical high street travel agency.

Activity

Using the list of travel agency functions given above as a guide, draw your own sketch plan of an 'ideal' travel agency, highlighting the different zones.

Equipment used in travel agencies

The equipment requirements of travel agencies can be grouped under four distinct agency functions, namely:

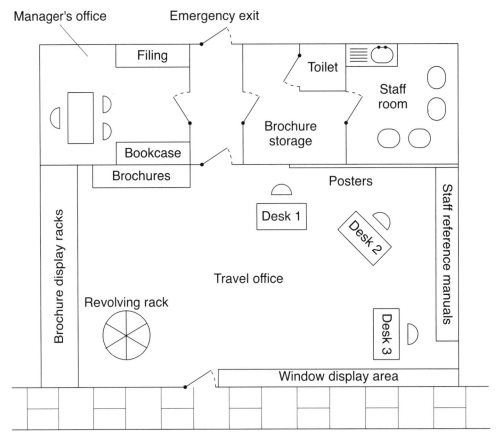

Fig. 16.3 Layout of a typical high street travel agency

1. Sales
2. Communications
3. Administration
4. Safety and security

Sales equipment

Most travel staff would agree that the most important piece of sales equipment is their computer keyboard and screen. Variously referred to as a VDU (visual display unit), computer terminal or viewdata system, these items are now commonplace in the vast majority of travel agencies in the UK. In the hands of trained staff, the VDU is a powerful selling tool, giving access to the central reservations systems (CRSs) of the major tour operators and airlines. The system allows staff to check availability, confirm prices and ultimately make bookings on behalf of their clients. The computer systems developed by the major tour operators, such as Thomson's TOP and Airtours' SPACE, allow agents to offer alternative holidays if the customer's first choice is unavailable. The principals' central reservations systems are accessed through a service provider, such as Fastrak, Istel or New Prestel (see the following section on communications equipment). Other equipment concerned specifically with sales of package holidays and other travel products and services includes:

- Telephone systems
- Reference manuals and atlases
- Calculators

Communications equipment

Equipment used in travel agencies for internal and external communication includes:

- Central reservation systems (CRSs), e.g. Galileo, Sabre, Worldspan, etc.
- Fax machines
- Telex
- Personal computers (PCs) with access to electronic mail (E-mail) and the Internet
- Viewdata sets, e.g. Istel, Fastrak and New Prestel (see Figure 16.4)
- Telephones
- Telephone answering machines
- Postal equipment, e.g. scales and franking machines

Figure 16.4 gives an example of the communications system of one of the major travel providers, Fastrak. Fastrak is a dial-up reservations and information service that allows travel agents to access various tour operators, flights, hotels, car hire, ferries and other travel-related suppliers. It allows users to check availability, create and confirm customers' bookings and provide travel information. Fastrak offers access to a variety of travel principals, which currently includes Airtours, Thomson, Kuoni, Cosmos, British Airways, Avis rent-a-car, First Choice and Swiss Travel Service.

Communication in travel takes place between agents and principals, as well as between agents and their customers, necessitating a range of communications equipment that is both cost-effective and reliable.

Administration equipment

Equipment for carrying out administrative functions in travel agencies includes personal computers, typewriters, agency stamps, photocopiers, franking machines, dictating machines, filing cabinets, etc., plus consumables (stationery items, paper clips, rubber bands, pencils, pens, etc.). The agency may use its computer for word processing, spreadsheets and databases, or perhaps a specialist software application concerning payroll or financial accounting.

Safety and security equipment

To ensure the safety and security of staff and customers, travel agencies should take precautions against theft, fire and injury, including keeping a first-aid kit and

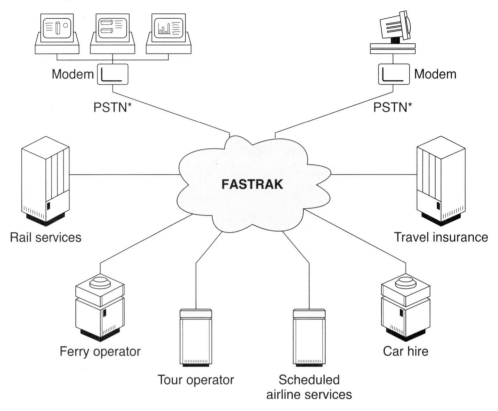

Travel agents' viewdata terminals

Modem

PSTN*

PSTN*

Modem

FASTRAK

Rail services

Travel insurance

Ferry operator

Car hire

Tour operator

Scheduled
airline services

*PSTN: Public Switched Telephone Network

Fig. 16.4 The Fastrak networked system

fire extinguishers on the premises and having smoke alarms fitted (local building regulations may impose conditions in relation to fire protection in the premises). The premises should be inspected by a crime prevention expert who will advise on any security equipment that should be installed, e.g. window and door locks, safes and closed-circuit television (CCTV) surveillance cameras. Element 16.3 looks at travel agency procedures concerned with security and confidentiality.

Activity

Carry out an equipment audit of a travel agency with which you are familiar, perhaps while on work placement or when working part time. Indicate whether each item of equipment is leased, purchased outright or bought on hire purchase.

Licensing and financial requirements

Newly established travel agencies, as well as those that have been trading for some time, are faced with an array of licensing and financial requirements, which seek to regulate business practices and ensure a high-quality service for the customer. Some of the most important are considered in the following paragraphs, including:

- Membership of ABTA
- Agency agreements
- IATA licensing
- Foreign exchange
- The Package Travel Directive

Membership of ABTA

The Association of British Travel Agents (ABTA) is the UK's leading trade body for the travel and tourism industry, representing the interests and business practices of both tour operators and travel agents. Although it is not compulsory for a UK travel agent to become a member of ABTA, membership does confer a range of benefits, including:

1. *Commercial* – use of the ABTA logo, bonding schemes, independent arbitration service, etc.
2. *Representation* – lobbying at Westminster and Brussels, plus regular dialogue with other important interest groups.
3. *Member services* – an information bureau giving advice to members, legal advisory service, legal seminars, annual receipt of the ABTA Members' Handbook and ABTA List of Members, monthly issues of ABTA News, ABTA's own viewdata service ABTEL, regional meetings of the Association, annual ABTA Convention, etc.
4. *Training* – ABTA's wholly owned subsidiary The Travel Training Company (formerly ABTA National Training Board) offers a range of courses for staff and management and supports the work of the Travel Industry Lead Body.
5. *Charity* – ABTA administers its own benevolent fund for members who need financial assistance.

Application for ABTA membership can take up to three months to process. Once an application has been received, and before any decision on its approval or otherwise is taken, the agency will receive an unannounced visit from an ABTA inspector, who will interview staff and inspect the premises. If successful, the applicant will be granted an ABTA licence number, which should be used on all publications and correspondence. Conditions of travel agency membership of ABTA are contained in its Articles of Association and the Travel Agents' Code of Conduct. The following are some of the current (1996) conditions that ABTA travel agents must adhere to:

1. *Staffing* – there must be at least one qualified person at each travel agent's office. To be considered as qualified, the person concerned must have had at least two years' relevant practical experience, or at least 18 months' such experience plus COTAC

Level I (General Section only) or ABTAC (Primary Level), or at least one year's such experience plus COTAC Level II (General Section only) or ABTAC (Advanced Level). 'Relevant practical experience' is judged to be those activities that an average travel agent would expect to acquire in the course of running a non-specialist agency, including procedures concerned with the full range of package tours.

2. *Premises* – although there are no specific membership conditions concerning travel agents' premises, the Travel Agents' Code of Conduct makes it clear that no ABTA agent should have any connection with a travel agency that falsely represents itself as a member of the Association.

3. *Identification* – all ABTA travel agencies must clearly show on their premises, note paper and other business literature their full company name and all other information required under the Business Names Act of 1985.

4. *Trading names* – members of ABTA must not use the name, or an imitation of the trading name, of any former member that has failed to meet its liabilities.

5. *Acceptability of directors, proprietors, partners and qualifying staff* – ABTA membership conditions state that all persons employed or concerned in the management of a travel agency must be respectable and honest individuals, none of whom is an undischarged bankrupt or is guilty of conduct unbecoming a member of the Association, as defined by the Travel Agents' Council.

6. *Financial stability* – all applicants for membership of ABTA travel agency class are required to provide financial protection to the Association in the form of a bond, as well as giving evidence of financial stability. The bond is a formal undertaking from an approved bank or insurance company to pay a sum of money to ABTA in the event of the member's financial failure, primarily for the purpose of reimbursing customers who would otherwise lose the money they had paid. The minimum acceptable financial standards for entry to the Association are currently:
   - There must be paid-up share capital or capital account balance of at least £50,000. Total net assets after deducting intangible assets should not be less than £50,000. There must be a working capital surplus of not less than £15,000.
   - The minimum bond level is £50,000.
   - Contribution to the Travel Agents' Bond Replacement Scheme is £400 for each head office and £40 for each additional branch, plus 2.5 per cent insurance premium tax.

   All members are required to submit audited accounts annually together with quarterly turnover statements. Additionally, management accounts must be supplied made up to a date six months after admission to membership.

7. *Fees and subscriptions* – ABTA currently levies a non-returnable registration fee of £387.75 payable at the time of applying for membership. The entrance fee is £1615.63 payable upon admission to membership. Annual subscription is £500 plus VAT per company plus £120 plus VAT for each additional branch office.

8. *Code of Conduct* – all applicants for membership of the travel agents' class of ABTA are required to declare their adherence to the Travel Agents' Code of Conduct.

9. *Change of address and opening of new branches* – all changes of address, plus the opening or acquisition of new branches, must be notified to ABTA within seven days of the event. Fees are charged for this service and members opening or acquiring additional branches are required to provide additional bonding.

(Information courtesy of ABTA)

ABTA – The Association of British Travel Agents

Introduction

ABTA is the trade body representing over 90 per cent of travel agents and tour operators in the UK. It was formed in 1950 with just 100 members, at a time which coincided with the dawn of a new era for British travellers, when new aircraft technology and greater personal freedom were giving people the means to travel further afield. Foreign travel came to be seen as a temporary escape from the drabness of post-war Britain and the mass market holiday boom was beginning to take shape. Today, holidays are the high point in the year for many millions of UK travellers, with travel for business purposes remaining an important element of the UK travel scene. In our fast-moving society, we have come to take ease of travel for granted, to the extent that some 11 million Britons book an overseas package holiday every year. Many millions will also take short breaks, holidays in the UK, trips by rail or ferry, or travel on business.

ABTA's aims

ABTA's main aims are to maintain the high standards of service among its members, as well as creating as favourable a business climate as possible for the industry. Specific objectives of the Association are:

- To establish an organisation which is fully representative of travel agents and tour operators in the UK.
- To promote and develop the general interests of all members of ABTA.
- To establish and maintain Codes of Conduct between members and the general public, with the object that membership of the Association will be recognised as a guarantee of integrity, competence and high standards of service.
- To discourage unfair competition without in any way interfering with initiative and enterprise based on fair trading.
- To promote friendly relations with others in the travel industry.
- To provide means for negotiations and liaison with other bodies concerned with the development of travel both in the UK and abroad.

How ABTA works

The Association is a self-regulatory body run by its membership. A network of Councils and Committees, appointed by member travel agents and tour operators, make up the policy-making and enforcing machinery of the Association and help to ensure that ABTA remains in close contact with the whole of its membership. The Association has an education and training function which is carried out by the Travel Training Company (formerly ABTA National Training Board), which liaises with validating bodies such as BTEC and City & Guilds to ensure that the industry has programmes of education and training that are appropriate to its needs.

Up until the end of 1993, ABTA legally operated a type of 'closed shop' arrangement known as the 'stabiliser', which stated that ABTA travel agents could only sell package holidays from tour operators who were themselves members of ABTA, and vice versa. The stabiliser was introduced 20 years ago to safeguard the public against unscrupulous agents and operators. The arrangement was dismantled in 1993, since it was considered to be a restrictive practice and also because, in theory at least, the introduction of the EC Package Travel Directive rendered the stabiliser obsolete.

Membership of ABTA

Those granted membership of ABTA are required to adhere to strict rules governing their business practice. These are contained in ABTA's Codes of Conduct, which regulate all aspects of tour operators' and travel agents' relationships with their customers and which have been drawn up in conjunction with the Office of Fair Trading (OFT).

The Tour Operators' Code of Conduct lays down the minimum standards for brochures, requiring that they contain clear, comprehensive and accurate descriptions of facilities and services offered. It details rules that govern booking conditions in brochures as they relate, for example, to the cancellation or alteration of tours, holidays or other travel arrangements by the tour operator. The Code also contains strict rules concerning the prompt handling of complaints and regulations relating to the business relationships between tour operators and travel agents.

Similar, stringent rules apply also to travel agents who are bound by their own Code of Conduct. The Travel Agents' Code of Conduct regulates all aspects of travel agents' relationships with their customers, covering their responsibility with regard to the standard of service they provide and the information they give to clients. It also lays down rules concerning travel agents' trading relationships with tour operators.

In addition, members of ABTA are required to adhere to precise financial specifications, overseen by ABTA's Financial Services Department, which checks all members' accounts at least once a year.

Protection and redress for the travelling public

In addition to its Codes of Conduct, ABTA seeks to protect the interests of travellers through its Consumer Affairs Department and its own Arbitration Scheme.

Staff in the Consumer Affairs Department offer a service for clients who have booked with an ABTA-registered travel agent or tour operator and who have reason to complain about some aspect of the service they have received. ABTA will look into the complaint and seek to redress the situation without recourse to law. If the dispute cannot be resolved through conciliation, the client may pursue the claim through ABTA's Arbitration Scheme, for which a fee is charged depending on the amount of the claim; current (1996) fees range from £64.63 for claims up to £1500 to £111.63 for claims between £3001 and £7500. These rates apply to groups of up to six people. The ABTA Arbitration Scheme, administered by the Chartered Institute of Arbitrators, gives the client the opportunity for redress without incurring high legal costs.

Tour operators and travel agent members of ABTA are required to provide bonds to protect their customers in the event of financial failure. The bond can take a number of forms, but is often an insurance policy for the amount required by ABTA, or a bank guarantee. The financial protection offered by the bonding system enables ABTA, in the event of a member's financial failure, to:

- Arrange for clients whose holidays are in progress at the time of the failure to continue their holidays, as far as possible as originally planned, and in any event to make certain that customers abroad are returned to the UK; and
- Reimburse customers whose holidays have not started, the money they paid for their holidays or to make alternative arrangements for the holidays to proceed.

(Information courtesy of ABTA)

Case study discussion questions

1. Why has ABTA developed its Travel Agents' Code of Conduct?
2. What is ABTA's principal aim?
3. What benefits are there to travellers who book through an ABTA-registered travel agent?
4. Why do ABTA travel agencies have to provide the Association with a 'bond'?
5. What training opportunities are offered by the Travel Training Company?

Agency agreements

All of the business conducted by travel agents on behalf of principals is strictly controlled by individual agency agreements. These contractual arrangements set out the obligations of each party to the agreement, the terms of trade and remuneration details. The most common agency agreement will be that between the travel agent and a tour operator, where the agent undertakes to sell the tour operator's products in return for a commission on sales. Other agreements may be made with coach operators, holiday centres, hotel groups, ferry companies, British Rail, National Express, car hire firms and a range of other travel and tourism companies. A standard written agency agreement between a travel agent and a tour operator will include details under a number of clauses, including:

- Accounting procedures for deposits and balances.
- Commission rates and arrangements for payment to the agent.
- Procedures for issuing tickets, vouchers and other travel documentation.
- Policy on refunds and cancellation of holidays by the client or tour operator.
- Handling of complaints made to the agent about the operator's products.
- Racking responsibilities of the agent in respect of the operator's brochures.
- Training and promotional support offered by the tour operator.

Such agreements are generally on a non-exclusive basis, i.e. many other travel agents will be selling the same products. It is only in the case of very specialised products that an agent may enter into an exclusive arrangement with an operator, although exclusive agreements in a particular geographical area are not uncommon.

IATA licensing

The International Air Transport Association (IATA) is an international trade body representing the interests of more than 80 per cent of the world's major airlines.

Its principal aim is to promote safe, regular and economic air travel. Travel agents in the UK, in common with agents world wide, can apply for an IATA licence to sell airline tickets and other services of IATA member airlines. Since these airlines only pay commission to approved IATA sales agents, an IATA licence is a much sought-after commodity. Applying for an IATA licence has similarities to an application for ABTA membership, in that the applicant has to meet certain minimum criteria and will be subject to an inspection and interview by an IATA representative. The criteria for approval are concerned with a number of factors, including:

1. *Nature of the premises* – the agency must be open for business on a regular basis and clearly identified as a travel agency.
2. *Security of premises* – premises must be adequately protected and a safe installed for the storage of airline tickets and other valuables.
3. *Staff qualifications* – staff selling the IATA tickets and services must be permanent employees and have relevant experience and qualifications, e.g. British Airways Fares and Ticketing Courses.
4. *Finances* – applicants must submit a full set of audited accounts for scrutiny by IATA personnel and meet certain minimum share capital/capital account amounts. Additionally, approved agents are required to submit a copy of their annual report and accounts within 6 months of the financial year end.
5. *Bonding* – a bank or insurance company bond will be required, based on a percentage of annual turnover.

On payment of a non-refundable application fee and an entry fee, the successful applicant will be granted an IATA licence to sell airline tickets and services of IATA member airlines.

Activity

Try to find out which travel agencies in your locality have an IATA licence. What do the non-IATA agents do when a client wishes to buy an airline ticket?

Foreign exchange

Some travel agents will want to offer their customers the full range of travel services by offering foreign currency and travellers' cheques. Competition between the main issuing companies, Thomas Cook and American Express, high street banks, building societies and even post offices, has reduced the commission rates earned by agents to such a low level that many have decided not to offer the service themselves, but rather use an existing provider in the locality. Those that do supply travellers' cheques and foreign currency will need to pay particular attention to security arrangements and insurance cover. Profit on the sale of foreign currency is made by selling it to the customer at a better rate than that at which it was bought.

The Package Travel Directive

Element 19.1 explains that the EU Package Travel, Package Holidays and Package Tours Directive was adopted in June 1990 and came into operation on 1 January 1993 in the Member States of the European Union. Its main aim is to give people buying package holidays more protection and access to compensation when things go wrong, while at the same time harmonising the rules covering packages operated throughout European Union countries. In the normal course of events, travel agents are not bound by the requirements of the Directive, since they are not the 'organiser' of the package, but the 'retailer'. The Directive defines these terms as follows:

1. *Organiser* – the person who, other than occasionally, organises packages and sells or offers them for sale, whether directly or through a retailer.
2. *Retailer* – the person who sells of offers for sale the package put together by the organiser.

In the UK travel and tourism industry the 'organiser' will normally be a tour operator and the 'retailer' a travel agent. There may, however, be occasions when a travel retailer does fall within the scope of the Directive. This will certainly be the case when the travel agent escorts his or her own tours for clients, since the contract for the holiday is between the agent and the customer, with no tour operator involved. Similarly, a travel agent who uses a range of reference materials to assemble a package for a client is likely to fall within requirements of the Directive. It is only when the customer enters into a contract directly with the tour operator, or other principal, that the travel agent will not be the 'organiser' as defined by the Directive. Happily for travel agents, this is the normal situation, and most agents are unlikely to become entangled in the complexity of the Package Travel Directive. To ensure that the position is clear, the agent should ensure that the customer signs the tour operator's booking form and receives an unaltered confirmation invoice from that party. Travel agents must be careful to ensure that correct documentation is passed from the principal, normally a tour operator, to the client.

Assignment 16.1

Examining the requirements for running a travel agency

Performance criteria satisfied: 16.1.1, 16.1.2, 16.1.3, 16.1.4, 16.1.5, 16.1.6

Core skills opportunities at level 3:   Communication   3.1, 3.2, 3.3, 3.4
                                         Information technology   3.1, 3.2, 3.3
                                         Application of number   3.1, 3.2, 3.3

Situation

You have recently taken up the post of projects assistant with your local Training and Enterprise Council (TEC). In response to an increasing number of enquiries from members of the public about working in the travel and tourism industry, the TEC is working with some local ABTA travel agents to put on a series of training seminars entitled 'Running your own travel agency'.

Tasks

Working as part of a small team, you are to contribute to the staging of one of these seminars, involving planning, collecting relevant material and making a presentation to the rest of your group. The content of the seminar should focus on:

- Factors that influence travel agency location
- The services offered by travel agencies
- The importance of design and layout in travel agencies
- The equipment used in travel agencies
- The licensing and financial requirements of travel agencies

Your presentation should include detailed information gathered from an in-depth investigation of a local travel agency. You should negotiate specific work tasks with the other members of your group to ensure equality of work load. You will be assessed on the content of the presentation and the quality of delivery.

Element 16.2 Investigate the personnel requirements of a travel agency

> **Performance criteria**
>
> 1. Describe skills and qualities needed by travel agency personnel.
> 2. Explain the training and qualifications which travel agencies require of their employees.
> 3. Explain how travel agencies deploy personnel.
> 4. Explain how trends in employment affect the personnel requirements of travel agencies.
> 5. Draw up a job description and person specification for a member of personnel in a travel agency.

Skills and qualities needed by travel agency personnel

The particular skills and qualities needed by travel agency personnel will depend on their role in the business and position in the organisation. Even in the smallest of agencies it is possible to identify three distinct types of staff roles, namely:

1. *Management* – undertaken by the manager or owner/proprietor.
2. *Supervisory* – undertaken by the senior travel clerk.
3. *Customer service* – undertaken by travel clerks.

Each of the three different staff roles will have distinct skills and qualities associated with it, the most important of which are:

- Management skills
- Communication skills
- Customer service skills

In addition to these skills, staff working in travel agencies must possess a variety of personal and professional qualities if they are to succeed at their jobs, including honesty, reliability, a smart appearance, enthusiasm for the industry, initiative and the ability to deal with customers of all types. There is no doubt that front line staff in travel agencies are given a great degree of responsibility, often at a very young age.

Activity

Interview the manager of a local travel agency and ask him or her to select the most important skills they use when carrying out their job. Are some skills more important than others?

Management skills

The manager or owner/proprietor of a travel agency will be responsible for overall control of the business, including the management of its physical, human and financial resources. As well as controlling the technical aspects of the business, such as monitoring financial performance or assessing security, the manager also has a motivational and leadership role, by creating a culture within which staff are encouraged to achieve optimum efficiency and effectiveness. Controlling the finances of the agency, whether by setting budgets, monitoring revenue or controlling costs, is vital to the long-term stability of the business. It follows, therefore, that managers need a wide range of skills, including:

- Communication skills – verbal and written
- Financial monitoring and control skills
- Decision-making skills
- Negotiation skills
- Sales and marketing skills
- Leadership and motivational skills
- Team-building skills
- Problem-solving skills

Some managers will develop these skills over time simply by working in the travel and tourism industry. Such experience is extremely useful to practising managers, but may need to be supplemented with periods of formal training, particularly for new entrants to management positions within the industry.

Communication skills

All three types of staff role, i.e. management, supervisory and customer service, will involve the development of excellent communication skills. Managers will liaise internally and externally, with staff, suppliers, principals, regulatory bodies, trade associations, tax authorities, banks, shareholders, area managers and a variety of other individuals and groups. Staff in a supervisory capacity will be responsible for the performance of employees under their direct control, involving a great deal of one-to-one communication on a daily basis. A senior travel clerk will also liaise with principals in the course of his or her normal daily duties. Travel clerks and other staff involved in front-line customer care need to develop a wide range of communication skills, since they will be in regular contact with customers and principals when carrying out their main role of selling holidays and other travel products. This will involve direct face-to-face contact, plus a variety of indirect communication methods, including:

- Telephone
- Fax
- Telex
- Electronic mail (E-mail)
- Viewdata
- Written correspondence

The importance of communication skills in travel agency operation cannot be over-emphasised. Staff must always remember that the way in which they communicate with customers is crucial to the success of the business. The highly competitive nature of the travel and tourism industry means that managers who do not invest in communications training for their staff are jeopardising the long-term future of the company.

Customer service skills

Travel clerks who are in regular contact with customers must develop a wide range of skills in order to fulfil their prime role of serving customers, meeting their needs and ultimately selling products and services (see Figure 16.5). These include:

1. *Product knowledge* – knowing the features and benefits of different holidays and other travel products is an essential prerequisite of successful customer service.
2. *Information retrieval* – travel staff must know where to find information on a wide range of matters related to holidays and travel, e.g. climate, time zones, health requirements, passport information, journey lengths, etc.
3. *Calculations* – of holiday costs, fares, journey times, time zone changes, mileages, etc.
4. *Communication* – with customers, principals, other members of staff, etc., by telephone, face-to-face contact, in writing, by fax, telex, viewdata, etc.

Fig. 16.5 Customer service skills are essential in travel agencies (reproduced courtesy of Thomson Travel Group)

5. *Keyboard skills* and computer literacy.
6. *Administration skills* – typing, filing, issuing documents, handling cash, etc.
7. *Selling skills* (see below).

Selling skills

Since the prime objective of travel agencies is to sell holidays and other travel products and services profitably, it goes without saying that the selling skills of an agency's staff are critical to its success. Selling is an essential component of the marketing process for travel agencies and should be seen as a continuous process that can help cement customer relationships, build customer loyalty and provide lasting benefits in an enhanced level of customer service.

Selling involves communication between a buyer and a seller, which is designed to persuade the customer to purchase the products or services on offer. It can be thought of as the culmination of all the marketing activities that have taken place beforehand in the company. It involves matching a customer's needs with the goods and services on offer; the better the match, the more lasting the relationship between the agent and the customer.

Not surprisingly, the prime objective of selling is to make a sale! This may seem a glaringly obvious statement, but there are likely to be other related aims to the selling process, including:

- Generating repeat business
- Meeting planned increases in sales volume
- Increasing customer satisfaction levels
- Increasing profitability
- Securing competitive advantage
- Targeting specific sectors of the market
- Raising awareness of a new product or service

Simply saying that the principal objective of selling is to make a sale, also masks the very complex nature of the sales process in travel agencies, involving the use of a whole set of principles, processes and techniques, linked to personal, social and interpersonal skills. The next section of this Element looks in detail at these skill areas in an investigation of the sales process in travel agencies.

The sales process in travel agencies

Successful selling is a structured activity, not just 'something that happens'. Figure 16.6 shows the six key stages of the sales process in travel agencies.

Raising customer awareness (stage 1) relates to the promotional techniques that travel agencies, and the principals whose products they are selling, use to inform customers about products and services. An agency will make full use of its premises to attract custom, with imaginative window displays, a prominent fascia board, late availability notices, posters and other point-of-sale materials. It may also advertise in the local press and on local radio, as well as mailing information to existing clients.

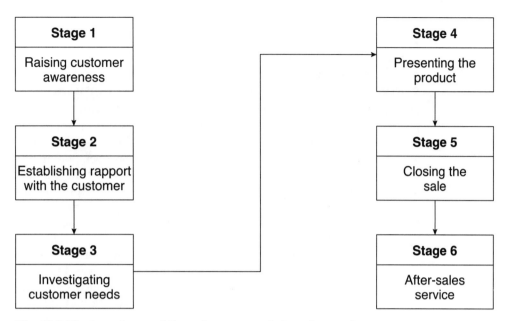

Stage 1		**Stage 4**
Raising customer awareness		Presenting the product

Stage 2		**Stage 5**
Establishing rapport with the customer		Closing the sale

Stage 3		**Stage 6**
Investigating customer needs		After-sales service

Fig. 16.6 The key stages of the sales process in travel agencies

Activity

Thinking of the last two holidays you went on, try to remember how you were made aware of the existence of the holiday in the first place. Are your own findings similar to those of other members of your group?

Once a customer has come through the door of the agency, it is necessary for staff to make an initial contact and establish a rapport (stage 2). In order to meet the objective of making a sale, this initial task of engaging the customer in conversation is important, since it gives the salesperson the opportunity to gain his or her trust and to discover the customer's needs. Some customers are suspicious of any attempts to sell them products, often preferring to make their own decisions on product selection and purchase. They may consider sales staff to be 'pushy' or arrogant, but even such reluctant customers can be put in the right frame of mind to buy a particular product or service if they receive a friendly and attentive level of service.

Stage 3 of the sales process gives the customer the opportunity to state his or her needs clearly, so that the travel clerk has the best chance of presenting a product or service that the client will want to buy. It is important for the member of staff to ask questions, both to solicit the necessary information and to keep the sales interview flowing. Although customers may not be in a position to answer all the questions put to them, the travel clerk will need to build up a picture of the client's requirements by asking such questions as:

- What is the size of the party travelling?
- Are there any children and, if so, what ages are they?
- When do you want to travel and for how long?

- Where do you want to go?
- Is there a particular company you prefer to travel with?
- How do you want to travel?
- How much do you expect to pay?
- Does anybody in the party have any special requirements?

Having determined the customer's needs, stage 4 of the sales process is to present the product to the customer, outlining its features, benefits and advantages. Product knowledge is crucial to the success of this part of the sales process, since the customer may wish to know extra information about the product on offer. Staff may also encounter objections from the customer at this stage, perhaps based on the price of the product or its availability and must be trained to handle these points in a positive fashion.

Closing the sale (stage 5) takes place when all objections have been overcome and the customer seems ready to make a commitment. Helping the customer move from 'I'd like' to 'I'll buy' is what this stage of the sales process is all about. Staff should be continually looking for buying signals from the customer to trigger the process of closing the sale. Statements such as 'that sounds fine' or 'yes, I like that' clearly indicate a desire on the part of the customer to buy. When such signals are evident, the member of staff should begin to finalise the deal, remembering that clients should never be forced into making a decision that they may later regret. Not every sales interview will necessarily end in a sale; what is important from the organisation's point of view is to end up with the best possible outcome to the process. For large purchases, customers may wish to consider the benefits in greater detail or discuss the sale with other people, before making a commitment to buy. In this situation, all sales staff can do is to ensure that the customer has been given excellent customer service throughout, thus increasing the chances of an eventual positive sales outcome.

Stage 6, after-sales service, is an appreciation that the sales process doesn't end when the customer has parted with his or her money. Just as we expect an after-sales service for consumer and household items we buy, travel agencies too must offer this service to their customers. Adding customers' details to a database should be the first step in developing a long-term relationship, that will hopefully benefit both the travel agent and the customer.

Activity

Working with a partner, role-play the situation of a member of the public who is looking to buy a package holiday to Turkey, but isn't sure which tour operator to book with. Ask another member of your group to evaluate how the person taking on the sales role performed in relation to each of the stages of the sales process.

Travel agency training and qualifications

Although it is not essential to have any formal qualifications to work in a travel agency, staff who are keen to improve themselves and their career prospects will certainly benefit from periods of study, either in their own time or with the support of their employers. There are a number of ways of categorising the training opportunities open to travel agency staff. One is to separate initial training for a first or new post, from ongoing career development. All staff will need to undergo a period of induction training when taking up a travel agency appointment for the first time or when moving from one agency to another. Well-planned induction training is so important to the effectiveness of an individual member of staff, although it is often not given the priority it deserves. Induction training can play an important part in reducing staff turnover and creating a successful team atmosphere in an agency.

Another way of categorising staff training is to divide it into that which takes place at work, referred to as 'on-the-job' training, and that undertaken elsewhere, known as 'off-the-job' training. For successful career progression in the travel and tourism industry, it is likely that a mixture of the two approaches will be needed.

On-the-job training

This is any type of staff training and development that occurs in the workplace. The initial induction training discussed above is a form of on-the-job training, where a manager and/or supervisor instructs a new entrant into the office procedures and routines. Induction should be a structured activity, including information on:

- The company, its history and objectives
- The names and duties of the other members of the team
- The new entrant's job roles and responsibilities
- Conditions of employment – hours of work, lunch arrangements, company rules, grievance procedures, etc
- Health, safety and security procedures
- Location of staff facilities

Other training in the travel agency will concentrate on the use of equipment, such as computerised booking systems, fax machines, computers, etc., telephone techniques, cash handling, using information sources, customer contact skills and a variety of other tasks. Some on-the-job training will be delivered by representatives of the holiday and travel companies whose products the agency sells. They are keen to provide information on their range of products as a way of improving customer service standards and promoting their company's products. Certain aspects of an employee's on-the-job training can give credit towards achieving National Vocational Qualifications (NVQs).

National Vocational Qualifications (NVQs)

NVQs (SVQs/Scottish Vocational Qualifications in Scotland) are qualifications introduced by the government to raise standards in the workplace, by creating a highly skilled, flexible and qualified workforce. They are designed to assess the skills and competences of employees, rather than their industry knowledge. NVQs are developed from occupational standards developed by industry-led bodies, who document appropriate tasks and skills for employees at different levels of experience. Staff working in travel agencies, and individuals hoping to gain employment in the travel industry, can study for Travel Services NVQs, accredited by the National Council for Vocational Qualifications (NCVQ) and developed jointly by the Travel Services Lead Body (TICK) and City & Guilds. Travel Services NVQs are assessed in the travel agency or in approved regional centres where work situations are simulated. They are currently offered at three levels, although qualifications at levels 4 and 5 are planned for the future.

Travel Services NVQs

NVQs in travel services are qualifications for people who want to follow a range of career opportunities in the travel industry, including travel agency sales staff, tour operations personnel, business travel clerks, travel guides, tour managers and customer services staff. They are designed for all types of people, from those who already have extensive travel experience to those who are entering the industry for the first time.

Travel Services NVQs are made up of a number of units, as shown in Figure 16.7. They concentrate on three interrelated leisure travel industry sectors, namely retail travel, tour operations and guiding/interpretation support services. The qualifications build on the work of other industry-led bodies, incorporating tasks from, for example, the Customer Service Lead Body and the Administration Lead Body.

Off-the-job training

As its name implies, off-the-job training is any training activity that takes place away from the normal place of work. Training away from work is sometimes preferred by staff and employers as a way of achieving a specific training objective or qualification. The recognised qualification for travel agency sales staff is ABTAC, which stands for ABTA Travel Agents Certificate, an examination-based qualification for those working, or wishing to work, in the travel industry. It was launched in 1994, following joint development by ABTA's Travel Agents Council and the Travel Training Company. The qualification is available at two levels, Primary and Advanced, which correspond to the former COTAC (General) Levels I and II. It will also provide much of the knowledge and understanding for NVQs levels 2 and 3 in Travel Services (see above). ABTAC Primary covers the knowledge that competent leisure travel clerks should have in order to do their work effectively, normally within approximately one year of starting work. ABTAC Advanced covers the knowledge required by travel clerks dealing with a wider range of enquiries, associated with a minimum of two years' experience. Unlike the former COTAC qualification, ABTAC does not have an air test paper as an integral part of the qualification. Staff can, however, study for separate qualifications to meet IATA requirements. ABTAC counts towards the staff qualifications requirement for ABTA retail membership and, as such, may exempt staff from up to one year's relevant, practical experience.

Courses leading to the ABTAC qualification are available at a number of approved centres in England, Wales, Scotland and Northern Ireland. These may be 'day release' courses or, more usually, evening classes in a local college.

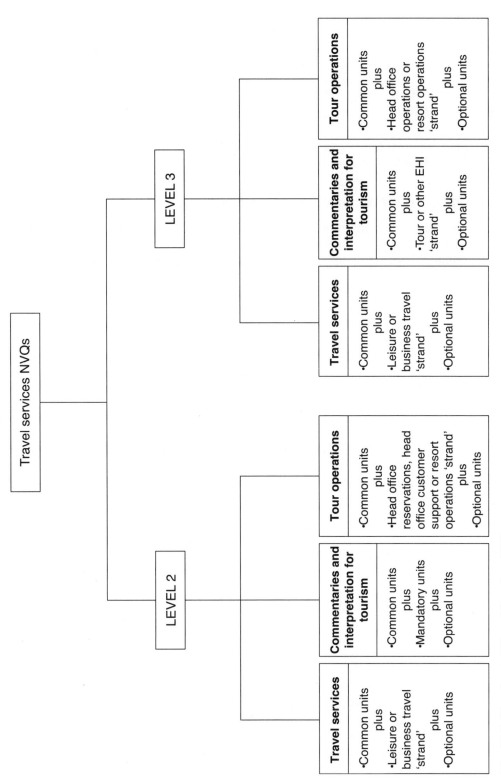

Fig. 16.7 Structure of Travel Services NVQs *(information courtesy of City & Guilds)*

The recognised industry qualification for managers in travel agencies has traditionally been COTAM, the Certificate of Travel Agency Management. With the introduction of Travel Services NVQs, managers now have the choice of this competency-based qualification route instead.

Activity

Find out what training opportunities for travel staff are provided in your locality. Do they tie in with the National Vocational Qualifications framework?

Other vocational and academic courses

There are increasing numbers of vocational and academic courses concerned with leisure, travel and tourism, reflecting the popularity of the subject in the eyes of the public. GNVQs (General National Vocational Qualifications) in Leisure and Tourism are new, work-related academic qualifications, designed to offer a choice of opportunities in employment or higher education. GNVQs in Leisure and Tourism are offered at a variety of levels, from Foundation to Advanced, and are based around mandatory, optional and additional units. Most Advanced GNVQ courses occupy two years, full-time study and are taken by 16–18-year-old students in colleges and schools. While GNVQs give students a broad understanding of the travel and tourism industry, they do not assess specific competences in the workplace, as is the case with NVQs. GNVQs are gradually replacing other vocational qualifications, including the BTEC National Diploma in Travel and Tourism.

Travel and tourism is increasingly being seen as a subject worthy of academic study in higher education as well. Many universities and colleges offer HNDs, Degrees and postgraduate qualifications, either through full- or part-time study, or by distance learning. Vocational higher level courses give students a thorough grounding in the basics of management in the industry, and equip them for a range of positions within travel and tourism.

Deploying staff in travel agencies

More than half of all ABTA travel agencies in the UK are small, family-run businesses employing two or three members of staff under the management of the owner/proprietor. With such an arrangement, there is little room for specialisation by individual members of staff, and all employees, including the owner, will be involved in the many tasks associated with selling holidays and travel products. The deployment of staff in an agency such as this is shown in Figure 16.8.

In the organisational structure shown in Figure 16.8, the owner/proprietor assumes overall day-to-day control of the agency, with the senior travel clerk deputising in his or her absence. The senior travel clerk will oversee the work of the two travel clerks, one a junior who may be on a training scheme operated by ABTA's Travel Training Company.

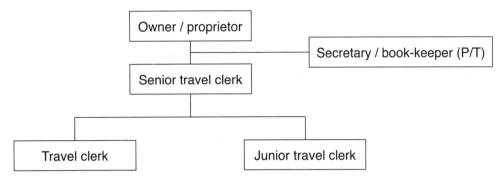

Fig. 16.8 Staff deployment in a small independent travel agency

The large travel agency chains have a more complex organisational structure, which is unsurprising given their scale of operations. Data from ABTA shows that, at the beginning of 1996, the top five multiples had the following number of branches nationwide:

1. Lunn Poly   796
2. Going Places   709
3. Thomas Cook   384
4. MTG (UK) Ltd   292
5. Co-op Travel   233

If we take the number one UK travel retailer in terms of number of branches, Lunn Poly, its organisational structure is given in Figure 16.9.

Figure 16.9 indicates that a sales consultant in a branch of the Lunn Poly chain is one part of a complex business structure. Lunn Poly is an operating division of the Thomson Travel Group, which in turn is part of the multinational Thomson Corporation of Canada. Eleven directors report to the managing director, including four sales directors covering the north, east, south and west of Britain. Area managers oversee the work of the branch managers and report directly to their appropriate area manager.

Trends in employment

The general trend in the UK employment sector away from permanent, full-time appointments to short, flexible, fixed-term contracts and freelance working, is beginning to have an effect on the retail travel industry. Positions that were previously full-time, permanent appointments are sometimes filled by part-time staff working on a contract basis, as a way of reducing overheads. The glamorous image of the industry tends to ensure a healthy response to any advertised post, but relatively low rates of pay can sometimes dissuade enquirers from applying.

Advances in technology have meant that staffing levels in agencies have not increased, even though business volumes have risen. Technology is not only affecting job roles inside the agencies; the large retail travel companies make

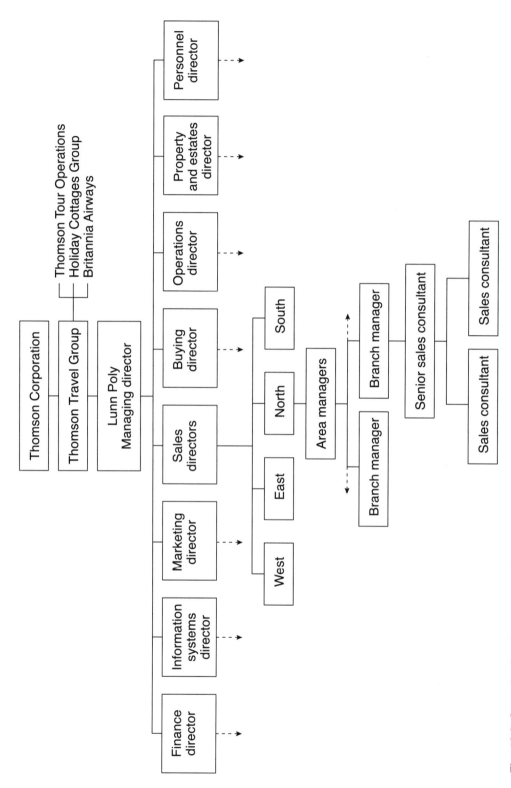

Fig. 16.9 *Organisational structure of Lunn Poly*

extensive use of new technology systems and equipment for their mobile sales teams, who may use laptop computers with modem access to head office systems. Financial control, too, is made easier with advances in spreadsheet software and payroll systems.

Job descriptions for travel agency staff

Travel agencies rely on job descriptions to define the boundaries of particular posts within the agency and clarify responsibilities and authority within the staffing and management structure. They are also essential for the purposes of recruitment, selection, staff promotion, training, reward systems, performance review, staff appraisal and personal development. Before a job description is written, there needs to be a thorough analysis of the post in question and what it entails. If it is an existing post to be filled, simply finding a set of old job details and reproducing them without considering if they are still relevant, is not good enough. The dynamic nature of the travel and tourism industry is such that an approach of this sort will not achieve the desired objective of filling the post with the best candidate. Information to be included in the job analysis can be obtained from the existing postholder, previous records, other members of staff and by direct observation. A job description can then be compiled, detailing the content of the job and areas of responsibility. A typical job description is likely to include:

1. *Title of the post* – including grade, post number, department/section, location, etc.
2. *Summary of the job* – outlining the key objectives of the post.
3. *Responsibilities* – clarifying the position in the organisational structure, detailing to whom responsible and for whom responsible.
4. *Detailed duties* – a list of all the relevant duties attached to the post.
5. *Conditions of employment* – general information on salary/wage, holiday entitlement, hours of work, pension arrangements, welfare and social facilities, trade union membership arrangements, training, etc.
6. *Date it was written* – this is important because duties and responsibilities may change over time.

Figure 16.10 shows an example of a fictitious job description for a travel clerk in a city centre branch of a multiple travel agency. It should be remembered that every travel agency, whether an independent retailer or part of a multiple chain, will have its own practices in relation to staff recruitment and selection. The job description in Figure 16.10 will, nonetheless, serve as a general guide.

Activity

Using the example in Figure 16.10 as a model, write a job description for the post of assistant manager in a branch of a major travel agency chain.

```
Sundown Travel PLC

Job Description

Title of post:        Travel clerk
Post no:              TC/9/96
Location:             Anytown branch
Responsible to:       Branch manager


Job summary

To work with the branch manager and other staff to provide previous and current
clients with a first-class standard of service in meeting all their travel needs.


Detailed duties

1.  Advising clients on the details and availability of a range of holidays and
    other travel products.
2.  Liaising regularly with travel principals in the  process of selling holiday
    products.
3.  Issuing tickets and other travel documentation.
4.  Maintaining brochure stocks, window displays and other promotional activities.
5.  Carrying out the range of duties by telephone, computer, VDU, direct contact,
    fax, telex, courier and post.
6.  Handling cash and completing non-cash transactions.
7.  Keeping up to date with the latest holiday and travel products through
    training and personal development.
8.  Helping to maintain a safe, friendly and welcoming environment for staff,
    customers and other callers.
9.  Other duties as detailed by the branch manager or other nominated senior
    staff member.


Special conditions

•   Hours of work will be from 9 am to 5.30 pm, five days per week.
•   Saturday working is compulsory, with a weekday off in lieu.
•   Staff are expected to work overtime by arrangement at busy periods of the
    year.
•   Some evening work will be necessary.
•   Salary is in accordance with the company's standard pay scales.
•   The post carries a  holiday entitlement of 20 days per year.
•   On and off-the-job training will be provided for the postholder.


Dated: 1 October 1996
```

Fig. 16.10 Job description for a travel clerk

Person specifications in travel agencies

A person specification, sometimes called a job specification, is normally drawn up at the same time as a job description. Its role is to identify the 'ideal' person for the job to be filled, in terms of experience, skills, character, attributes, qualifications, etc. Figure 16.11 shows an example of a fictitious person specification for the travel clerk's post shown in Figure 16.10.

Person specifications sometimes indicate which selection criteria are essential and which are desirable for any particular post. It may be essential, for example, for an applicant to meet the minimum ABTA staff requirement of two years' relevant experience, but only desirable if he or she has a recognised travel and tourism qualification. In addition to indicating the particular skills and qualities that a successful candidate will need, some person specifications also show how an individual candidate who meets the criteria will be assessed. Qualities such as attention to detail and honesty, for example, may be assessed from references, whereas personal appearance and diction will be gauged at interview. Standards of numeracy and literacy may be assessed with the aid of a written test at interview.

Person specifications are clearly very helpful when recruiting new staff, but they can also help identify gaps in knowledge and skills of existing personnel, highlighting areas for staff training and development.

Assignment 16.2

The personnel requirements of a travel agency

Performance criteria satisfied: 16.2.1, 16.2.2, 16.2.3, 16.2.4, 16.2.5

Core skills opportunities at level 3:   Communication   3.1, 3.2, 3.3, 3.4
Information technology   3.1, 3.2, 3.3
Application of number   3.1, 3.2, 3.3

Situation

You have recently taken up the post of personnel assistant with a major travel agency chain. Part of your induction training is an investigation of the personnel requirements of travel agencies.

Tasks

You are to prepare a written report entitled 'The personnel requirements of travel agencies' for your line manager, Rachel Jones, the senior training officer. In the report, you should:

- Describe the skills and qualities needed by travel agency personnel.
- Explain the training and qualifications available to travel agency staff.
- Explain how travel agencies deploy personnel.
- Explain how trends in employment affect the personnel requirements of travel agencies.

Sundown Travel PLC

Person Specification

Title of post: Travel clerk
Post no: TC/9/96
Location: Anytown branch

Personal qualities

- Good appearance and diction.
- In a good state of health.
- Enthusiasm and willingness to learn.
- Attention to detail.

Character

- Honest and reliable.
- Able to work under pressure and meet deadlines.
- A team player.

Previous experience

- Previous experience of working in an ABTA travel or a retail environment.
- Previous experience of IATA practices.

Qualifications

- Recognised travel and tourism qualifications, e.g. COTAC/ABTAC, BA Fares and Ticketing, BTEC National Diploma, GNVQ Leisure and Tourism.

Skills

- Good numeracy and literacy skills.
- Keyboard skills.
- Good interpersonal skills.
- Sound administrative skills.

Fig. 16.11 Person specification for the post of travel clerk

● Draw up a job description and a person specification for a member of staff in a travel agency.

Your report should be word processed and include relevant charts, diagrams and statistics.

Performance criteria

1. Describe the types of, and explain the need for, filing systems in a travel agency.
2. Describe means of receiving correspondence, and its subsequent distribution.
3. Explain the need for security and confidentiality.
4. Describe the handling process of brochure stocks.
5. Explain how in-store displays should be organised.
6. Describe the processing of customer bookings in a travel agency.

Travel agency filing systems

Staff in travel agencies must be able to respond quickly to enquiries, whether they are from a client, a tour operator or another principal. This calls for an efficient system of filing client documentation and other information, such as country fact sheets and file copies of brochures, timetables, etc. Most agencies still operate manual filing systems, but the popularity of computerised filing systems based on database software is growing rapidly. A filing system can be arranged alphabetically, numerically or in date order. Information on countries, office copies of brochures, timetables, etc., are best filed alphabetically. Numerical filing is favoured by some agencies for clients' bookings, each being assigned a unique reference number and filed accordingly. The majority of agents, however, prefer to organise their client files in date order based on the date of departure. One drawback of this method is that the peak travel months of July and August generate a great deal of paperwork, making it necessary to devote extra space to these months. Filing by date of departure is, nonetheless, preferred by most travel agencies.

Some agencies further refine their client filing system according to the status of the booking, with separate sections for:

1. *Initial enquiries* – written record of a client's first contact.
2. *Options* – details of a client who has taken out an option on a booking.
3. *Confirmations* – clients who have paid a deposit.
4. *Final payments* – bookings on which the balance has been paid.
5. *Awaiting tickets* – clients who are awaiting their tickets and vouchers.
6. *Refunds due* – any clients who are due a refund on their payments.

With this system, clients' files are moved from one section to another according to their current status. This way, a member of staff can see at any one time the progress of a client's booking. Client files are normally kept for up to two years, although new rules for self-assessment of income tax insist on longer periods of time. Files that are no longer current are referred to as 'dead files' or 'closed files' and are stored in an archive in case they are needed for any claims that may be made.

Storage of files

The most common method of storage is in filing cabinets with suspension files. These are excellent for paper documents, such as copies of booking forms, receipts, options forms, etc. Bulkier material, including maps and country information, is best stored in strong box files on shelving. Contact telephone numbers and addresses of clients are sometimes stored on index cards, filed by client surname. These can be actual cards stored in a box or details entered on a card file on a computer.

Activity

Carry out some research in a travel agency with which you are familiar and find out what filing systems they use and the types of material stored in each system.

Receiving and distributing correspondence

Travel agencies receive and generate a wide variety of correspondence in the course of their normal trading activities, including:

- Brochures
- Other promotional materials, e.g. posters, leaflets, price lists, etc.
- Booking forms
- Invoices
- Letters
- Notifications of special offers, late availability, etc.

Much of this will arrive via the postal service, although brochure stocks will normally be delivered by specialist courier and distribution companies, such as BP Travel Trade Services (see case study in Element 22.2 on page 314). On-screen information, fax transmissions and electronic mail (e-mail) are also popular ways of receiving and distributing information, particularly between agents and principals. All staff should be briefed on current offers and products so that they can provide the best possible service to their customers. The travel supervisor will generally be responsible for distributing information to the relevant members of staff. Correspondence relating to clients' holiday and travel plans will be dealt with accordingly, with copies being placed in the appropriate office files.

Security and confidentiality in travel agencies

Like all commercial enterprises, travel agencies need to constantly monitor their operations in respect of security threats and breaches of confidentiality. It is important for the owners and managers of agencies to address a number of security hazards, relating to the security of premises, systems for handling and storing money and other valuables, the safety of staff and customers, and the security of information. Government legislation on health and safety at work places a duty on the operators of travel agencies to provide a safe environment for staff, customers and all other people visiting their premises.

All retail premises need to be made secure against burglars, and travel agencies are no exception. Attention to external security is very important and may include:

- Fitting security locks to doors and windows, and window bars to high-risk areas such as equipment stores.
- Using closed circuit television (CCTV) or employing security personnel to monitor large areas including car parks and staff and public entrances and exits.
- Installing invisible beams and pressure pads in passageways and entrances to activate alarms.
- Fitting intruder alarms which, for large organisations, should be capable of alerting a central monitoring station which operates 24 hours a day.
- Introducing card access control using PIN systems to identify which parts of a building are for staff access only.
- Installing security lighting, particularly in high-risk areas.
- Providing panic alarms for staff.

Inside the premises, attention will need to be paid to the secure storage of money, passports, travellers' cheques, foreign exchange, travel tickets and other valuables, as well as staff possessions and confidential information about clients, whether held manually or on computer. A strong safe is an essential item of security equipment for all travel agencies and is often a requirement for the granting of an agency licence with a principal or association, e.g. IATA.

Handling money

Staff in travel agencies handle cash and other forms of payment on a regular basis. Common methods of paying for holidays and other travel products include the use of credit cards, charge cards, debit cards and cheques, supported by cheque guarantee cards. When handling cash, staff should always follow these simple procedures:

- Count the amount in front of the customer.
- Take care to give the right amount of change; it is good practice, when a note is given in payment, to leave it outside the till until the change has been given, to avoid claims that a higher value note was tendered.
- Check that notes are genuine; some travel agencies have now installed equipment to detect fake notes.
- Ensure that tills and cash boxes are not left unattended for long periods.

- Make sure that tills are emptied overnight and that cash is locked securely in a safe or deposited in a bank.

When accepting payment by cheque, it is important to reduce the risk of fraud by checking:

1. That the date on the cheque is correct.
2. That the amount in words and figures agree.
3. That the amount is within the cheque guarantee card limit.
4. That the signature on the cheque matches that on the cheque guarantee card.
5. That the code numbers on the cheque and the cheque guarantee card are the same.
6. That the cheque is signed in front of the payee.
7. That the cheque guarantee card has not expired.

Increasingly, customers in travel agencies are using credit and debit cards in preference to cash and cheques, for reasons of security and convenience. Once again, simple procedures should be followed by staff, including checking that:

- The card is one that is accepted by the agency.
- The card has not expired.
- The card is not on a list of stolen or lost cards.
- The card has the same name as the customer.
- Whether the card requires authorisation from the credit/debit card company before use.
- That details on any vouchers completed by staff are correctly entered.
- That the customer's signature matches that on the card.

Security of information

All travel agencies carry a variety of sensitive and confidential information about their clients, employees and business operations. In the competitive world of travel and tourism, guarding commercially sensitive business information is an important consideration. No travel agent in a town would want his or her competitors to know about sales performance and revenue. It is for this reason that contracts of employment often contain a clause about not disclosing commercial information to third parties. This point should be reinforced at staff induction sessions.

The two main security hazards associated with client information and business records are fire and theft. Twenty years ago, all business records would have been held entirely on paper. Today, information is held on a variety of other formats including microfiche, computer disks, photographic materials and audio/video tapes. These are all vulnerable to the twin threats of fire and theft and do not inherently offer any greater security than paper. Computers, however, do give the option of storing information on 'floppy disks', which can be stored securely away from the main computer terminal, thus reducing the risk of losing information in the event of theft or fire. All computer and other sensitive information should be routinely locked in safes or fire-proof data protection cabinets kept in controlled access rooms.

The storage of information on computers raises the issue of the Data Protection Act 1984. This Act was introduced to safeguard the public from problems relating to the inaccuracy of any information held about them on computer records.

Data Protection Act

This government legislation was introduced in 1984 to safeguard the public from problems relating to the inaccuracy of any information held about them on computer records. Under the terms of the Act, all organisations that hold data about individuals on automated systems must register with the Data Protection Registrar and comply with a series of Data Protection Principles, which are a set of good practice guidelines. Individuals who have computer data held on them have a number of rights in civil law, including right of access to the data, rights to compensation for inaccuracy of data or its wrongful disclosure, and rights to have any inaccuracies in the data rectified. Travel agencies that hold client details on computer databases are likely to fall within the scope of the Act and must abide by the Data Protection Principles. One of the Principles states that the information held on computer must not be disclosed to third parties. This means that a travel agent who holds information on clients on a computer cannot sell the data to another company without being in contravention of the Act.

Activity

While on work experience, carry out an investigation of your travel agency to find out what security measures are in place in relation to the premises, the staff, taking payments and the security of information.

Brochure stocks

Elements 19.2 and 22.2 show us that brochures play a vital role in the promotion and sale of holidays and other travel products sold in agencies. The brochure is the travel agent's prime sales tool and is the mechanism by which a customer's enquiry is, hopefully, turned into a sale. The high costs of designing, printing and distributing brochures means that tour operators and other principals keep firm control on which agencies receive brochure stocks and in what quantities. The agencies with the best track record of selling a company's products will receive regular bulk supplies and command special treatment, including extra incentives for travel agency staff and management to encourage even more sales. Agencies with smaller sales volumes will still be sent brochure stocks, but on a smaller scale. In all cases, the tour operator will ensure that the agency has a file copy of the latest brochure as soon as possible after printing, in advance of the bulk supplies being delivered.

Bulk supplies of brochures are sent to agents in a variety of ways. The mass market tour operators generally have their own distribution departments and networks, whereas smaller operators may use specialist distribution firms, such as BP Travel Trade Services (see case study on page 314). Brochure distribution is sometimes graded on a regional basis, where agencies close to airports used by a tour operator are handled separately.

When bulk brochure supplies arrive at the agency, there is often a problem in deciding where to store them. All agencies will have an area set aside for storage, but at certain times of the year this may be overloaded. An alternative 'overflow' area should be identified, bearing in mind the safety of staff and customers. Either way, there should be a workable method of storing the brochures, using an alphabetical system that will enable staff to locate a particular brochure when required. Brochures should never be left in piles on the floor of the main selling area of the travel agency. Apart from looking very untidy, there are clear issues concerning fire regulations and health and safety legislation.

Agencies sometimes delegate the task of brochure stock control and re-ordering to a specific member of staff, in order to minimise the chances of running out of supplies. Agencies should, without fail, always keep an office copy of every brochure they sell so that, should the bulk supplies run out, staff will at least have one copy for reference. Nowadays, brochure re-ordering is often handled via the viewdata screens, but brochures can also be ordered by fax and over the telephone.

In-store displays

Point-of-sale materials, such as window displays and free-standing displays in the main body of a travel agency, play an important role in promoting holidays and other travel products. They should be changed on a regular basis to provide customers with a new 'focal point' and as a way of alerting clients to new products and special offers. Displays should, at all times, look professional and tidy. The use of handwritten signs and posters should be avoided, since they do little to enhance the image of the product being sold or the agency as a whole.

Activity

Working in teams of two, visit some travel agencies in your local area and study their window displays. Make a note of any good features you notice and any points that would benefit from improvement. Suggest ways in which the improvements could be carried out.

Processing bookings

Travel agencies sell a wide variety of holidays and other travel products, including airline tickets, short breaks, car hire, coach holidays, holiday centres, rail tickets, etc. Travel agencies will have contractual agreements with a range of principals whose products they sell. Each principal will have its own methods of accounting and handling bookings, although there are common elements to the processing of bookings by travel agencies, as shown in Figure 16.12.

Figure 16.12 indicates that the process starts with an initial enquiry to the agent from

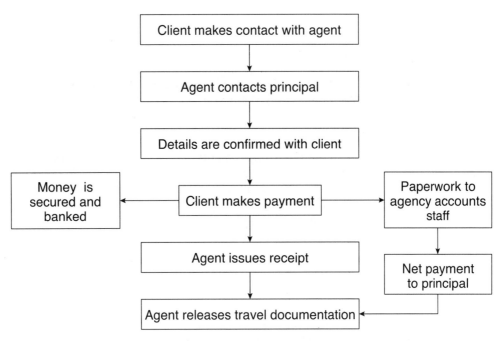

Fig. 16.12 Stages in the processing of customer bookings

a customer. This may be face-to-face in the agency or over the telephone; a small number of enquiries may also come by fax. Except in the case of certain products that an agent can sell without contacting the travel company (known as 'freesale'), e.g. some coach tickets, theatre tickets, rail tickets, etc., the next stage in the booking process will be for the agent to contact the principal to check availability. This may be by telephone, but nowadays more commonly by computer, especially with package holiday bookings and airline flights. Details are next confirmed with the client who, if happy with the details, makes a payment to the agent. Depending on when the client is due to travel, this may be the full amount or a deposit. Payment may be made by cash, credit card, charge card, debit card, banker's draft, money order or cheque accompanied by a cheque guarantee card, for which a receipt is issued by the travel agent. The relevant paperwork is sent for processing by the accounts staff in the agency, while the payment and/or counterfoil is secured for banking. The net payment is sent to the principal, which releases the travel documents to the agent for distribution to the client. Copies of all relevant documentation will be filed for future reference.

Assignment 16.3

Administrative procedures in travel agencies

Performance criteria satisfied: 16.3.1, 16.3.2, 16.3.3, 16.3.4, 16.3.5, 16.3.6

Core skills opportunities at level 3:   Communication   3.1, 3.2, 3.3, 3.4
                                        Information technology   3.1, 3.2, 3.3
                                        Application of number   3.1, 3.2, 3.3

Situation

You have recently joined a travel company that has 23 branches spread throughout Scotland. You are employed as a junior executive in the training section, working with the training manager Josie Murray, who has overall responsibility for the training and personal development of some 95 staff, including head office personnel.

Tasks

Josie has asked you to research and compile a training booklet for new staff working in the company's travel agencies. The booklet will focus on the administrative procedures followed by travel agencies in general and will provide a useful first step in how the company handles this part of its work. Specifically, the booklet should:

- Describe the need for filing systems in a travel agency and explain the different types available.
- Describe the means of receiving correspondence and its subsequent distribution.
- Explain the need for security and confidentiality in travel agencies.
- Describe how brochure stocks are handled in a travel agency.
- Explain how in-store displays are organised.
- Describe how customer bookings are handled in travel agencies.

Your booklet should be written in a lively style appropriate to the intended audience and should include relevant tables, diagrams and statistics.

Unit 17

LEISURE TRAVEL SERVICES

Element 17.1
Investigate the development and structure of leisure travel services

Element 17.2
Investigate the package holiday and its market

Element 17.3
Investigate the process of making a package holiday booking in a retail travel agency

Element 17.1 Investigate the development and structure of leisure travel services

> **Performance criteria**
>
> 1. Explain the structure of the leisure travel industry.
> 2. Describe, with examples, the principal products and services provided by the leisure travel services industry.
> 3. Explain the key activities of a UK tour operator.
> 4. Explain the key activities of a UK retail travel agency.

The structure of the leisure travel industry

The leisure travel industry is an important sector of the UK travel and tourism industry that exists to meet the travel needs of people travelling for leisure, as opposed to business, purposes. It includes the multiple travel agency chains, such as Lunn Poly and Going Places, independent travel agencies, major tour operators, including Airtours and First Choice Holidays and specialist tour operators, plus a range of other professionals who provide support services to the sector, such as ground handling agents and tour guides. A good way of illustrating the breadth of the leisure travel industry is to consider the wide variety of employment opportunities it offers, which include:

- Travel consultants in travel agencies
- Reservations staff in tour operators
- Green Badge (local) and Blue Badge (regional) Guides working in UK towns and cities
- Overseas resort representatives
- Children's couriers
- Product managers for tour operators
- Stewards on a leisure travel airline
- Tour managers based in the UK or overseas
- Owners of incoming tour operating businesses

These jobs show that, in most instances, people working in the leisure travel industry are primarily concerned with providing intermediary services to the travelling public. The structure of the leisure travel industry is shown in Figure 17.1, which demonstrates that the leisure travel industry comprises three interrelated elements: travel agencies, tour operators and the providers of a variety of support services.

The multiple travel agencies are the high street chains, for example Lunn Poly, Going Places, Thomas Cook and A T Mays. 'Miniple' agencies are those with a small

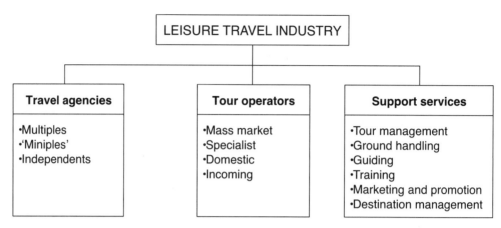

Fig. 17.1 The structure of the leisure travel industry

number of branches, e.g. British Airways Travel Shops with 19 branches and STA travel with 23 outlets. Miniples are sometimes clustered in the same region, for example West Midlands Co-op with 25 branches. The remainder of the 7000 travel agency branches found in the UK are independent agencies, usually with a single retail outlet under the direction of the owner/proprietor. Travel agents are in business to sell the holidays of the tour operators and a range of travel products from a variety of other principals, e.g. airline tickets, car hire, coach tickets, theatre tickets, travel insurance, etc. The majority of UK travel agents are members of ABTA (the Association of British Travel Agents), a self-regulating trade body (see case study in Element 16.1 on page 15).

Tour operators assemble the components of a holiday and offer the final product direct to the customer or through a travel agent. Their most popular product is the package holiday, sometimes referred to as an inclusive tour (IT), which combines accommodation, transportation and other travel services for an all-inclusive price (see Figure 17.2).

Mass market operators, such as Thomson, Inspirations, Airtours and First Choice Holidays, provide the bulk of the holidays bought by British travellers. The three biggest operators, Thomson, Airtours and First Choice, together account for 60 per cent of the total market for inclusive tours by air (AITs). A larger number of smaller, specialist tour operators provide a variety of products for individual markets, e.g. self-drive camping holidays on the continent, winter ski programmes, adventure travel and heritage tours. AITO (the Association of Independent Tour Operators) is the trade body representing the interests of smaller, independent operators (see case study in Element 19.2 on page 163). Domestic operators offer holidays and other travel products in the UK, including coach holidays, packages to UK hotels, short breaks, activity and special interest tours and farm holidays. Incoming tour operators specialise in meeting the travel needs of the increasing numbers of overseas visitors to Britain. There are some 300 incoming tour operators in this country that offer a range of services, from complete package tours of the UK to a 'meet and greet' service on behalf of an agent or operator. Examples of incoming tour operators based in the UK are British Heritage Tours, Frames Rickards and Evan Evans Tours. A third of all UK incoming tour operators are members of BITOA (the British Incoming Tour

Fig. 17.2 Inclusive tours by air are the tour operators' main product (reproduced courtesy of Airtours)

Operators' Association), an independent organisation that aims to provide a forum for the exchange of information and ideas, to follow an accepted code of conduct and to act as a pressure group in dealing with other bodies in the UK with a common interest in tourism matters.

The range of support services in the UK leisure travel industry includes tour management and ground handling, when companies or individuals provide a service to tourists on behalf of tour companies. e.g. transfers from airport to hotels and sightseeing tours of major towns and cities. Registered guides offer tours of town and country areas by coach, car or on foot. Private and public sector organisations offer training opportunities for staff working in the leisure travel industry, including courses leading to National Vocational Qualifications (NVQs). Marketing and promotion services are provided to support the work of travel agencies and tour operators by merchandising companies, market research specialists, distribution companies, advertising agencies, PR specialists, exhibition companies, etc. Public sector bodies have a responsibility to provide a clean, safe and secure environment for tourists once they have reached their chosen destination area.

Activity

Carry out some research to find out the names of variety of UK domestic tour operators and the details of the products they sell.

Position in the UK travel and tourism industry

We have highlighted the various components of the leisure travel industry in the UK, but it is important to illustrate where leisure travel fits in the overall travel and tourism industry. The very broad nature of travel and tourism makes any illustration of the linkages between its different components difficult, given the many different industry sectors. Figure 17.3 shows that the leisure travel industry works in conjunction with the core components of the travel and tourism industry – namely, accommodation, transportation, attractions and destinations – to provide tourists with a range of leisure travel products and services.

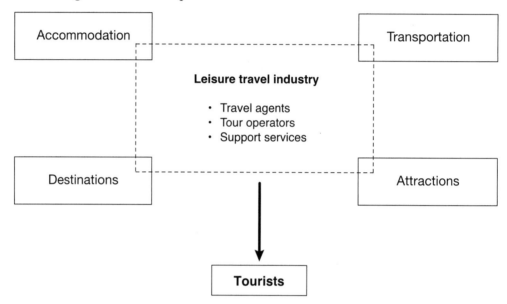

Fig. 17.3 The position of the leisure travel industry

Leisure travel products and services

Glancing at the wide variety of brochures in travel agencies, not to mention the travel advertisements in newspapers, magazines and on television, it is easy to assume that there is a travel company somewhere that will provide a product or service to meet any need, no matter how unusual. Everything from ballooning across the Victoria Falls to mountain biking in Majorca, scuba diving in the Seychelles to sampling whisky in Scottish distilleries, are all available to UK travellers, as long as they know where to look! This is where the expertise of the tour operator and skill of the travel agent come into their own. Both fulfil a number of important functions, for example:

● They offer specialist knowledge and advice – in the same way that you might ask a plumber to fix a leaking pipe rather than trying to do it yourself, travel agents and tour operators are specialists in their field, many with years of valuable experience about countries, health requirements for travellers and the various travel options open to the client.

- They have access to up-to-date information – by using reference manuals and computer databases, they can quickly find information on travel services that is not readily available to members of the general public. New technology gives travel agents direct access to the computer systems of airlines and tour operators.
- They have the ability to negotiate discounts – in return for a guaranteed volume of business with the suppliers of travel services, travel agents and tour operators can offer reduced rates to their clients, for such items as hotel and airline bookings.
- They offer security to their clients – companies that are registered with industry associations such as the Association of British Travel Agents (ABTA) or the Association of Independent Tour Operators (AITO) offer travellers financial security in the event of a company failure.
- They offer an 'after-sales service' – most good travel agents and tour operators understand that their service does not finish when the product has been sold. A travel agent, for example, may well contact clients soon after their return from holiday, to find out if everything went according to plan. Apart from anything else, this is good PR for the agency.

Travel agents, tour operators and the providers of travel support services work in partnership to provide a wide variety of leisure travel products to meet customer needs. The main products offered by tour operators are package holidays and flight-only sales. These are looked at in more detail in Element 19.2. Travel agents are in business to sell the tour operators' products, including package holidays and short breaks, but they also offer a wide range of other services, including:

- Foreign exchange
- Visa and passport information
- Car hire
- Travel insurance
- Coach tickets
- Theatre tickets
- Rail tickets
- Hotel bookings
- Holiday centre products

These products and services were investigated in Element 16.1.

Activity

While on work experience in a travel agency, make a list of the leisure travel products and services on offer. How have these changed in the last 10 years?

Key activities of UK tour operators

Unit 19 looks in detail at the role and structure of the different types of UK-based tour operators and how they carry out their functions, both in the UK and abroad. The key activity of a tour operator is to organise inclusive tours (ITs) to a variety of domestic and international destinations, and sell them at a profit. In the travel industry, they take on the role of a wholesaler, since they buy their 'raw materials' in bulk, e.g. aircraft seats and hotel bedspaces, and break the bulk into manageable products, i.e. the package holidays themselves. These are then sold to customers by travel agents, the retail outlets. Some operators, known as direct sell, do not make their products available through travel agents, but prefer to sell direct to the public. The main types of tour operators found in the UK are:

- Mass market operators – e.g. Thomson, First Choice Holidays, Airtours, etc.
- Specialist operators – e.g. Vacances Franco-Britannique (VFB), Himalayan Kingdoms
- Domestic operators – companies that specialise in tours in Britain, e.g. Rainbow Holidays, YHA Holidays, etc.
- Incoming tour operators – companies that specialise in tours of Britain for overseas visitors, e.g. Evan Evans, British Heritage Tours, etc.

Many UK tour operators are members of trade associations, including the Association of British Travel Agents (ABTA), Association of Independent Tour Operators (AITO) or the British Incoming Tour Operators' Association (BITOA).

A typical mass market outbound tour operator will have a main UK head office, regional offices and overseas offices. The UK head office will be organised on a departmental basis in order to carry out the following key activities:

1. *Marketing* – staff employed in the marketing department will be responsible for planning and developing products, which will be aimed at particular segments of the market. They will focus on the selection of resorts, choice of accommodation and selection of regional UK departure airports. Typical segments of the market include:
   - Singles
   - Families
   - Couples without children
   - Disabled travellers
   - Groups
   - Business travellers
   - Youth market
   - Elderly travellers
2. *Market research* – a great deal of background research is undertaken to ensure that the products have the best chance of meeting their sales potential. Sources of research material include internal sales data, external sales data available from commercial sources, analysis of competitors' programmes, analyses of customer satisfaction questionnaires (CSQs) and financial analyses
3. *Contracting* – once the structure of the programme is finalised, staff in the contracts department will negotiate with accommodation providers to finalise the number of beds and names of accommodations required.
4. *Flights* – teams working on different programmes and products liaise with the flight or aviation department over how many seats they will need, which regional airports are to be used and whether day or night flights are required. The flight department must make optimum use of its resources.

5. *Brochure production* – the brochure is the most visible part of the tour operator's sales and marketing process. Teams working in the marketing department will work with brochure production staff to finalise design, copy and photographs. Some brochures are printed outside the UK to save on costs.
6. *Brochure distribution* – sales staff will make decisions about how many brochures are required and to which travel agents they will be distributed. Agents with the best 'track record' for sales will receive regular bulk supplies and preferential sales treatment from the tour operator.
7. *Promotion* – marketing staff will plan and co-ordinate a range of activities including advertising, direct mail, sales promotion, merchandising and PR.
8. *Reservations* – systems are developed by computer operations personnel and sales staff are fully briefed on the features of products included in the brochure before they go on sale.
9. *Agency sales support* – sales representatives will regularly visit agencies and offer product training and POS (point-of-sale) materials, such as posters and window displays.
10. *Administration* – the administration department is responsible for producing invoices, receiving payments and issuing tickets and other documentation to agents for distribution to clients.
11. *Customer services* – this department will be responsible for handling complaints and queries from agents and members of the public. They will try to ensure that all matters are dealt with quickly and efficiently in order to retain goodwill.

The overseas office of a major tour operator will be responsible for:

- Feeding back to head office any formal or informal research findings.
- Organising transfers to and from the accommodation and airport.
- Selling and arranging excursions and other 'extras' such as car hire.
- Finalising contracts with hoteliers and transport operators.
- The well-being, training and deployment of representatives.
- The handling of complaints and emergencies.

A tour operator's main source of income is the payment it receives from clients for its products. This revenue may come direct from the customer if it is a 'direct sell' company, or, more usually, through a travel agent that sells the holiday on behalf of the operator. A large tour operator such as Airtours may have a number of separate operating divisions, each of which will contribute to overall group profits; Airtours owns its own airline, runs camping holidays under the EuroSites brand and operates a chain of travel agencies under the Going Places banner. Mass market tour operators will usually offer a range of holiday products catering for different sectors of the market. Although this range will vary from time to time in response to fluctuating demand, there are likely to be a series of brochures, which may include:

- A main summer sun programme
- A winter sun programme
- A winter ski programme
- City breaks
- Flight-only packages
- Programmes featuring particular countries or regions, e.g. the Caribbean, Greece, Turkey, etc.

- Holidays geared to the youth market
- Programmes for 'seniors'
- Budget holidays
- Specialist programmes, e.g. golf, cruising or sailing

Activity

Working with another member of your group, investigate the range of holiday and travel products offered by a major, mass market tour operator of your choice.

Other sources of income to tour operators include:

1. *Interest on money held in account* – deposits for holidays are sometimes paid up to 12 months before departure and balances settled 6–8 weeks before the start of the holiday. This money accumulates for the tour operator and attracts interest.
2. *Commission on 'extras'* – commission for items such as car hire, insurance, flight-only and excursions is generally paid direct to the tour operator. Most operators will offer their own insurance and car hire in their brochures, hoping to benefit from the high commission levels that these two products attract.
3. *Currency dealing* – large operators may buy foreign currency in advance if rates are favourable to use later for payments to suppliers. Surplus funds can be invested to provide a return.
4. *Vertical integration* – tour operators that have financial interests at more than one level of the distribution chain, can generate income from a greater number of sources and spread costs, e.g. duty-free sales on aircraft and hotel bar sales.
5. *Charges* – tour operators levy charges for cancellations and amendments to holiday arrangements.

Key activities of UK travel agencies

We saw in Unit 16 that the prime objective of travel agencies is to sell holidays and other travel products and services profitably, while maintaining the highest standards of customer care. There are more than 7000 ABTA travel agency branches in the UK, some part of multiple chains, others owned and managed as independent units. In recent years, there has been a significant growth in multiple travel agencies at the expense of independent agents. Lunn Poly is an excellent example of this so-called 'march of the multiples' (see Figure 17.4).

At the time of writing, the 'big three' multiple agencies in terms of number of branches are:

1. Lunn Poly
2. Going Places
3. Thomas Cook

Thomson Travel estimates of the market shares of the top five travel agency chains are given in Figure 17.5.

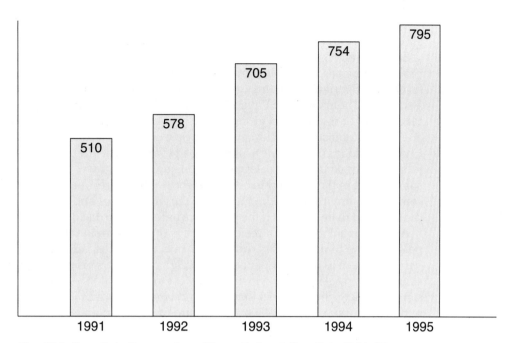

Fig. 17.4 Growth in the number of Lunn Poly retail outlets 1991–95 (source: Thomson Travel Group)

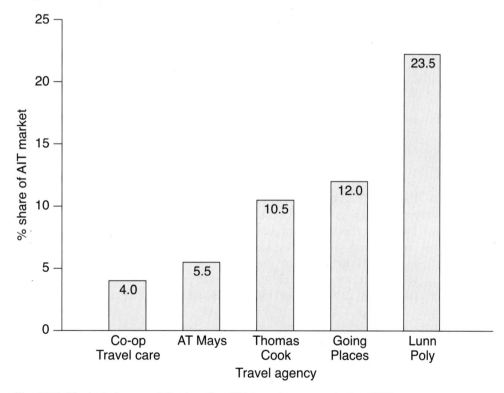

Fig. 17.5 Market shares of the top five UK travel agency chains 1995 (source: Thomson Travel Group)

The statistics in this figure indicate that Lunn Poly has nearly twice the share of the air inclusive tour (AIT) market of its nearest rival, Going Places.

Each of the 'big three' multiples has a close alliance with a major tour operator, a process known as vertical integration (one company having control of more than one level of the distribution chain). Lunn Poly is part of the Thomson Travel Group, which also owns Thomson Tour Operations, the UK's number one tour operator; Going Places, part of the Airtours group, is the new trading name for the former Pickfords and Hogg Robinson agencies; and Thomas Cook has a 'strategic alliance' with First Choice Holidays (formerly Owners Abroad). Vertical integration of this sort, when a tour operator controls the sales policy of its own retail travel agencies, is thought by some people in the industry to be against the public interest, as it could lead to an anti-competitive environment. In such cases the Monopolies and Mergers' Commission can be asked to investigate if the public are indeed being disadvantaged.

A travel agent's main source of income is the commission it receives from principals, such as tour operators, hotels, car hire companies, airlines, etc. Commission varies between as little as 1 per cent on foreign currency transactions up to as much as 40 per cent on sales of travel insurance. Most tour operators pay 10 per cent commission on package holidays, so that an agent would receive £150 for booking a holiday with a brochure price of £1500. This figure of £150 is not clear profit for the agent, however, since it does not take account of overheads such as staff costs, heating, postage and telephone charges. Once these costs have been accounted for, most travel agents will make on average only 1 per cent net profit over the course of a year's trading. Put another way, an independent travel agent who has recently set up in business and is hoping to make a net profit which is equivalent to the salary of £18,000 per year that was earned in his or her last job, would need to achieve sales of £1,800,000.

Although commission is by far the biggest source of income, travel agents can also earn revenue from arranging their own tours. This practice is becoming an increasingly common way of injecting extra income into the business, while at the same time giving clients a more personal service than they might receive on a standard package tour. It is important to remember, however, that such activities fall within the scope of the EU Package Travel Directive, since the travel agent is, in effect, becoming the organiser of a tour (see Element 19.1 for more on the Package Travel Directive).

Another important source of funds for travel agents is the interest gained on any money held on behalf of principals. Deposits and balances paid by clients may stay in the agent's account for some time, thus accruing interest. It is generally in the agent's interest to negotiate a credit rather than cash arrangement with principals. This gives the agent the benefit of simpler administrative procedures and, more importantly, credit agents can hold on to clients' payments longer. Some agents supplement their income in other ways, for example, by selling luggage and other travel goods, running training courses or teaching on evening classes, writing a regular column in a local paper, appearing on local radio or selling maps and guide books.

Assignment 17.1

The development and structure of leisure travel services

Performance criteria satisfied: 17.1.1, 17.1.2, 17.1.3, 17.1.4

Core skills opportunities at level 3:   Communication   3.1, 3.2, 3.3, 3.4
Information technology   3.1, 3.2, 3.3
Application of number   3.1, 3.2, 3.3

Situation

While on work experience with Jimmy Booth, the regional sales manager of a major travel agency chain, you have been asked to help him prepare for a speech he is due to make to his local Rotary Club.

Tasks

You are asked to prepare the draft of the speech for Jimmy on the subject 'The development and structure of leisure travel services'. Your draft should focus on:

- The structure of the leisure travel industry.
- The main products and services provided by the leisure travel industry.
- The key activities of UK tour operators.
- The key activities of UK retail travel agencies.

You should also produce a detailed diagram of the structure of the leisure travel industry, for use as a visual aid during the speech.

Element 17.2   Investigate the package holiday and its market

> **Performance criteria**
>
> 1. Explain the development of the package holiday market in the UK.
> 2. Describe the components of a package holiday.
> 3. Explain, with examples, market segmentation for package holidays.
> 4. Describe the needs of a package holiday customer.

The development of the package holiday market

Vladimir Raitz of Horizon Holidays (now part of Thomson Tour Operations) is credited with having organised the first modern package holiday from the UK, when he carried a party of holidaymakers to Corsica in 1950. This first modern inclusive tour included full-board accommodation in tents and travel in a 32-seater DC3 aircraft; things have moved on a lot since those days! Not that package holidays were totally new in the 1950s. The pioneering work of Thomas Cook, who in 1841 organised an excursion from Leicester to Loughborough for his local Temperance Association, was an early indication of things to come. Within 15 years of this first excursion, Cook was running a fully commercial travel company arranging tours and excursions both at home and overseas, including the Great Exhibition in London in 1851 and inclusive tours to the Paris Exhibition in 1855. In 1872, Thomas Cook offered a round the world trip, including stopovers at India, Singapore and Hong Kong, and using a variety of travel methods, including paddle steamer, steam ship across the Atlantic, stage coach and rail. His son, John Cook, took over the business in 1879 and, with his three grandsons, carried on the business into the twentieth century.

Developments after 1945

The ending of the Second World War heralded the beginning of a positive climate for the development of travel for leisure purposes in general, and package holidays in particular, in the UK. A number of factors contributed to this situation, including:

- Increased prosperity once the war had ended.
- Greater exposure to mass media, including television, creating a desire to travel.
- Increased paid holiday entitlements for workers.
- Better standards of education.
- The end of rationing in 1954.

These factors, coupled with technological improvements in aircraft design and spare aircraft capacity, led to a surge in demand for overseas travel. Much of this demand could not be met initially, resulting in the growth of holidays and day trips in the UK, where holiday camps and seaside resorts prospered. The introduction of the Boeing 707 jet aircraft in 1958, however, led to a surge in scheduled and charter flights, the latter being combined with accommodation and other travel services to form the package holiday that is so familiar to us all in the 1990s.

The growth in the package holiday market

From the first modern inclusive tour to Corsica in 1950, the demand for package holidays grew steadily in the 1960s. By 1965, there were more than 1 million air inclusive tours (AITs) from the UK to European destinations and this number had risen to more than 3 million at the beginning of the 1970s. There were, however, some casualties resulting from the growth. Fiesta Tours was declared bankrupt in 1964, leaving its clients stranded in Spain, and Omar Khayyam Tours went bust in 1965. In response to the growing problem of company failures brought on by fierce price cutting, a group of the leading tour operators established the Tour Operators' Study Group (TOSG) in 1967 to protect members' interests and discuss matters of common concern. In 1970, the members of the TOSG, which incidentally still exists today under the umbrella of ABTA, decided that bonding should be introduced to offer holidaymakers a degree of protection when an operator collapsed.

The most significant event of the 1970s in the tour operating industry was the collapse of Court Line in 1974, taking the Clarkson and Horizon brands with it. The fact that the number one tour operator of the time had gone into liquidation sent shock waves through the industry and the travelling public alike. The collapse was an early, and stern, test of the bonding system recently put in place. Notwithstanding these company failures, demand for package holidays grew steadily in the 1980s and has continued into the 1990s (see Figure 17.6). The failure of the International Leisure Group (ILG) in 1991, best known for its Intasun tour operating division, was a further stark reminder of the fragility of the ex-UK tour operating industry.

Activity

Carry out some further research into the reasons for the rapid growth in the number of package holidays taken by British people since the 1980s.

Components of a package holiday

The providers of package holidays assemble their constituent components into a saleable product that meets the needs and expectations of the customer. All package holidays will differ in their make-up, but we can identify three distinct components:

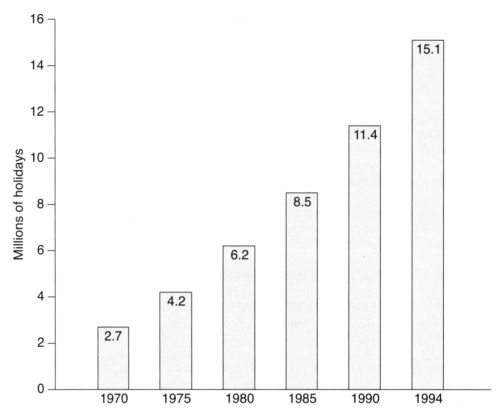

*Fig. 17.6 **Overseas package holidays taken by UK residents*** *(source: ABTA Information Bureau)*

- Accommodation
- Transportation
- Other travel services

Each of these elements will be considered in the following sections.

Accommodation

The accommodation component of the tour operator's package can be either serviced or self-catering. There has been a steady growth in the demand for self-catering holidays over the last 10–15 years, with a rise from 27 to 38 per cent of the summer package holiday market between 1989 and 1995, according to data from Stats MR, an independent market research organisation. Serviced accommodation is usually in a hotel that can offer a range of meal arrangements, including:

- Full board (sometimes called American plan), which means that three meals are provided.
- Half board (or modified American plan), which on overseas package holidays usually refers to breakfast plus either a midday or evening meal.
- Bed and breakfast (sometimes called Continental plan).

Hotels in some parts of the world do not include any meals in their standard room rates, an arrangement sometimes known as European plan. This is common in certain parts of Europe, the USA and the Far East. Customers can usually request a room with extra facilities or a particular aspect for the payment of a supplementary charge, e.g. a room with a sea view or a ground floor room.

Self-catering can be in a wide range of accommodation, such as:

- Studios
- Villas
- Apartments
- Tents
- Caravans/mobile homes
- Boats

Self-catering accommodation will usually come complete with cooking facilities and utensils, although many people often choose to eat out and avoid household chores. Some self-catering accommodation will include a maid service, either included in the price or on payment of a supplement.

Transportation

The transport element of a package holiday can be travel by:

- Air
- Coach
- Rail
- Ship
- Self-drive car

Whichever type of transport is used, the tour operator will be offered preferential, discounted rates, known as inclusive tour (IT) rates. Depending on the volume of business generated, a ferry company, for example, can offer a tour operator prices that may be discounted by as much as 50 per cent of their standard tariff. It is increasingly common for tour operators to offer their clients free or discounted travel on public transport within the UK to their departure point.

Three-quarters of all package holidays sold in the UK use air travel to transport clients to their chosen destinations. These air inclusive tours (AITs) use either chartered or scheduled services; package holidays that use seats on charter aircraft are known as inclusive tours by charter (ITC), while those based on scheduled services are referred to as inclusive tours by excursion (ITX). Aircraft may be chartered for specific flights or for blocks of time, usually a whole year or for the duration of a season. This is known as time series charter and is financially more attractive than 'ad hoc' arrangements. Many tour operators will charter their aircraft on a flight series basis, contracting for the same time and destination each week, for example. By using flight series charters and setting very high load factors for each flight (the percentage of seats that needs to be filled before the operator starts to make a profit), tour operators have been able to keep prices down and stimulate demand. It is not uncommon for an operator to set a break-even load factor as high as 85-90 per cent.

One disadvantage of flight series charters is that there will inevitably be an empty flight home at the beginning of the season and an empty flight out at the end of the season. These flights are referred to as 'empty legs'. In order to maximise capacity, some travel companies will operate a 'bus stop' arrangement, whereby an aircraft will take off from one UK airport, say Manchester, but stop at another, perhaps East Midlands, to pick up passengers, before flying on to its final destination airport. If bookings from one particular regional airport are low, the tour operator may decide to consolidate, i.e. cancel the flight altogether and transfer the passengers by coach to another departure airport.

Other travel services

Apart from accommodation and transport, package holidays will usually include other services, which may include:

● Transfers to and from accommodation and point of entry (see Figure 17.7).
● The services of a representative
● Car hire
● Excursions
● Equipment hire, e.g. skis, hammocks, bicycles, etc.
● Insurance

Depending on the number of passengers, transfers will be by taxi, minibus or, most commonly nowadays, coach. Operators will schedule flight arrivals so that maximum use can be made of coaches, without undue delay being caused to clients.

Fig. 17.7 Transfer coach at Palma Airport (reproduced courtesy of Airtours)

Resort representatives ('reps') will provide information and support for their clients, deal with any emergencies, arrange excursions and generally ensure the smooth running of the holiday while the clients are in the resort. Many reps will only be employed for the duration of the season, either summer or winter, with some returning to work at head office out of season.

Activity

Carry out a small-scale survey to find out what people like and dislike about package holidays. Based on the results of your survey, how might the component parts of overseas and domestic package holidays be improved?

Market segmentation

Everybody's idea of their perfect holiday will be different; for some it will be a sun-drenched and remote Caribbean island, while others will look for the cultural stimulation of a visit to the great art galleries and museums in Paris; some people will indulge themselves at a Swiss spa resort or enjoy a big game safari in Kenya. To the tour operator, these all represent segments of the total market for package holidays and other travel products. The process of subdividing the total market for a product or service into clearly identifiable sectors that share similar characteristics is known as market segmentation. It is an important tool for tour operators, since it allows them to clearly identify the needs of their customers and provide products to meet their particular needs, through targeted promotional activities.

Tour operators spend considerable sums of money on undertaking and commissioning market research in order to understand the market in which they operate and the needs of their customers. Markets can be segmented in a number of ways, for example, according to age, social class, regional distribution, leisure habits, lifestyle, etc. Mass market operators produce a wide range of package holiday products aimed at three distinct market segments, namely:

● Youth market
● Family market
● 'Empty nesters'

The youth market ranges from those holidaymakers with restricted income, e.g. students and those who are in paid employment for the first time, to sophisticated singles and couples with good jobs and a high level of disposable income. Holiday products to meet the needs of these diverse markets include package holidays in budget accommodation and up-market tours to long-haul destinations (see Figure 17.8).

Families occupy the biggest share of the outbound package holiday market, with many of the summer sun and winter sun products geared to their needs. Tour operators select accommodation and resorts that have 'family appeal' and the facilities to

Fig. 17.8 Young people are an important market segment for tour operators *(reproduced courtesy of Airtours)*

meet their needs, e.g. children's clubs, children's reps, early evening meals, safe beaches, quiet resorts, etc. The mass market operators stimulate early demand for their products by offering a restricted quantity of free child places on their programmes.

'Empty nesters' describes couples whose children have left home ('flown the nest'). Without the financial burden of children at home, and fewer other financial commitments, they have considerable discretionary spending power and are a major market for tour operators. Given the fact that UK citizens are generally living longer, the future potential of this market is also of interest to the major travel companies. Most UK tour operators cater well for the needs of empty nesters, providing a variety of winter sun and summer sun packages in accommodation and resorts that meet their particular needs. They are also an important market sector for cruise operators and coach companies.

Element 19.2 includes an example of how one mass market tour operator, Thomson, segments its market and provides products to suit all tastes (see page 160).

Activity

Study a range of tour operators' brochures and draw up a chart of which sectors of the market each is trying to attract. Include in your chart examples of the products they sell to the particular market sectors.

The needs of package holiday customers

We can consider the needs of package holidaymakers from two viewpoints. Firstly, there are motivational needs, i.e. the psychological reasons why people choose to go on a package holiday in the first place. Secondly, having chosen a particular type of holiday and selected a destination, the holidaymakers have a number of different information needs, relating to the booking process, the area they are to visit, the components of the package, the travel details, etc. Motivational needs are explored in the following section, while information needs are dealt with in Element 17.3 (see page 67).

Motivational needs

Package holidays provide a relatively inexpensive way for people to get away from their normal daily routine, perhaps swapping it for a different environment, language and culture, and giving them the chance to meet new people and enjoy fresh experiences. All human beings have different needs, desires and aspirations, a principle that Maslow developed into his famous 'hierarchy of needs' (see Figure 17.9)

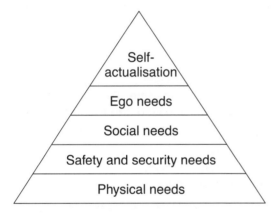

Fig. 17.9 Maslow's hierarchy of needs

The starting point for Maslow's hierarchy is that we all have basic physical needs, such as food and water. Above these are safety and security needs, such as personal protection and protection of property. Social needs include affection, love, friendship and understanding. We all have ego needs (some more than others!), such as self-respect, self-esteem and status. Finally, we have a need for self-actualisation, i.e. spiritual needs and the feeling of being at one with the world. We can relate Maslow's theory to the demand for package holidays as follows:

1. *Physical needs* – e.g. food, sleep and drink at the resort.
2. *Safety and security needs* – e.g. safe means of transportation, safe destination, secure accommodation.
3. *Social needs* – e.g. meeting new people, socialising, taking part in activities.
4. *Ego needs* – e.g. going to a fashionable resort, travelling in style on Concorde.

5. *Self-actualisation* – e.g. learning a new skill on holiday, becoming spiritually enlightened, getting back to nature, exploring a new region.

Package holidaymakers are commonly classified into those who seek an active holiday and those who want a relaxing holiday. To some extent this distinction is related to age, although there are many senior citizens who enjoy active pursuits, such as walking, tennis, swimming and cycling.

Assignment 17.2

The package holiday and its market

Performance criteria satisfied: 17.2.1, 17.2.2, 17.2.3, 17.2.4

Core skills opportunities at level 3:   Communication   3.1, 3.2, 3.3, 3.4
                                        Information technology 3.1, 3.2, 3.3
                                        Application of number   3.1, 3.2, 3.3

Situation

You are spending three weeks on work experience with the travel editor of your local newspaper. She is currently compiling information for an article about package holidays taken by British people.

Tasks

In order to provide the editor with an overview of package holidays, she has asked you to write a detailed report with the title 'The package holiday and its market'. Your report should be word processed and focus on:

- The development of the package holiday market.
- Components of package holidays.
- Market segmentation for package holidays.
- The needs of package holiday customers.

Your report should include examples of UK package holiday companies and their products, plus relevant charts, diagrams and statistics.

Element 17.3 Investigate the process of making a package holiday booking in a retail travel agency

Information needs of package holiday customers

Package holidaymakers will need information at a number of different stages in their holiday plans:

- The initial planning stage
- The booking stage
- The destination stage

The initial planning stage

The length and complexity of the planning stage will depend on the type of package holiday chosen and the nature of the person booking the holiday. Holidays to long-haul destinations invariably involve more prior planning, given the extra health, passport, visa and foreign requirements that may be needed, as well as extra effort involved in finding out about lesser known destinations and cultures. People will approach the planning stage in different ways; some will put a great deal of time and effort into researching a destination and its surroundings, while others will plan as little as possible. The planning stage is likely to involve comparisons between the holidays offered by different tour operators, looking at the range and quality of accommodation, travel arrangements, facilities at resorts and, not least, the prices on offer. Travellers may also be concerned about the financial security of the tour operator, perhaps choosing to book with a company that is a member of the Association of British Travel Agents (ABTA) or the Association of Independent Tour Operators (AITO). All holidaymakers should look for the ATOL (Air Travel Organisers' Licence) number of the operator, indicating financial protection through the Civil Aviation Authority (CAA).

The booking stage

Having selected a destination and a preferred tour operator, the customer is now in a position to proceed with a booking. This may be through a travel agent or direct with the tour operator. Either way, the holidaymaker will be looking for answers to a number of questions, such as:

- What is the full price of the holiday?
- How much deposit is required?
- When has the balance to be paid?
- What's included in the price?
- What's not included in the price?
- Are there any discounts or special offers?
- What about insurance?
- Is there car parking at the airport?
- Can I hire a car in the resort?
- Does the accommodation have a lift?
- Which airline will I fly with?
- What activities are there for children in the resort?

Customers will rely on the travel specialists to supply accurate information in answer to their questions.

The destination stage

Having arrived safely at their destination, package holidaymakers will quickly want to familiarise themselves with their new surroundings, so as not to waste any precious time abroad. Their information needs while in the destination will focus on four principal areas, namely:

- The attractions that the resort and surrounding area has to offer.
- The location of restaurants, bars and other eating places.
- How to travel around the resort.
- Where to go in the event of an accident or emergency.

Some of this information may have been gleaned before travel, but the majority will be found in the destination resort.

Activity

Interview a cross-section of people of different ages and find out their main information needs when in an overseas holiday resort. Present your findings as a bar chart, based on age categories.

Information sources

All sales staff working in travel agencies must be able to refer to a wide variety of information sources when dealing with package holiday bookings. They will use tour operators' brochures as a starting point for reference when handling enquiries, but will need access to other printed and computer-based information in order to provide a complete service to customers. Although viewdata-based information sources are growing in popularity, a good range of travel manuals and timetables is essential for the professional travel agent.

Trade manuals

Manuals provide travel agency staff with general resort information, hotels and travel requirements. Some of the most common in use in agencies are:

● *Guide to International Travel*
● *Official Hotel Guide* (OHG) – formerly *Official Hotel and Resort Guide* (OHRG)
● *Travel Trade Directory*
● *World Travel Guide* and *World Travel Atlas* (see Figure 17.10)
● *ABC Guide to International Travel*
● *Hotel and Travel Index*
● *Agents Hotel Gazetteer*
● *Apartment Gazetteer*
● *ABC summer and winter holiday guides*

Fig. 17.10 **Word Travel Guide** *and* **World Travel Atlas** *(reproduced courtesy of Columbus Press)*

Timetables

Access to timetables is very useful for staff putting together itineraries for clients and can save the time of contacting a number of individual carriers. A basic set of time-tables in any travel agency should include:

- *Thomas Cook European Rail Timetable*
- *Thomas Cook Overseas Timetable*
- *ABC Rail Guide*
- *British Rail Timetable*
- *ABC Shipping Guide*
- *ABC World Airways Guide*
- *Official Airline Guide* (OAG)
- Individual airline timetables

Other information sources

The National Tourist Offices (NTOs) of overseas destinations are happy to provide travel agents with country information in the form of brochures, maps, posters and videos. The UK tourist boards are also keen to promote the sale of British holidays through travel agents and produce an annual *UK Handbook of Commissionable Holidays*. The travel industry press, including *Travel Trade Gazette*, *Travel Weekly* and *Travel Agency*, also has valuable information for agents. As technology develops it is likely that more travel information will be available on CD-roms and via the Internet. Already Thomas Cook is experimenting with CD-rom screens in a selection of its agencies, giving clients the chance to look inside their 'virtual' hotel bedroom!

Activity

Make a list of some of the main consumer reference sources that a package holidaymaker could look through before contacting a travel agency to make a booking.

Booking a package holiday

The starting point for a package holiday booking will be when a client makes contact with a travel agent, either in person or by telephone (see Figure 17.11).

If the client has a definite departure date, holiday company and resort in mind, the agent will quickly be able to check availability on the computer screen. If there is availability, the booking can proceed. If not, or if the client is unsure about which resort to choose, some further advice and help will be needed from the agent. The tour operators' reservation systems are designed to be able to search by date, resort, hotel, type of holiday, etc., so the client's needs should be satisfied eventually. Once the holiday is chosen, the agent takes out an option, giving the client the chance to think about the choice before making any commitment. The option will be entered on the screen and normally lasts for 24 hours, after which time it lapses and the holiday is put on sale again. If the client returns within the 24 hours and pays a deposit, then the booking is

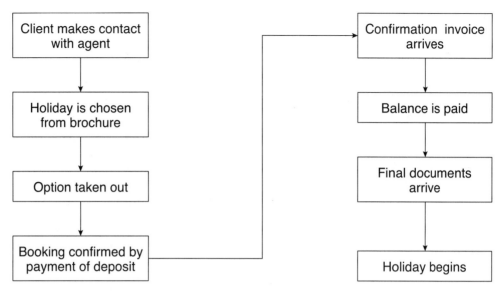

Fig. 17.11 Stages in the booking of a package holiday

confirmed. The client will be issued with a receipt for the deposit payment and a new file started.

Normally within two weeks of making the booking, a written confirmation invoice will be sent from the tour operator, giving precise details of the client's travelling, the booked holiday and travel details. The balance is normally paid eight weeks before departure, but if the holiday is booked within eight weeks of departure the full amount must be paid. Two to three weeks before the holiday starts, final tickets and documentation are received by the agent and passed to the client. This is a good point at which to try some 'cross-selling' by asking clients if they need any foreign currency or travellers' cheques for their holiday.

Documentation used in package holiday bookings

One of the most important documents found in travel agencies is the form that is used to record the details of an initial enquiry from a customer. This may be called the enquiry form, office booking form or option form and it becomes the first item of a client's office file, to which other documentation is added later if the booking progresses. Whether the customer makes contact by telephone or in person, the enquiry form gives a travel clerk the opportunity to record basic client information and holiday details. This will be invaluable when the client wishes to proceed with the booking or the agent needs to contact the client to seek clarification. The form also acts as a reminder to staff, ensuring that the necessary information is obtained and recorded correctly. Figure 17.12 gives an indication of the sort of information that appears on an enquiry form.

The enquiry form shown in Figure 17.12 gives a member of staff the opportunity to

Out and About Travel		TEL: 014 682 595			

Client details

Names	Address				Tel. No.
1.					
2.					
3.					
4.					
5.					
6.					

Holiday details

Holiday company:	Thomson ❏	Airtours ❏	First Choice ❏	Other..... ❏	
Booking ref.:	Holiday no.:	Option exp. date:	Date confirmed:	Agency ref.:	
Resort:	Dep. date:	Duration:	Dep. airport:	Insurance: Y/N	
Hotel / Self-cat.:	Accom. details:	Special requests			

Flight details | Airline: | | Ref.: | | |

	Date	From	To	Flight no.	Dep. time	Arr. time
Outward						
Return						

Other travel requirements

Notes / costing		Agency ref.:
		Taken by:
		Date of booking:

Fig. 17.12 Example of a travel agent's enquiry form

record client information, such as name, address and telephone numbers, plus details of their chosen holiday or other travel arrangements. There is space at the bottom for the agent to make some price calculations on behalf of the client.

Confirmation invoice

Once a holiday has been booked, the first document the client receives will be a confirmation invoice giving precise holiday details, including:

- Holiday reference/booking number
- Inclusive dates of the holiday
- Name and address of lead person
- Names of all clients travelling (including ages of children and infants)

- Details of travel arrangements for the outward and return journeys
- Details of the accommodation booked
- Details of other items booked, e.g. car hire
- Full holiday costing

The confirmation invoice will also indicate when any balance of moneys is due for payment. Any discrepancies noticed by the client or agent should be rectified at this stage. An example of a package holiday confirmation invoice is shown in Figure 17.13.

Final travel information form

Two or three weeks before the holiday begins, the clients will receive their final travel details and documents. This will include their travel tickets, accommodation vouchers, insurance details, car hire details (if applicable), baggage labels, customer satisfaction questionnaire and a printed travel information form that duplicates some of the details on the original confirmation invoice (see Figure 17.14). These are the documents that the clients will need to take with them on holiday as proof of purchase when boarding their flights and checking into the accommodation.

Assignment 17.3

Making a package holiday booking in a retail travel agency

Performance criteria satisfied: 17.3.1, 17.3.2, 17.3.3, 17.3.4

Core skills opportunities at level 3:   Communication   3.1, 3.2, 3.3, 3.4
                                         Information technology   3.1, 3.2, 3.3
                                         Application of number   3.1, 3.2, 3.3

Situation

In your new role as personnel assistant with a major travel agency chain, you have been asked to develop a training factsheet for use in all the company's branches nationwide, in order to standardise the procedures concerning bookings for package holidays.

Tasks

Working to the personnel and training officer, Frank Graves, you are to prepare a detailed factsheet entitled 'Making package holiday bookings'. The factsheet should:

- Describe the information needs of package holiday customers.
- Explain the main information sources used in making package holiday bookings.
- Explain the procedures for booking a package holiday.
- Describe the types of documentation used during a package holiday booking.

Your factsheet should be written in a lively style appropriate to the intended audience and should include relevant tables, diagrams and statistics.

Back Out Travel
Oildrum Lane, Anytown, UK

TEL: 018 759 28762
FAX: 018 759 28763

Booking details

Booking Nos.	: 12345
Issue date	: 1/2/96
Sales advisor	: JENNY
Holiday type	: VILLA INCLUSIVE
Membership No.	: -
Party size	: 2Ad 2Ch 01nf

Holiday Details COSTA BLANCA

Provisional Travel Details - subject to alteration - local timings

```
SATURDAY    18-MAY-96 BRISTOL   -ALICANTE    1425 / 1750 AIH707 AIRTOURS
SATURDAY    01-JUN-96 ALICANTE  -BRISTOL     1840 / 2000 AIH708 AIRTOURS
        PROVISIONAL FLIGHT TIMINGS        NON SMOKING AIRCRAFT
```

Accommodation

```
Property:        VILLA PAELLA  Reserved: SATURDAY 18-MAY-96 to 01-JUN-96 (14 nights)
                       3 BEDROOMED VILLA FOR UP TO 6. OWN POOL

No. of cots: 0      Overseas taxi transfers to property: 0  From property: 0
```

Car & Boat Hire, Motorail, Hotel, etc.

```
GROUP [A]          18-MAY-96 AIRP  01-JUN-96 AIRP  Roof-rack:  N Requests-Babyseat:   0
                                          "          "         "            0
```

Notes / Requests

```
            INV. DEPOSIT REFUNDABLE ON 16-JUN-96
```

CONFIRMATION & INVOICE TO

MR J Brown
10 St. John Street
Anytown
AN1 7HQ

We have pleasure in confirming your holiday arrangements. Please check the details carefully and notify us by return if there are any discrepancies. Where special requests have been made, details are shown above. We will endeavour to fulfil them but no guarantee can be given. If you have any queries or require further information, please do not hesitate to contact us.

Message

Holiday costing

	1	2	3
Basic holiday cost:	389.00	344.00	0.00
Regional airport/port supplement:	0.00	0.00	0.00
Other: SEASONAL SUPPLEMENT	15.00	15.00	0.00
Insurance:	25.00	12.50	0.00
Cost per person	£429.00	£ 371.50	£0.00
Number of clients (excl. accom.only)	2	2	0
Total columns 1, 2, & 3		£1601.00	
Infant:		0.00	
Other:		0.00	
		0.00	
PROPERTY DEPOSIT		100.00	
Car hire: 2 X 111		222.00	
Reductions: 1 WEEK FREE CAR HIRE		-111.00	
Total		£1812.00	
Payment received:		£1812.00	
Balance due for payment by:		£ 0.00	

Passenger Details Note - Only clients named below may travel or occupy the property

		Age	Sex	Ins			Age	Sex	Ins
1 MR	BROWN		M	Y	2 MRS	BROWN		F	Y
3 MISS	BROWN	13	F	Y	4 MSTR	BROWN	6	M	Y

Registered in England No. 123456789

Fig. 17.13 Package holiday confirmation invoice

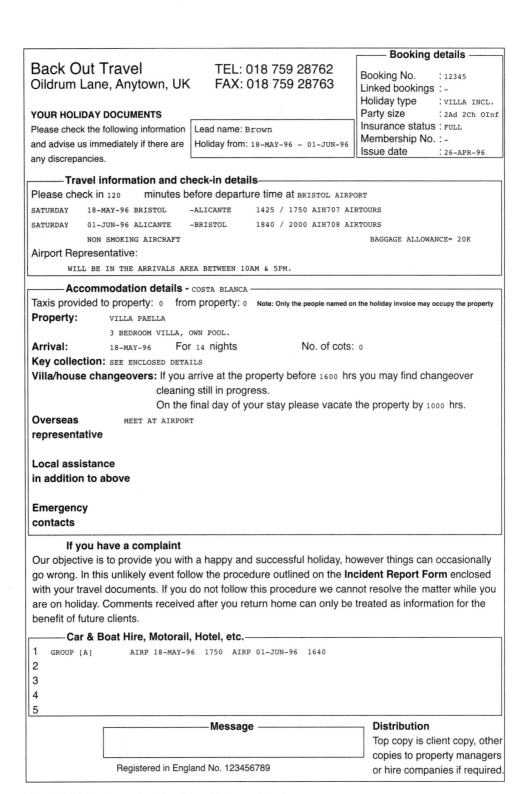

Back Out Travel
Oildrum Lane, Anytown, UK

TEL: 018 759 28762
FAX: 018 759 28763

┌─ **Booking details** ─────┐
Booking No.   : 12345
Linked bookings : -
Holiday type   : VILLA INCL.
Party size   : 2Ad 2Ch OInf
Insurance status : FULL
Membership No. : -
Issue date   : 26-APR-96

YOUR HOLIDAY DOCUMENTS
Please check the following information
and advise us immediately if there are
any discrepancies.

Lead name: Brown
Holiday from: 18-MAY-96 - 01-JUN-96

─── **Travel information and check-in details** ───
Please check in 120   minutes before departure time at BRISTOL AIRPORT

SATURDAY   18-MAY-96 BRISTOL   -ALICANTE   1425 / 1750 AIH707 AIRTOURS

SATURDAY   01-JUN-96 ALICANTE   -BRISTOL   1840 / 2000 AIH708 AIRTOURS

NON SMOKING AIRCRAFT   BAGGAGE ALLOWANCE= 20K

Airport Representative:
WILL BE IN THE ARRIVALS AREA BETWEEN 10AM & 5PM.

─── **Accommodation details -** COSTA BLANCA ───
Taxis provided to property: 0   from property: 0   Note: Only the people named on the holiday invoice may occupy the property

Property: VILLA PAELLA
                 3 BEDROOM VILLA, OWN POOL.

Arrival: 18-MAY-96   For 14 nights   No. of cots: 0

Key collection: SEE ENCLOSED DETAILS

Villa/house changeovers: If you arrive at the property before 1600 hrs you may find changeover
                             cleaning still in progress.
                             On the final day of your stay please vacate the property by 1000 hrs.

Overseas   MEET AT AIRPORT
representative

Local assistance
in addition to above

Emergency
contacts

If you have a complaint

Our objective is to provide you with a happy and successful holiday, however things can occasionally
go wrong. In this unlikely event follow the procedure outlined on the **Incident Report Form** enclosed
with your travel documents. If you do not follow this procedure we cannot resolve the matter while you
are on holiday. Comments received after you return home can only be treated as information for the
benefit of future clients.

─── **Car & Boat Hire, Motorail, Hotel, etc.** ───
1   GROUP [A]   AIRP 18-MAY-96 1750 AIRP 01-JUN-96 1640
2
3
4
5

┌─── **Message** ───┐

│   │

Registered in England No. 123456789

Distribution
Top copy is client copy, other
copies to property managers
or hire companies if required.

Fig. 17.14 Package holiday travel information form

Unit 18

WORLDWIDE TRAVEL DESTINATIONS

Element 18.1

Investigate major overseas destinations for UK originating tourists

Element 18.2

Analyse the appeal to UK originating tourists of overseas destinations

Element 18.3

Investigate overseas destinations for UK originating business travellers

Element 18.1 Investigate major overseas destinations for UK originating tourists

Element 18.2 Analyse the appeal of overseas destinations to UK originating tourists

Introduction

This section looks in detail at the location and the appeal of major overseas destinations visited by British tourists, the twin subjects of Elements 18.1 and 18.2 of Unit 18. Given the common nature of many of the features and development of overseas destinations, the section combines the content of Element 18.1 with that of Element 18.2, while still retaining separate Element assignments.

What are the major overseas destinations for UK tourists?

We shall see in Element 19.2, in relation to package holidays, that Spain is the most popular short-haul destination and the USA the most popular long-haul destination for UK tourists in 1994 (see Tables 19.5 and 19.6 on pages 153 and 155). If we look at <u>all</u> holiday travel abroad for the same year, statistics from the International Passenger Survey (IPS) allow us to chart the top six short-haul overseas holiday destinations as follows:

1. Spain
2. France
3. Greece
4. Portugal
5. Italy
6. Cyprus

Using the same criteria, the top six long-haul destinations in 1994 were:

1. USA
2. Commonwealth Caribbean
3. Africa (excluding North Africa and South Africa)
4. Canada
5. Middle East
6. Australia

Activity

Mark the top six short-haul and top six long-haul destinations for UK tourists on an outline map of the world.

The remainder of this element looks in detail at the characteristics of a range of these popular destinations, focusing on location, principal tourist areas, climate and transport routes.

Spain

Location

Spain is situated in south-western Europe and has borders with Portugal, France and Andorra. Its northern coastline fronts the Bay of Biscay, while the southern coastal resorts are bathed by the warmer waters of the Mediterranean Sea (see Figure 18.1).

Spain is the most popular holiday destination with British tourists, who enjoy the warm climate and attractions of its Mediterranean coastline at resorts along the Costa Brava, Costa Dorada, Costa Blanca and Costa del Sol, as well as its other coastal areas. Interior Spain is also gaining in popularity, with Madrid, the country's capital, attractive to both long-stay tourists and those on short breaks from the UK. Spain's northern

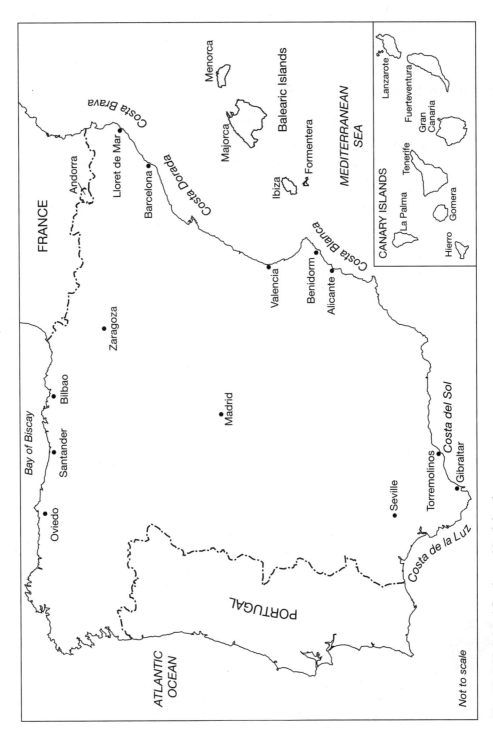

Fig. 18.1 Mainland Spain and its islands

coastline is relatively undiscovered, but extra promotion of regions such as the Asturas, Galicia and Cantabria are opening up their tourist potential to visitors.

The Canary Islands and the Balearic Islands are Spain's two principal island destinations (see Figure 18.1). Majorca, the largest of the Balearics, is the number one Spanish destination for UK tourists, while the Canaries attract visitors all year round, particularly in the winter season.

The main tourist areas in Spain

Spain can be divided up into a number of different holiday areas, as follows:

- Mediterranean Spain – resorts along the east-facing Mediterranean coast.
- Southern Spain – areas along the country's southern coastal strip.
- Green Spain – northern regions bordering the Bay of Biscay and the Atlantic Ocean.
- Inland Spain.
- The Balearic Islands – Majorca, Menorca, Ibiza, Formentera and Cabrera.
- The Canary Islands – Gran Canaria, Lanzarote, Fuerteventura, Tenerife, La Palma, Gomera and Hierro.

Mediterranean Spain

Mediterranean Spain stretches from the French border to the north to the Costa Calida in the south, and includes the well-known tourist areas of the Costa Brava, Costa Dorada and Costa Blanca (see Figure 18.2). All the major mass market tour operators, and many smaller specialist companies, offer package holidays to the most popular resorts in these areas, including Lloret de Mar, Tossa de Mar, Salou, Sitges, Benidorm, Calpe and Javea.

Southern Spain

This region includes the well-known resorts of the Costa del Sol, such as Torremolinos, Marbella, Fuengirola and Nerja, stretching east along the Mediterranean from Gibraltar, and the Costa de la Luz on the Atlantic shores of southern Spain (see Figure 18.3).

Green Spain

This is the name given to the region in the north-west of the country fronting the Bay of Biscay (see Figure 18.4). Its name derives from the nature of the landscape, with wooded valleys and lush meadows, although the Spanish National Tourist Office promotes the area as a 'green tourism' destination, in contrast to the mass tourism in the south of the country.

Activity

Carry out some further research to discover which tour operators feature the regions of Green Spain in their programmes. Don't forget to investigate the ferry companies' brochures.

Fig. 18.2 Mediterranean Spain

Inland Spain

The Spanish National Tourist Office has been working in partnership with cities, towns and rural areas to increase the marketing and promotion of Spain's interior, as a way of spreading the economic benefits of tourism. Madrid occupies the geographical centre of the Iberian Peninsula and is a popular leisure and business travel destination. Other important tourist centres include Toledo, Zaragoza, Seville, Pamplona, Salamanca and Guadalajara. The introduction of Paradores, state-operated tourist accommodation in a variety of historic buildings, has helped many parts of inland Spain to develop their tourist potential. Visitors to the interior are attracted by the dramatic scenery, rich cultural heritage and regional customs.

Fig. 18.3 Southern Spain

Fig. 18.4 Green Spain

The Balearic Islands

The Balearic island chain is located in the Mediterranean Sea off Spain's eastern shore, some 240 kilometres from Valencia (see Figure 18.1 on page 81). With its warm climate, picturesque beaches and excellent facilities for visitors, the Balearics form one of Spain's foremost tourist areas. The four principal Balearic islands are Majorca, Menorca, Ibiza and Formentera (see Figure 18.5).

Palma de Majorca (known to the British simply as Palma) is the capital of the archipelago and an important port in the Mediterranean. Among its architectural treasures are the Gothic cathedral, the fourteenth-century Bellver Castle and the ancient market area. The island as a whole is the most popular overseas holiday destination for British tourists, who frequent a number of resorts in the south and north of Majorca, including Magaluf, Palma Nova, Santa Ponsa, Cala d'Or, Alcudia and Puerto Pollensa. Menorca is regarded as a quieter holiday island than Majorca, boasting a variety of resorts – such as Cala Galdana, S'Algar and Santo Tomas – used by the major tour operators. Mahon is the capital of Menorca and has a layout and architecture that combines typical island features with British characteristics, the result of a long relationship with the UK dating back more than 250 years. Ibiza is the capital of the island of the same name, with resorts ranging from the lively San Antonio in the west of the island to quieter, more sophisticated areas in the north and south, including Playa d'en Bossa and Puerto San Miguel. Formentera is a small, uncrowded island with access from Ibiza by ferry.

The Canary Islands

Volcanic in origin, the Canary Islands are a popular winter sun destination for the British, including those on cruises. The islands are located some 1500 kilometres south-east of the Spanish mainland in the waters of the Atlantic Ocean. There are seven islands in the chain and they are divided administratively into two provinces:

- Las Palmas – which includes the islands of Gran Canaria, Fuerteventura and Lanzarote.
- Santa Cruz de Tenerife – governing the four islands of Tenerife, La Palma, Gomera and Hierro.

Figure 18.6 shows the position of the seven islands and a selection of popular resort areas. Tenerife is the biggest of the Canary Islands and boasts a number of resorts used by the major tour operators, including Puerto de la Cruz and Playa de las Americas. It has two international airports, one in the south and one in the north of the island.

Activity

Analyse the brochures of a range of tour operators that feature the Canary Islands. Identify the products they offer and illustrate how these relate to the needs of different sectors of the market.

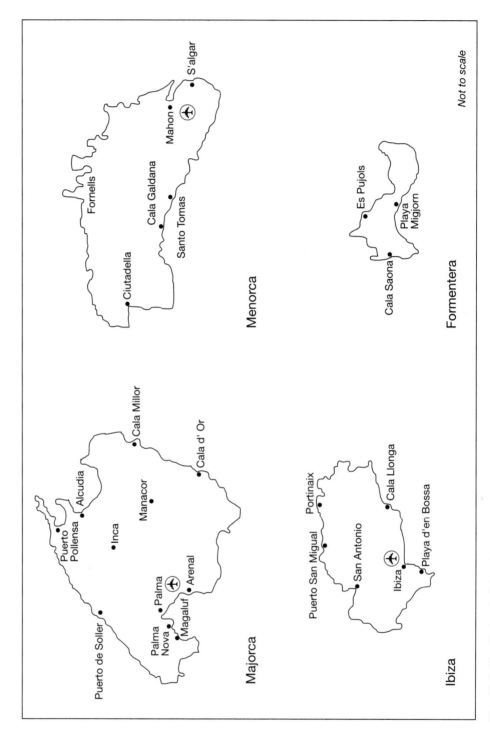

Fig. 18.5 The Balearic Islands

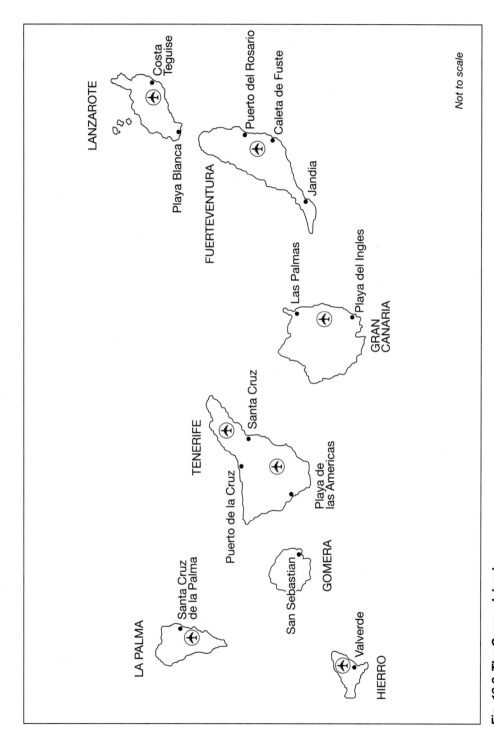

Fig. 18.6 The Canary Islands

Climate

The climate in mainland Spain varies from temperate in the north to dry and hot in the south. The warmest months are from April to October, although it can become excessively hot in the peak summer months of July and August throughout the country, except for the coastal regions. The Balearic Islands enjoy a temperate, Mediterranean climate throughout the year. The cooling influence of the sea ensures that, even in high summer, temperatures do not become excessive. Mild winters make the island resorts, and the south of the Spanish mainland, popular off-season destinations. The climate in the northern Canary Islands is subtropical, while the southern islands tend to be hotter and drier, although rainfall is generally low throughout the islands. Table 18.1 shows the annual temperatures throughout mainland Spain and the islands.

Transport routes

The great majority of British tourists travelling to Spain do so by air, arriving at one of the principal airports shown in Figure 18.7. The Balearic Islands and the Canary Islands are also well served by airports, as shown in Figures 18.5 and 18.6 respectively, making them particularly accessible to UK tourists.

Travel from the UK to Spain by ferry is possible, using either the 24-hour Plymouth to Santander Brittany Ferries service or the slightly longer Portsmouth to Bilbao service operated by P&O. For those visitors wishing to drive from the UK to Spain, the route is via France. If using autoroutes, access to the north of Spain is via Toulouse or Bordeaux, while travellers to eastern Spain should head for Toulouse or Barcelona. Rail travel to Spain is again via France, with direct routes from Paris to both Barcelona and Madrid. Some coach operators, for example Eurolines, operate scheduled coach services to Spain from London, with connections elsewhere in the UK.

France

Location

France is the largest country in Europe, lying on the western edge of the European land mass and has boundaries with Belgium, Luxembourg, Germany, Switzerland, Italy, Andorra and Spain. It also has jurisdiction over the Mediterranean island of Corsica. France has more than 3000 kilometres of coastline, fronting the Atlantic Ocean to the west, the English Channel to the north and the Mediterranean Sea to the south (see Figure 18.8).

Figure 18.8 also shows a selection of the most popular holiday regions in France, although some might say that the whole of the country is the perfect holiday destination given the variety of its scenery, climate, gastronomy and cultural attractions. France is the second most popular holiday destination for British people and with the opening of the Channel Tunnel and the introduction of the Eurostar rail service from London to Paris, its popularity is set to grow.

Table 18.1 Average temperatures in Spain

Town and area		Jan		Feb		Mar		Apr		May		Jun		Jul		Aug		Sep		Oct		Nov		Dec	
		F	C	F	C	F	C	F	C	F	C	F	C	F	C	F	C	F	C	F	C	F	C	F	C
Cape Bagur: Costa Brava	Max.	57	14	57	14	61	16	63	17	68	20	74	23	80	27	78	26	77	25	69	21	62	16	59	15
	Min.	43	6	43	6	46	8	49	9	55	18	60	16	65	18	69	21	62	17	55	13	49	9	45	7
Barcelona: Costa Dorada	Max.	56	13	58	14	61	16	65	18	70	21	77	25	83	28	83	28	77	25	70	21	61	16	56	13
	Min.	43	6	45	7	49	9	52	11	58	14	65	18	70	21	70	21	66	19	59	15	52	11	47	8
Valencia: Costa del Azahar	Max.	59	15	61	16	65	18	68	20	74	23	79	26	84	29	84	29	81	27	74	23	66	19	61	16
	Min.	43	6	43	6	47	8	50	10	56	13	61	16	66	19	68	20	65	18	59	15	50	10	45	7
Alicante: Costa Blanca	Max.	61	16	63	17	68	20	72	22	78	26	84	29	90	32	90	32	86	30	77	25	70	21	63	17
	Min.	44	7	43	6	47	8	50	10	56	13	61	15	66	19	68	20	65	18	59	15	50	10	45	7
Murcia: Costa Calida	Max.	59	15	61	16	65	18	67	19	74	23	77	25	84	29	84	29	81	27	75	24	68	20	63	17
	Min.	41	5	41	5	47	8	49	9	56	13	63	17	68	20	68	20	65	18	58	14	50	10	45	7
Malaga: Costa del Sol	Max.	63	17	63	17	67	19	70	21	74	23	81	27	84	29	86	30	84	29	74	23	68	20	63	17
	Min.	49	9	49	9	52	11	56	13	59	15	66	19	70	21	72	22	68	20	61	16	54	12	49	9
Cádiz: Costa de la Luz	Max.	59	15	58	14	65	18	70	21	74	23	81	27	84	29	86	30	84	29	74	23	68	20	63	17
	Min.	47	8	45	7	52	11	54	12	59	15	65	18	68	20	68	20	66	19	59	15	54	12	49	9
Santander: Cornisa Cantabrica	Max.	54	12	54	12	59	15	59	15	63	17	67	19	72	22	72	22	70	21	65	18	59	15	54	12
	Min.	45	7	45	7	47	8	50	10	52	11	58	14	61	16	64	18	59	15	54	12	50	10	47	8
Pontevedra: Galicia	Max.	58	14	59	15	61	16	65	18	68	20	75	24	77	25	79	26	75	24	68	20	61	16	58	14
	Min.	38	3	40	4	41	5	45	7	50	10	54	12	56	13	56	13	54	12	49	9	43	6	41	5
Madrid: Castilla	Max.	49	9	52	11	59	15	65	18	70	21	81	27	88	31	86	30	77	25	66	19	56	13	49	9
	Min.	34	1	36	2	41	5	54	12	50	10	58	14	63	17	63	17	58	14	50	10	41	5	36	2
Sevilla: Inland Andalucia	Max.	59	15	63	17	69	21	74	23	79	26	90	32	95	35	97	36	90	32	79	26	68	20	61	16
	Min.	43	6	43	6	49	9	52	11	56	13	63	17	69	21	68	20	65	18	58	14	50	10	45	7
Mallorca: Baleares	Max.	58	14	59	15	63	17	67	19	72	22	79	26	84	29	84	29	81	27	74	23	65	18	59	15
	Min.	43	6	43	6	48	8	50	10	56	13	63	17	66	19	68	20	65	18	58	14	50	10	47	8
Las Palmas: Canarias (East)	Max.	70	21	70	21	72	22	73	23	74	23	76	24	77	25	79	26	79	26	80	27	75	24	72	22
	Min.	61	16	61	16	61	16	63	17	65	18	66	19	70	21	72	22	72	22	70	21	65	18	63	17
Tenerife: Canarias (West)	Max.	68	20	70	21	72	22	74	23	76	24	79	26	83	28	84	29	83	28	79	26	75	24	70	21
	Min.	58	14	58	14	59	15	61	16	63	17	66	19	68	20	70	21	70	21	66	19	63	17	61	16

Source: Spanish National Tourist Office

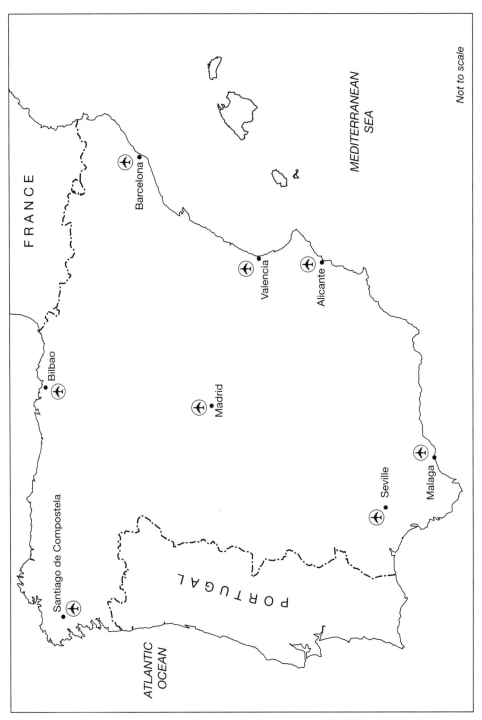

Fig. 18.7 Principal airports of mainland Spain

Fig. 18.8 Holiday regions in France

The main tourist areas in France

Brittany

Occupying the north-western tip of France, Brittany is a popular destination for British tourists who want to be near the coast. The landscape is not dissimilar to England's west country, with its ragged coastline and rocky headlands. Inland lie lush, green fields that support Brittany's agricultural economy, and reminders of the area's Celtic traditions. Fishing ports are found all round Brittany's coastline, from St Malo in the north to Concarneau on the Atlantic coastline. The area is popular with British campers and caravanners, who do not have to venture too far from home to experience the French way of life. Important tourist resorts include Quimper, Benodet and Carnac.

The Loire Valley

The Loire river rises in the Massif Central and flows in a westward direction to meet the Atlantic Ocean at La Baule. This is one of the most popular tourist regions in France, noted for its chateaux, vineyards and gently undulating valleys. The main concentration of chateaux lies between Angers and Orleans, often located in prominent hilltop positions overlooking the river. The Loire is also popular with garden lovers, with many chateaux and country houses with landscaped gardens open to the public. The region of Western Loire, where the river flows into the Atlantic, marks the boundary between the temperate climate of the north and the warmer maritime climate of the south of the country.

The French Alps

The highest point in the French Alps is Mont Blanc in the Savoy Alps, rising to 4807 metres above sea level. From this high point in the Alpine region the mountains slope gently to the south, terminating in the Basse Alps in Provence close to the Mediterranean coastline. Thus the area welcomes visitors all year round, attracting skiers in the winter and tourists in the summer months to the coastal resorts and hinterland. Popular ski resorts in the French Alps include Courcheval, Chamonix, Val d'Isere, Meribel and Alpe d'Huez.

The Mediterranean coast

France's Mediterranean coastline stretches from its border with Italy in the east to the boundary with Spain in the west. It includes the famous Côte d'Azur located between the Italian border and Marseille, with its sophisticated resorts such as Cannes, Nice and St Tropez. Further east along the coast near Marseille is the Camargue, an area known throughout the world for its wild horses, bulls and flocks of pink flamingos. The coastline east of Marseille is less popular with foreign tourists, although French people enjoy its landscape of marshy lowlands and shallow lagoons. The whole of the Mediterranean coastline of France is a haven for the sailing fraternity, from the multi-million pound craft found in the up-market resorts of the Côte d'Azur to the small pleasure boats found in the western area.

The Pyrenees

The Pyrenees is a 400 kilometre chain of mountains running along the border between France and Spain. The area is important for summer tourists, who are attracted by the area's landscape of deep gorges, wooded valleys and fast-flowing streams. The mountains rise to over 3000 metres and have sufficient snow cover in the winter to support a healthy winter ski market. Popular ski resorts in the Pyrenees include Font Romeu, Cauterets, Luchon and La Mongie. The area also benefits from hot thermal springs, a fact that is reflected in many of the place names, e.g. Les Eaux Bonnes, Aulus-les-Bains and Ax-les-Thermes.

Main cities

Paris is one of the world's finest cities, famed for its variety of attractions including the Arc de Triomphe, Eiffel Tower, Pompidou Centre, the Louvre and Notre Dame, to name but a few. Paris is a very popular short break destination for UK tourists who have the choice of travelling by air, rail, ferry, coach or taking their own car. Many large and small tour operators feature a range of accommodation in the capital. Twenty miles east of the city is Disneyland Paris, accessible by air, autoroute and rail services. Other cities in France popular with UK tourists include Bordeaux, Calais, Dijon, Lyon, Marseille, Nantes, Nice, Perpignan, Poitiers, Rennes, Strasbourg and Toulouse.

Activity

Carry out some further research and list the principal attractions of the main French tourist cities listed above.

Climate

France's climate varies between cool temperate in the north of the country to a Mediterranean climate in the south. The Jura Mountains have an alpine climate, while Lorraine is relatively mild due to its sheltered position. In the south, the mountainous areas are cooler with heavy snow in winter in the Alps. The climate of the western coastal regions is influenced by the Atlantic Ocean, giving relatively mild, temperate conditions with rainfall distributed throughout the year. Summers can be very hot and sunny. The holiday regions in the French Riviera and Provence enjoy a Mediterranean climate, although strong winds can occur throughout the region, the most famous being 'the Mistral'. Table 18.2 shows the average temperatures during the year throughout a number of French regions.

Transport routes

There are a host of ferry companies competing on the cross Channel routes between England and France, including Sea France, Brittany Ferries, Sally Line, Hoverspeed, P&O Ferries and Stena Line. Add to this the vehicle shuttle service operated through the Channel Tunnel (*Le Shuttle*), and the permutations of date and time of travel for those travelling to France in their own cars are seemingly endless. The main Channel ferry points of entry into France include:

- Roscoff
- St Malo
- Cherbourg
- Caen
- Le Havre
- Dieppe
- Boulogne

Table 18.2 Average temperatures in France

Average air temperature (°C)	Jan	Feb	Mar	Apr	May	Jun	Jul	Aug	Sep	Oct	Nov	Dec
Paris/Ile-de-France	7.5	7.1	10.2	15.7	16.6	23.4	25.1	25.6	20.9	16.5	11.7	7.8
Alsace	5.5	5.3	9.3	13.7	15.8	23.0	24.1	26.3	21.2	14.9	7.6	4.7
Aquitaine	10.0	9.4	12.2	19.5	18.0	23.7	27.2	25.7	24.2	19.7	15.4	11.0
Auvergne	8.0	6.4	10.1	15.9	17.1	24.2	27.0	24.5	23.3	17.0	11.0	8.3
Brittany	9.3	8.6	11.1	17.1	16.0	22.7	25.1	24.1	21.2	16.5	12.1	9.3
Burgundy	6.1	5.9	10.3	15.3	15.8	23.8	25.8	26.1	21.2	15.5	9.1	6.2
Champagne-Ardenne	6.2	5.6	8.9	13.8	15.1	22.5	23.8	24.9	19.3	15.0	9.6	6.2
Corsica	12.9	12.2	14.1	16.5	21.0	25.5	28.1	27.9	25.7	21.5	18.1	14.5
Franche-Comté	5.4	4.8	9.8	14.6	15.5	23.0	25.0	26.5	21.8	15.2	9.6	5.8
Languedoc-Roussillon	12.4	11.5	12.5	17.6	20.1	26.5	28.4	28.1	26.1	21.1	15.8	13.5
Limousin	6.1	6.1	9.6	16.1	14.9	22.1	24.8	23.6	21.0	16.2	12.8	8.5
Lorraine	5.5	5.3	9.3	13.7	15.8	23.0	24.1	26.3	21.2	14.9	7.6	4.7
Midi-Pyrénées	10.0	9.0	12.3	18.3	19.1	26.4	27.6	27.2	25.0	19.3	15.5	9.8
Nord/Pas-de-Calais	6.6	5.6	8.3	13.7	14.9	21.5	22.7	24.0	19.3	15.3	8.3	6.9
Normandy	7.6	6.4	8.4	13.0	14.0	20.0	21.6	22.0	18.2	14.5	10.8	7.9
Picardy	6.6	5.6	8.3	13.7	14.9	21.5	22.7	24.0	19.3	15.3	8.3	6.9
Poitou-Charentes	10.0	8.7	11.7	18.2	16.4	22.4	25.3	24.6	22.0	18.4	14.0	9.8
Provence	12.2	11.9	14.2	18.5	20.8	26.6	28.1	28.4	25.2	22.1	16.8	14.1
Rhône Valley	7.4	6.7	10.8	15.8	17.3	25.6	27.6	27.6	23.5	16.5	10.4	7.8
Riviera/Cote d'Azur	12.2	11.9	14.2	18.5	20.8	26.6	28.1	28.4	25.2	22.2	16.8	14.1
Savoy & Dauphiny Alps	3.1	3.7	7.9	13.8	15.7	22.4	26.8	25.7	22.7	15.9	10.7	6.3
Val de Loire	7.8	6.8	10.3	16.1	16.4	23.6	25.8	24.5	21.1	16.2	11.2	7.0
Western Loire	9.9	8.6	11.3	17.7	16.7	23.3	25.7	24.6	21.8	16.9	12.4	9.5

Source: French Tourist Office

- Calais
- Dunkirk

France has an excellent internal rail service, including the TGV (*Train de Grande Vitesse*) linking major cities, plus a network of provincial services. Access from the UK is via the Channel Tunnel on the Eurostar service from Waterloo to either Paris or Lille. Motorail services carry cars, motorbikes and passengers overnight from Calais, Lille and Paris to all the main holiday areas. Bicycle and car hire are available at many stations in France.

Principal international airports for those flying from the UK on charter or scheduled services include:

- Bordeaux
- Lille
- Lyon
- Marseille
- Nantes
- Nice

- Paris (Charles de Gaulle)
- Paris (Orly)
- Toulouse

A scheduled coach service between the UK and France is offered by Eurolines, operating over 70 services to Calais, Amiens, Perpignan, Strasbourg, Toulouse and Tours. Hoverspeed also operates a London to Paris coach service as part of their hovercraft operation.

Activity

Draw the main French Channel ports on an outline map of the country and indicate alongside each port which ferry company services the route. Locate also the principal international airports of France on the same map.

USA

Location

The United States of America is one of the largest countries in the world, covering the greater part of the North American continent, and has borders with Canada to the north and Mexico to the south. Its eastern seaboard fronts the Atlantic Ocean, the west coast faces the Pacific Ocean, while the southern shores are bathed by the warm waters of the Gulf of Mexico and the Caribbean Sea (see Figure 18.9). The state of Alaska is separate from the rest of the USA, being located adjacent to Canada in the north-west corner of the continent. The island state of Hawaii is found more than 2000 miles from mainland USA in the Pacific Ocean. The total population of the USA is more than 250 million.

The country has a wide diversity of terrain, including the gentle landscape of the New England states, the grandeur of the Rocky Mountains, the deserts and canyons of Arizona, the Everglades in Florida, the Great Lakes on the northern border and the fertile plains of the Mid West. As well as the country's natural attractions, tourists from all over the world are drawn by such famous cities as New York, Las Vegas, San Francisco, New Orleans, Boston, Los Angeles and Washington DC. Popular man-made attractions include Walt Disney World, Universal Studios, the Golden Gate Bridge, the Statue of Liberty and the White House, to name but a few.

The main tourist areas in the USA

Florida

The popularity of Florida with British tourists has contributed greatly to the USA becoming the number one long-haul destination for UK travellers. Located in south-eastern USA, 100 miles north of the Tropics, Florida's east coast borders the Atlantic

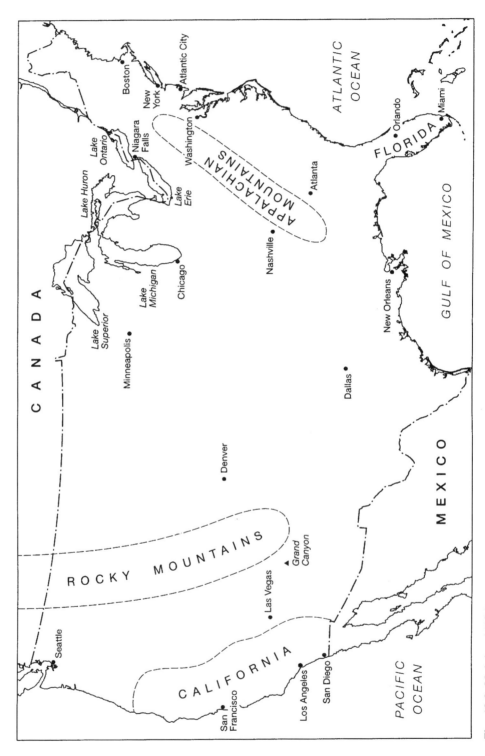

Fig. 18.9 Mainland USA

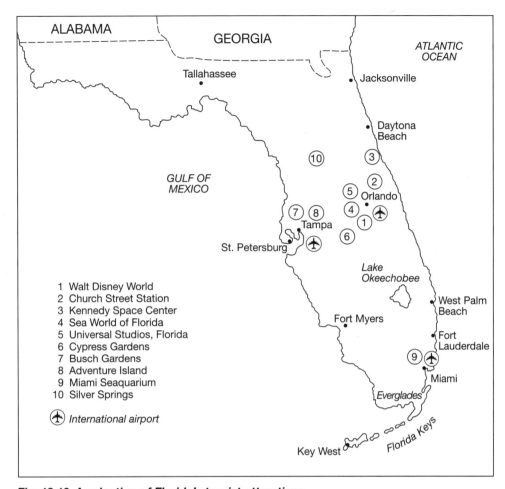

Fig. 18.10 A selection of Florida's tourist attractions

Ocean, while its western shores are bathed by the waters of the Gulf of Mexico. Tourism is the state's largest industry, generating more than $30 billion in 1992 and employing 657,000 people across a range of sectors including accommodation, attractions and transportation.

Florida offers visitors a blend of natural, scenic beauty coupled with an array of tourist attractions that any country in the world would find hard to beat. Orlando is the centre of the state's tourist attractions and is home to the world famous Walt Disney World, attracting more than 20 million visitors every year. Some of Florida's best-known tourist attractions are shown in Figure 18.10.

Florida offers visitors a variety of terrain, including more than 10,000 freshwater lakes, over 1800 miles of coastline, swamps, hills, forests, countless small islands and 1000 miles of sandy beaches. Miami and Miami Beach are twin gateways to the Florida peninsula, as well as being the world's biggest cruise port. They offer tourists year-round attractions, including the nearby Everglades National Park. The world famous Florida Keys stretch for nearly 200 miles, terminating in Key West with its unique wildlife and architecture.

Fig. 18.11 The Eastern Seaboard of the USA

Sometimes referred to as 'the sunshine state', climate is a key feature of the state's success, with long summers and mild winters. Average annual temperatures in summer are around 27 °C and in the winter approximately 12 °C. It is, however, affected by hurricanes and less severe tropical storms, giving heavy rainfall during the months of July and October.

Activity

Investigate which major UK tour operators and airlines offer programmes to Florida and draw up a comparative chart outlining price, features, resorts used, departure/arrival airports and accommodation offered.

The eastern seaboard

The cities and states on the east coast of the USA are important destinations for UK visitors for long holidays and, increasingly, short breaks. The area includes the New England states of Maine, Vermont, New Hampshire, Massachusetts, Connecticut and Rhode Island, and the cities of New York, Boston, Philadelphia, Washington DC, Baltimore, Pittsburgh, Cleveland and Newport. Inland, the area has a wealth of natural attractions, including the Great Lakes, Niagara Falls, the Appalachian Mountains, the Adirondacks and Catskill ranges, plus a number of National Parks (see Figure 18.11).

New York is the largest city in the USA and third largest in the world. Among its numerous attractions are the Statue of Liberty, the Empire State Building, Broadway, the World Trade Center, the Lincoln Center, the United Nations and Greenwich Village, to name but a few. The city is famous for its ethnic quarters, including Chinatown and Little Italy in Lower Manhattan, and Germantown along 86th Street. Boston is the state capital of Massachusetts and the gateway to New England. It is the cradle of American democracy, home of the Boston Tea Party that began the move towards the declaration of independence in 1776. It is the oldest of US cities and has a distinctly British atmosphere. Washington DC (District of Columbia) is the capital of the USA and offers a variety of tourist attractions, including the White House, the Lincoln Memorial, Arlington Cemetery, the Capitol Building, the Washington Monument, Potomac Park, the Smithsonian Institute and the Jefferson Memorial.

The climate of the eastern seaboard and its hinterland provides opportunities for both coastal, summer tourism and winter sports activity in the mountains. Much of the region experiences warm, sunny conditions from May to October, with average temperatures peaking at 22 °C in July and August. Winters are cold, with temperatures generally below freezing between December and March.

The west coast

The west coast of the USA runs from the border with Canada in the north to the Mexican boundary in the south (see Figure 18.12).

The region includes the state of California, the most populous state in the USA and the country's leading tourist area, famous for its sunny climate, excellent beaches, cosmopolitan cities, wine growing areas, mountain ranges and National Parks. Known as the 'golden state', on account of its sunny climate and links with pioneering for gold, California is also synonymous with glamour and the film industry, being the home of Hollywood, the location of the most famous film studios in the world. The west coast also has some of the world's leading cities, including Los Angeles, San Francisco, Las Vegas and Seattle.

Los Angeles is the principal gateway to southern California and has the second highest population of any city in the USA. It is best known for the Hollywood film studios, exclusive Beverly Hills community and the original Disneyland theme park at Anaheim, some 25 miles south of Los Angeles centre. The city also has a number of excellent swimming and surfing beaches, including Laguna Beach, Long Beach, Malibu Beach and Redondo Beach.

San Francisco acts as the main gateway to northern California, Nevada and Oregon. The city has developed on a peninsula, with the Pacific Ocean to the west and San Francisco Bay to the east, the entrance to the Bay being spanned by the famous Golden Gate Bridge. The Chinatown district of the city has the largest Chinese community outside Asia, with a variety of theatres, museums and authentic eating places. The former prison island of Alcatraz in San Francisco Bay has been transformed into a major attraction for visitors. There are a number of natural attractions close to the San Francisco metropolis, including Sequoia, Kings Canyon and Yosemite National Parks, each with a mixture of pine forests, glacial valleys and waterfalls.

Las Vegas is the largest city in Nevada and one of the major gambling and entertainment centres in the world. Hotels, casinos, restaurants, night clubs and entertainment venues are found on 'the Strip', a section of Las Vegas Boulevard South. Lake Tahoe

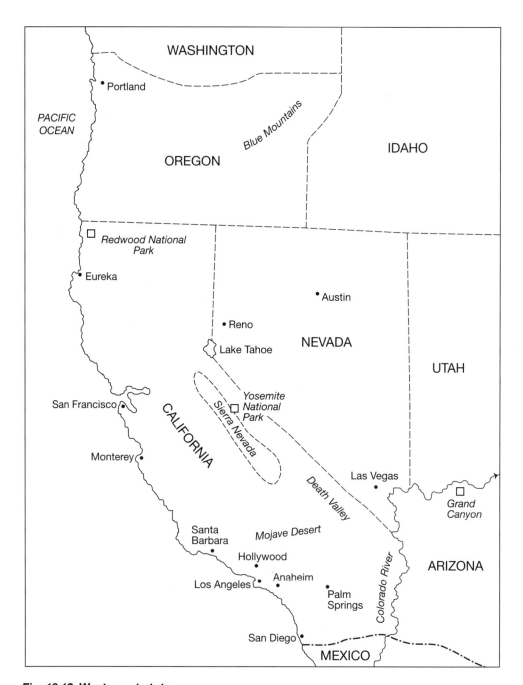

Fig. 18.12 West coast states

spans the state boundary between Nevada and California, and is located in one of the USA's main mountain resort areas, with year-round attractions and activities.

Seattle, in the north-west corner of the USA, is the principal international gateway to the state of Washington and the Pacific north-west region of the country, as well as being close the city of Vancouver in British Columbia, Canada. The city is surrounded by the waters of Lake Washington and Puget Sound, with a backdrop of the Cascades and Olympic Mountains. The Seattle Center is the cultural heart of the city, the home of opera, ballet and theatre. Seattle is also well known for its associations with the sea, with harbour tours and fishing trips available to visitors.

Climate

The size of the US land mass, and its varied topographical structure, results in wide variations in the country's climate. The north-east of the country, including the New England states, has warm summers, with temperatures close to 30 °C in the warmest months, but experiences cold winters with freezing temperatures. Rainfall in this area is spread evenly throughout the year and humidity is generally high in August and September. The southern states of the USA, including Florida, Georgia and Alabama have hot summers and mild winters. Heavy rainfall in the summer months is not uncommon and the area can be very humid at this time of year. California and other south-western states have hot summers and mild winters, with rainfall generally confined to the winter months. Humidity is high in the summer months, especially May, June, July and August. The desert regions of the interior are hot and dry throughout the year, while mountain regions, including the Rockies, experience very low winter temperatures.

Transport routes

The great majority of UK visitors travelling to the USA arrive by air. There are currently 20 international 'gateway' airports spread throughout the country, located in or close to the following cities:

- Atlanta
- Boston
- Dallas/Fort Worth
- Detroit
- Los Angeles
- Minneapolis/St Paul
- Orlando
- Phoenix
- Seattle
- Tampa

- Baltimore
- Chicago
- Denver
- Houston
- Miami
- New York/Newark
- Philadelphia
- San Francisco
- St Louis
- Washington

Activity

Locate the international airports listed above on an outline map of the USA, including the full name and three-letter code of each airport.

The network of internal air services in the USA is very comprehensive and competition between airlines has kept prices low for domestic travel. The size of the country and often long distances between major population centres, has meant that air travel has become the accepted way to travel for Americans, whether for business or leisure purposes. The US passenger rail network is not extensive across the whole country, but there are good services in the densely populated north-east of the country.

The Caribbean

Location

The Caribbean is one of the fastest growing long-haul destinations for UK tourists, attracted by its warm climate, unspoilt beaches and relaxed lifestyle. The major tour operators now offer cut-price package holidays and charter flights to the Caribbean, which is also a major centre for cruising. The area also has a significant VFR (visiting friends and relatives) market from the UK. The Caribbean islands are located along a 2500-mile-long arc in the Caribbean Sea in the western Atlantic Ocean, sweeping eastwards from Florida to the coast of Venezuela in South America (see Figure 18.13). The islands were colonised from the sixteenth century onwards by a number of European countries, including Britain, France, Spain, Portugal and the Netherlands. Many of

Fig. 18.13 The Caribbean Islands

the islands retain the character and customs of their colonising countries, making visitors feel immediately at ease when on holiday. Each island is very different in character, from bustling destinations to undiscovered island paradises well away from the pressures of modern life. As well as their natural attractions, the Caribbean islands offer visitors a variety of water-based sports and activities, including scuba diving, sailing, wind surfing and fishing.

The main tourist areas in the Caribbean

The Bahamas

The Bahamas are a group of more than 700 islands spread across a 750-mile stretch of the Atlantic Ocean from Florida to Haiti. Many are low lying and are covered with lush vegetation. The beaches in the Bahamas are among the finest in the world, attracting tourists throughout the year from all parts of the globe. Most visitors to the Bahamas stay in the main resort areas on New Providence and Grand Bahama Islands, including the capital Nassau. The islands are also a magnet for cruises, being the first port of call for many ships that set sail from Florida. Watersports are well catered for in the Bahamas, with sailing, parasailing, powerboat racing, diving, swimming, snorkelling and water skiing all widely available.

Barbados

Barbados is the most easterly of the Caribbean islands and is part of the Windward Islands chain. The western coast of Barbados has sheltered, coral beaches of fine, white sand, while along the east of the island there is a lively surf that pounds a rocky shoreline. It is a predominantly flat island with fertile plains supporting a variety of crops including sugar cane (see Figure 18.14).

Bridgetown, the capital of Barbados, has a decidedly English appearance and character, the result of its former British sovereignty. There is even a miniature Trafalgar Square with a statue of Lord Nelson! The island is equally popular with staying tourists and cruise visitors, who enjoy its fine beaches and crystal clear waters that offer a wide range of water-based activities such as swimming, scuba diving, jet skiing and water skiing. Other sports on offer include cricket, golf, tennis, horse riding and horse racing.

Jamaica

Jamaica is the third largest island in the Caribbean, located to the south of Cuba and west of Haiti. Most of the island is forested and mountainous, rising from 1000 metres in the west to the Blue Mountains in the east reaching 2256 metres in height. Most of the beaches are found on the north and west coasts of the island where the principal resorts of Montego Bay, Ocho Rios, Negril and Port Antonio are located. Montego Bay is one of the world's great resorts and is the jewel in the crown of Jamaica's tourism industry. The island's capital, Kingston, is on the south coast and is the site of one of Jamaica's two international airports. It is the largest English-speaking city in the Caribbean and an important business and administrative centre (see Figure 18.15)

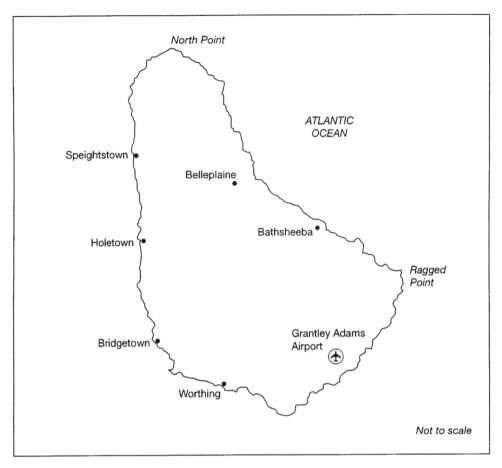

Fig. 18.14 Barbados

Like many Caribbean islands, Jamaica welcomes both staying and cruise tourists, who enjoy its varied nightlife, relaxed way of life and numerous sporting opportunities.

Activity

Carry out some further research to investigate which UK tour operators and airlines offer tour programmes to either Jamaica or Barbados. Make detailed notes on the tourist attractions of the most popular resorts featured in the programmes of your chosen country.

The Dominican Republic

The Dominican Republic occupies the eastern part of the island of Hispaniola, which it shares with Haiti, and is the second largest of the Caribbean states (after Cuba). Its

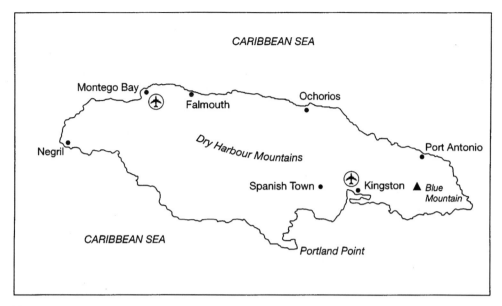

Fig. 18.15 Jamaica

popularity with visitors from the UK is growing rapidly, with many of the larger tour operators promoting the Dominican Republic as an all-year-round destination, with package holidays and regular charter flights. Its main tourist attractions are its unspoilt beaches, for example, around Puerto Plata with the popular resort of Sosua and along the Samana Peninsula, both on the north coast (see Figure 18.16). Inland, the landscape is forested and mountainous, with many valleys, plains and plateaux. The capital, Santo Domingo, was founded in the fifteenth century and the old, colonial part of the city has been restored to its former glory. The modern part of the capital is a bustling port city, offering visitors a variety of nightlife and cultural experiences.

Tourism has developed much later in the Dominican Republic than in other Caribbean destinations. Consequently, many of its tourist facilities and tourism infrastructure are not fully developed.

Trinidad and Tobago

Trinidad and Tobago are sister islands situated off the coast of Venezuela in the southern Caribbean. Trinidad is the larger of the two islands with its capital, Port of Spain, dominated by mountainous terrain. Elsewhere, inland Trinidad is a relatively flat, agricultural landscape with unspoilt beaches on its north and east coasts. Tobago is a very small island with quiet, sandy beaches and a mountainous interior with lush, tropical vegetation. The islands, particularly Trinidad, are renowned for their carnivals and music festivals, and boast a good selection of restaurants serving local delicacies. The islands are also noted for their flora and fauna, with more than 600 species of butterfly and 700 varieties of orchid. Hummingbirds are found in abundance in Tobago.

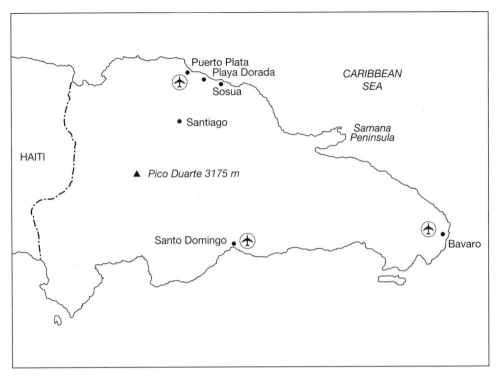

Fig. 18.16 The Dominican Republic

St Lucia

St Lucia is the second largest of the Windward Islands (after Dominica), located in the eastern Caribbean between St Vincent and Martinique. It is rich in tropical vegetation and has a mountainous interior. One of its main attractions are its unspoilt, palm-fringed beaches surrounded by the warm, clear Caribbean Sea. The island has a great variety of plant and animal life, including orchids and parrots. The mountains are intersected by rivers that form broad fertile valleys in some parts of the island. The capital, Castries, is a busy, land-locked harbour surrounded by hills. It is a major port of call for cruise ships, which dock at Pointe Seraphine. St Lucia has two international airports, Vigie and Hewanorra, 2 and 42 miles respectively from Castries.

Climate

The Caribbean enjoys a tropical climate that is dominated by the easterly trade winds that blow from the mid-Atlantic towards Mexico. Temperatures throughout the Caribbean generally average over 25 °C, peaking at more than 30 °C in mid to late summer. The islands in the east experience the greatest cooling effect of the prevailing wind. Elsewhere, relative humidity is high at more than 70 per cent. The so-called wet season varies across the islands, but is generally between the months of June and November. Hurricanes are a problem in the Caribbean, particularly affecting the northern and eastern islands. The incidence of hurricane activity is greatest in the wet season, notably between July and October. Given these climatic conditions, it is not surprising that the main tourist season in the Caribbean is in the winter, between January and April, although there is a summer peak in July and August despite the threat of adverse weather.

Transport routes

Tourism in the Caribbean is dominated by two types of transportation, air travel and cruise ships. Travel by air dominates the staying visitor market in the Caribbean; indeed the growth of tourism in the Caribbean islands has occurred as a direct result of the development of aircraft routes and their associated infrastructure. All the popular island destinations have at least one international airport, generally offering direct scheduled flights from the UK with British Airways or the national airline of the country concerned, e.g. Bahamasair, Air Jamaica, British West Indian Airways, etc. Charter flights are increasingly on offer to a number of popular Caribbean destinations with the major UK tour operators, including Thomson (Britannia Airways), Airtours (Airtours International) and First Choice Holidays and Flights (Air 2000).

Miami and Puerto Rico tend to be the principal centres of cruise tourism in the Caribbean, attracting mainly US-based tourists. The majority of UK cruise visitors to the Caribbean buy a fly-drive holiday and start their cruise at an island port such as Bridgetown in Barbados, San Juan in Puerto Rico or Montego Bay in Jamaica. Alternative starting points include Miami and Fort Lauderdale in Florida.

Activity

Carry out some further research and draw up a list of the Caribbean islands that have an international airport. Plot these airports on an outline map of the Caribbean and include the appropriate international three-letter codes.

Australia

Location

Australia is a huge continent, as big as the whole of Europe and only slightly smaller than the USA. From Sydney in the east to Perth in the west is a distance of nearly 2500 miles, while a journey from Darwin on the north coast to Adelaide in the south covers more than 2000 miles. Australia is located in the southern hemisphere, with the Pacific Ocean to the east and the Indian Ocean to the west. To the north are the Timor Sea and the Torres Strait, which separates Australia from Papua New Guinea. Tasmania is located off the south-east tip of Australia, separated from the mainland by the Bass Strait (see Figure 18.17).

Australia's terrain is extremely varied, ranging from the wilderness and deserts of the west and central plains to lush green rain forest in the east. The landscape consists

Fig. 18.17 Australia

mainly of a low central plateau skirted with coastal mountain ranges, highest in the east of the country with the Great Dividing Range. Its beaches and surfing are world-renowned, and other natural attractions, such as Ayers Rock and the Great Barrier Reef, are magnets for overseas and domestic tourists. The country boasts 11 World Heritage Sites, as shown in Figure 18.18. Australia also has enormous snow fields the size of Switzerland. The ancient cultural history of the Aboriginal people, plus the vibrant way of life found in its bustling cities, also serve to attract visitors to Australia from all over the world. The VFR market from the UK is important, with many British people combining visits to friends and relatives with a tour of the most popular regions of the country.

Australia's share of world tourist arrivals is increasing, due to its natural attractions and favourable climate, backed up by effective marketing and promotion. Although travel times from the UK to some parts of Australia can exceed 24 hours, it is an increasingly popular destination for the British, tempted by low-cost package holidays now offered by a variety of tour operators in the UK. The growth in the number of Australian television programmes shown in Britain has also increased the country's appeal.

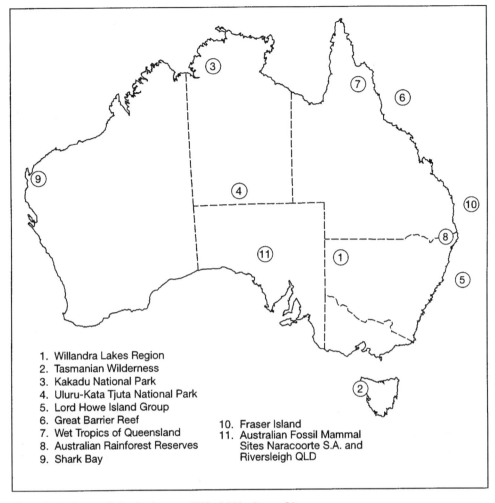

Fig. 18.18 Australia's designated World Heritage Sites

1. Willandra Lakes Region
2. Tasmanian Wilderness
3. Kakadu National Park
4. Uluru-Kata Tjuta National Park
5. Lord Howe Island Group
6. Great Barrier Reef
7. Wet Tropics of Queensland
8. Australian Rainforest Reserves
9. Shark Bay
10. Fraser Island
11. Australian Fossil Mammal Sites Naracoorte S.A. and Riversleigh QLD

Activity

Investigate which UK tour operators and airlines feature Australia in their programmes. Carry out a comparative analysis of the companies in terms of price, product features, resorts used, quality of accommodation, special offers and convenience of travel arrangements.

The main tourist areas in Australia

Queensland

Queensland is located in the north-eastern corner of Australia and is bisected by the Tropic of Capricorn. The state's terrain is a mixture of vast inland, fertile plains, long stretches of sandy beaches, coral reefs, rain forests, forested mountains and expanses of wilderness. It is known as the 'sunshine state' and boasts probably the best beach area in the country at the Gold Coast, close to Brisbane, the state capital. The Gold Coast is made up of 26 miles of white surfing beaches, including the world famous Surfers' Paradise beach, now a lively, sophisticated resort. Queensland has within its borders one of the world's foremost natural wonders, the Great Barrier Reef. The Reef stretches for more than 1200 miles along the Queensland coast, from the Cape York peninsula to the Tropic of Capricorn, and supports unique animal and plant life.

Brisbane is the economic hub of Queensland and is the gateway to the tourist resorts of the Gold Coast and the Sunshine Coast. The city has grown rapidly in recent years, due to the popularity of the region with home and overseas visitors. Further north along the Queensland coast are Cairns and Townsville, both with international airports forming gateways to the Great Barrier Reef.

Western Australia

Western Australia is the largest of the country's states, covering one-third of Australia's land area. It is larger than western Europe, yet has a population of less than 2 million. It is bordered in the east by South Australia and the Northern Territory. Its northern shores are surrounded by the Indian Ocean, while the south coast fronts the Southern Ocean. The terrain of Western Australia is predominantly desert and the state has rich oil and mineral deposits, including iron, diamonds and gold; Kalgoorlie in the south of the state is well known to tourists as a gold-mining ghost town. The only significant concentration of population is in the south-east corner around the capital Perth, which has a number of fine beaches, including Port, Cottesloe, City and Scarborough. All-year-round sunshine makes Perth Australia's sunniest capital. Western Australia has several National Parks and wildlife reserves, including Kalbarri, Yanchep and Nambung to the north of Perth. Shark Bay, at the western tip of the state, is one of Australia's 11 designated World Heritage Sites.

Northern Territory

The Northern Territory is a true wilderness area and is closest of all states to the popular image of the Australian 'outback'. It covers one-sixth of the Australian land-mass and can be divided topographically into the tropical north, with the capital Darwin as its hub, and the southern red desert ranges dominated by Ayers Rock in the Uluru National Park. This ancient monolith is steeped in Aboriginal mythology and is one of Australia's most important tourist attractions. The starting point for tours to Ayers Rock is the nearby town of Alice Springs, a popular base for exploring the outback, which is located in the geographic centre of the continent. Darwin, found on the north coast, is a modern, provincial city and a good base from which to explore the area's many natural attractions, including the Kakadu National Park.

Victoria

Victoria is Australia's second smallest but most densely populated state and the country's principal producer of agricultural and industrial products. It is located in the south-east of the country, bordered by South Australia to the west and New South

Wales to the north, along the route of the famous Murray River. Its mild, temperate climate has given rise to the title of 'the garden state', with a varied landscape consisting of mountains, rain forests, deserts, snow fields, market gardens and agricultural plains. Melbourne, the capital, is located in the south of the state at the mouth of Port Philip Bay. It is a modern, cosmopolitan city of some 3 million people and is the home of the National Gallery, which houses Australia's greatest collection of fine art. As well as its cultural heritage, Victoria has a variety of natural attractions, including fine beaches, snow-covered mountain ranges and a number of National Parks.

South Australia

South Australia is the country's driest state, sparsely populated apart from around its capital, Adelaide. It is a region of rocky plains and desert landscape, broken by the fertile wine-growing area of the Barossa Valley. The terrain ranges from the beach resorts of the Adelaide suburbs to the expanses of desert outback, from the lush banks of the Murray River to the craggy mountains of the Flinders Range. Offshore from Adelaide is the popular resort of Kangaroo Island, a natural wildlife sanctuary noted for its fishing and colony of seals. Adelaide itself is a modern, coastal city nestling in the foothills of the Mount Lofty Ranges.

New South Wales

New South Wales is located in the south-eastern corner of Australia and has borders with Queensland to the north, South Australia to the west and Victoria to the south. Its eastern boundary is bathed by the waters of the South Pacific Ocean. The terrain ranges from the subtropical north of the state to the Snowy Mountains in the south, home of Australia's highest peak, Mount Kosciusko at 2230 metres. The interior of the state is typical Australian outback and there are more than 800 miles of coastline with fine, sandy beaches, plus the famous Darling and Murray rivers. New South Wales attracts visitors throughout the year, whether for skiing in the season between June and September, swimming off Sydney's beaches, including the world famous Bondi Beach, or exploring the natural attractions of the interior at places such as the Blue Mountains, the vineyards of the Hunter Valley or the Warrumbungle National Park. Sydney, the capital of New South Wales, is best known for its Opera House and Harbour Bridge.

Canberra

Canberra is located in the Australian Capital Territory (ACT) in the south of New South Wales. Canberra was conceived in the early 1900s in order to create a capital city in a federal state separate from any of the other uniting states of Australia. It is built around Lake Burley-Griffin and has many fine attractions, including the National Library, Parliament House and the Royal Australian Mint.

Tasmania

Tasmania is located off the south-east corner of Australia, separated from the mainland by the Bass Strait. It is an island of rugged mountains that are snow capped in winter, dense bush land, farmland plains, fine beaches and sand dunes. The more sheltered eastern coastline offers a variety of water sports opportunities, including swimming, surfing, sail boarding and fishing. Hobart, the capital of Tasmania, is Australia's second oldest city after Sydney and is found on the south side of the island. It is characterised by strong links with the sea, still maintaining much of its colonial architecture and ambience.

Climate

Australia's location in the southern hemisphere means that its seasons are the opposite of those in the UK, i.e. the winter in Australia takes place during our summer season, their summer is our winter, and so on. The climate varies from tropical, humid and wet in the north of the country, with a dry season between May and October, to hot, dry desert conditions in the central area. The southern states generally have milder weather than those in the north, enjoying a Mediterranean style climate. The west coast spans a wide range of climatic conditions, but is generally drier than the east of the country. Table 18.3 gives an indication of the seasonal variations in temperature and rainfall in a selection of cities and towns throughout the country.

Table 18.3 Average temperatures and rainfall in Australia

Area	Summer		Autumn			Winter			Spring		Summer	
	Jan	Feb	Mar	Apr	May	Jun	Jul	Aug	Sep	Oct	Nov	Dec
Adelaide												
Max.	29	29	26	22	19	16	15	17	19	22	25	27
Min.	17	17	15	12	10	8	7	8	9	11	14	16
Rainfall	19	8	33	47	68	75	84	67	58	44	28	28
Rainy days*	4	4	5	9	13	15	16	15	13	11	8	6
Alice Springs												
Max.	36	35	32	28	23	20	19	22	27	31	33	35
Min.	21	21	17	13	8	5	4	6	10	15	18	20
Rainfall	36	42	37	14	17	15	16	12	8	21	26	37
Rainy days	5	5	3	2	3	3	3	2	2	5	6	5
Brisbane												
Max.	29	29	28	26	23	21	20	22	24	26	28	29
Min.	21	21	19	17	13	11	10	10	13	16	18	20
Rainfall	171	177	152	86	84	82	66	45	34	102	95	123
Rainy days	13	14	15	11	9	8	7	7	8	9	10	12
Cairns												
Max.	31	31	30	29	28	26	26	27	28	29	31	31
Min.	24	24	23	22	20	18	17	18	19	21	22	23
Rainfall	413	435	442	191	94	49	28	27	36	38	90	175
Rainy days	18	19	20	17	14	10	9	8	8	8	10	13

continued

Table 18.3 continued

Area	Summer		Autumn			Winter			Spring		Summer	
	Jan	Feb	Mar	Apr	May	Jun	Jul	Aug	Sep	Oct	Nov	Dec
Canberra												
Max.	28	27	24	20	15	12	11	13	16	19	23	26
Min.	13	13	11	7	3	1	0	1	3	6	9	11
Rainfall	59	58	53	49	49	38	40	48	52	68	62	53
Rainy days	8	7	7	8	9	9	10	12	10	11	9	8
Darwin												
Max.	32	31	32	33	32	30	30	31	32	33	33	33
Min.	25	25	24	24	22	20	19	21	23	25	25	25
Rainfall	409	353	311	97	21	2	1	7	19	74	143	232
Rainy days	20	20	19	9	2	1	0	1	2	6	12	17
Hobart												
Max.	22	21	20	17	14	12	11	13	15	17	19	20
Min.	12	12	11	9	7	5	4	5	6	8	9	11
Rainfall	48	40	47	53	50	56	54	52	52	63	56	57
Rainy days	11	10	11	13	14	14	15	15	15	17	14	13
Melbourne												
Max.	26	26	24	20	17	14	13	15	17	20	22	24
Min.	14	14	13	11	8	7	6	7	8	9	11	13
Rainfall	48	47	52	57	58	49	50	59	59	66	60	59
Rainy days	8	7	9	11	14	14	15	15	14	14	12	10
Perth												
Max.	30	30	28	25	21	19	17	18	20	21	25	27
Min.	18	18	17	14	12	10	9	9	10	12	14	16
Rainfall	8	12	19	45	123	184	173	136	80	54	21	14
Rainy days	3	3	4	8	14	17	18	17	14	11	6	4
Sydney												
Max.	26	26	25	22	19	17	16	18	20	22	24	25
Min.	18	19	17	15	11	9	8	9	11	13	16	17
Rainfall	103	113	134	126	121	131	101	81	69	79	83	78
Rainy days	13	13	14	13	13	12	11	11	11	12	12	12
Celsius to Fahrenheit												
C	0	5	10	15	20	25	30	35	40	45	50	55	60
F	32	41	50	59	68	77	86	95	104	113	122	131	140

˙*Rainy day = min. 0.2mm*

Source: Australian Tourist Commission

Transport routes

Air travel dominates travel to and within Australia. The size of the country means that air travel is as common as travel by train and bus in the UK. International airports are located in the following cities and towns:

- Canberra
- Sydney
- Adelaide
- Melbourne
- Darwin
- Perth
- Brisbane
- Hobart
- Townsville
- Cairns

Activity

Locate the international airports listed above on an outline map of Australia. Include also the main resort areas discussed in the state descriptions given above, plus the state boundaries and capitals.

The major airlines operating scheduled services between the UK and Australia include Qantas, the national carrier, Singapore Airlines and British Airways. Britannia Airways and Airtours International also operate charter flights at certain times of the year. Australia has an internal airline network of more than 95,000 miles, covering the whole continent. The major domestic airlines include Ansett, Qantas and East West, serving the major resorts and cities throughout Australia.

Australia has only one rail service running from coast to coast, although there is an extensive network across the country. The Indian Pacific service runs between Sydney in the east and Perth in the west, covering the 2500 mile journey in three days. Bus companies, including Greyhound Pioneer, offer a network of services between all major destinations.

Assignment 18.1

Major overseas destinations of UK tourists

Performance criteria satisfied: 18.1.1, 18.1.2, 18.1.3, 18.1.4, 18.1.5

Core skills opportunities at level 3:   Communication   3.1, 3.2, 3.3, 3.4
                                        Information technology 3.1, 3.2, 3.3
                                        Application of number   3.1, 3.2, 3.3

Tasks

You are to prepare a detailed written report entitled 'Major overseas destinations for UK tourists'. In particular, it should:

- Identify major overseas tourist destinations for UK tourists.
- Classify six major overseas destinations and match to market types.
- Describe which aspects affect the choice of overseas destinations by UK tourists.
- Identify transport routes and major gateways to overseas destinations.
- Assess the suitability of transport routes for three different types of UK tourists.

Your report should be word processed and include relevant charts, maps, diagrams and statistics.

Assignment 18.2

The appeal of overseas destinations to UK tourists

Performance criteria satisfied: 18.2.1, 18.2.2, 18.2.3, 18.2.4

Core skills opportunities at level 3:   Communication   3.1, 3.2, 3.3, 3.4
                                        Information technology   3.1, 3.2, 3.3
                                        Application of number   3.1, 3.2, 3.3

Situation

You are on work experience in the marketing department of a medium-sized, specialist outbound tour operator based in Edinburgh. You are working with Zoe Bell, who is responsible for the forward planning of tour programmes for the company.

Tasks

To help her in her work, Zoe has asked you to prepare a report entitled 'The current and future appeal of overseas destinations to UK tourists'. Working with a colleague in your group, you are to prepare a detailed, written report that will:

- Explain the appeal of major overseas destinations to UK tourists.
- Explain the reasons for the selection of major overseas destinations by different types of customers.
- Analyse the factors that have influenced the recent growth or decline of two selected overseas destinations.
- Analyse the likely future trends in the appeal of overseas destinations to UK tourists.

Your report should be word processed and include relevant charts, maps, diagrams and statistics.

Element 18.3 Investigate overseas destinations for UK originating business travellers

Performance criteria

1. Locate and assess the importance of major overseas destinations for UK business travellers.
2. Explain the main features of major overseas destinations that determine their appeal to UK business travellers.
3. Identify and locate major gateways and transport routes between the UK and major overseas destinations used by UK business travellers.
4. Assess the suitability of transport routes and transport modes for given UK business travellers.

What is business travel?

Travel for business purposes is one of the most profitable and fastest growing sectors of the UK travel and tourism industry. Figures from the International Passenger Survey (IPS) show that business travel accounted for nearly 12 per cent of all visits abroad by British residents in 1994, with total spending on overseas business travel for the same period estimated at £5.7 billion, a 9 per cent growth over the 1993 figure. Business travel within the UK is also an important industry sector worth more than £2 billion to the UK economy, with 12.5 million business trips made in the UK in 1994, 11 per cent of all trips made by British people for leisure and business purposes.

Business travel is concerned with travel for a variety of work-related activities, including:

- Business meetings
- Exhibitions
- Conferences
- Trade fairs
- Sales missions
- Incentive travel

Travel for business purposes is considered to be high-value tourism, since business travellers often have to travel at short notice, thereby incurring the higher fares charged on scheduled airline and other travel services. Limited flexibility also means that they are not always able to take advantage of reduced rates for hotel accommodation. There is also a link between the class of travel and accommodation used by business travellers, and the image they portray to their clients. Many business people believe that they have a better chance of securing a deal with a client if they are seen to be staying in the best accommodation and travelling first class to their appointment. Whether this belief is real or perceived is open to debate, but there is little doubt that travel for business purposes is one of the most effective ways of doing business, exchanging ideas, securing contracts, gathering market intelligence and generally communicating with colleagues and customers alike.

Travel for business purposes is also important since it is much less seasonal than leisure travel. Business travel takes place throughout the year, providing valuable revenue for tourist businesses out of the peak holiday seasons. Indeed, the promotion of business travel is an effective way of reducing the traditional peaks and troughs of tourism demand in holiday destinations.

Major overseas destinations for UK business travellers

The principal overseas destinations for UK business travellers are shown in Figure 18.19. Advances in transportation mean that no major, global destination is more than 24 hours' travel from the UK. The USA remains the number one global destination for international conferences and conventions, closely followed by France and the United Kingdom. Paris plays host to more international conventions than any other world city, with London in second place and Brussels third.

Although international travel for business purposes is growing in the mid-1990s, there is evidence that the industry is still taking time to recover from the major setback suffered at the beginning of the decade, with the Gulf War of 1990-91 and the worldwide recession of the early 1990s. The Gulf War, and the associated threat of terrorism in international travel, caused major multinational corporations to reconsider their approach to global business travel. Some questioned whether their past business travel activity was really necessary, given that they had managed quite well during the period of the Gulf War. Others began to investigate alternatives to global travel for their personnel, including video conferencing and teleconferencing. The post-Gulf War business travel scene is one where companies are altogether more sceptical when it comes to justifying international business trips, and one where business travel agents, accommodation providers and transport operators are having to be more inventive with their marketing, levels of service quality and pricing strategies, in order to retain their business travel clients. There is, however, some cause for cautious optimism, with a recent American Express survey showing that business travel spending in the UK increased by 9 per cent to $30 billion between 1993 and 1994.

Activity

Make notes on the importance of either the Middle East, Africa or South America as business travel destinations. Give an indication of the various travel routes between the UK and your chosen area.

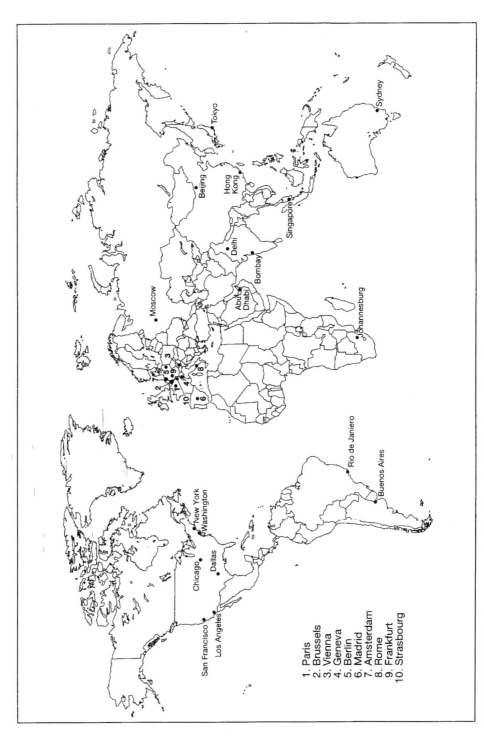

Fig. 18.19 Principal overseas destinations for UK business travellers

1. Paris
2. Brussels
3. Vienna
4. Geneva
5. Berlin
6. Madrid
7. Amsterdam
8. Rome
9. Frankfurt
10. Strasbourg

Paris

Paris is the world's leading city for international conferences and conventions, with total seating for more than 100,000 delegates. In 1990, the capital city attracted 361 international conferences, approximately 100 more than its nearest rival London. Brussels, with 194 international conventions, was third in the league table in 1990. Paris has a wide range of accommodation for business travellers, spread throughout the city and surrounding suburbs. *Hotêls de Tourisme* are officially graded establishments, with five categories fixed by government regulation; these are:

- 4 Star L (luxury)
- 4 Star (deluxe)
- 3 Star (first class)
- 2 Star (standard)
- 1 Star (budget)

The appeal of Paris to business travellers

The popularity of Paris with business travellers lies in its high-quality business and conference facilities, good accessibility, variety of city attractions and its location as the capital city of one of Europe's most culturally diverse countries. In world terms, Paris has a stable political and economic climate, and is currently considered to be a safe city for business travellers attending conferences, making sales presentations or simply making new business contacts. France has a wide industrial and commercial base, and a fast-growing service sector, including one of the most dynamic tourism industries in the world. It is also western Europe's leading agricultural nation, with over half of its land area given over to farming. The variety of history, culture, landscapes and gastronomic delights make Paris and the whole of France ideal locations for post-conference tours and excursions, a factor that contributes greatly to the success of Paris as an important business travel destination. Its close proximity to the UK makes Paris an ideal 'springboard' for British business dealings with the rest of the European landmass.

Transport links to Paris

Paris has two international airports, Charles de Gaulle and Orly, located respectively 15 miles north and 9 miles south of the city, and both with extensive regular taxi, rail, bus and coach links to the city centre. The average flight time from London to Paris is around one hour. Travel by train from London to Paris takes three hours on the Eurostar service from Waterloo, with connections to other principal cities in the UK. For business travellers using their own transport there are many short Channel crossings linking the English motorways with the French *autoroutes*, for example the popular Dover–Calais service. *Le Shuttle*, the vehicle-carrying service through the Channel Tunnel, is also available, with a crossing time of 35 minutes. Paris has one of the best internal transport networks in the world. The *Métro* is the ideal way to travel around the city and there are fast and frequent suburban rail and bus services.

Brussels

The growth of Brussels as a business travel destination has been closely linked to its role as the home of the European Commission and one of the two cities that houses the European Parliament, an honour it shares with Strasbourg. Brussels is also the headquarters of NATO, the North Atlantic Treaty Organisation, as well as being the European base of many multinational corporations.

The appeal of Brussels to business travellers

The appeal of Brussels as a destination for conferences and business meetings lies principally in the fact that it is at the heart of European decision making, by virtue of its links with the European Commission and European Parliament. This makes it an important business travel destination for both public and private sector organisations and individuals keen to influence European policy, forge links in Europe and expand their business operations. The city's location – close to many of the major trading nations of Europe, including Germany, France and the UK – also contributes to its popularity as a business travel destination.

Transport links to Brussels

Brussels is just 55 minutes' flying time from London, with arrivals at Brussels Zaventem airport, some 8 miles north-east of the city centre. There are frequent train, bus and coach services to the centre of the city. Brussels is also one of the three continental destinations for Eurostar services from the UK through the Channel Tunnel, together with Paris and Lille. The journey time from London Waterloo to Brussels is approximately 3¼ hours. The Belgian port of Ostend is the nearest cross-Channel entry point from the UK, with regular sailings from Ramsgate with Sally Ferries. North Sea Ferries also operates a service from Hull to the port of Zeebrugge.

New York

With a population of more than 7 million, New York is the most populous of any of the US cities and the third largest city in the world. As well as being the tourist gateway to many of the eastern seaboard states of the USA and the Great Lakes, it is also one of the leading business travel destinations in the country, attracting some 2 million delegates per year to conferences and conventions alone. Manhattan Island, with its dramatic skyline of soaring skyscrapers, is the business heart of the city, home of the United Nations, World Trade Center, Pan Am Building, Chrysler Building, the Stock Exchange and numerous other corporate headquarters.

New York's appeal to business travellers

New York's location on the east of the country makes it an obvious focus for business travellers from the UK and elsewhere in Europe. Approximate flying time to London is 7 hours, or just over half this length of time on Concorde. The concentration of financial, legal and corporate services in New York make it an ideal base for business clients to meet and finalise transactions. The city also benefits from one of the most vibrant entertainment scenes of any city in the world, from the heart of the theatre district on Broadway to jazz bars in Greenwich Village, where convention delegates and other business people can relax after a hard day's work. Shopping is also an attraction for conference delegates and their spouses, from the elegant shops on Fifth Avenue to ethnic goods in Chinatown.

Transport links to New York

The vast majority of business travel arrivals in New York are by air, with most international flights using John F. Kennedy (JFK) International Airport, 15 miles south-east of central Manhattan. Some flights from London also land at Newark, while the bulk of domestic arrivals use La Guardia airport, 8 miles east of Manhattan. Inter-airport transfers are available by helicopter, coach, limousine or taxi. Travel from the airports to central New York is available by bus, coach, rail or taxi. For travel around the city, the New York subway operates 24 hours a day, 7 days a week, offering a fast, efficient and cheap service to business and leisure travellers, and there are extensive bus services throughout the city.

Hong Kong

Hong Kong is a small, British colonial territory located at the south-eastern tip of the People's Republic of China. It consists of Hong Kong Island, 235 other islands and a section of the Chinese mainland known as the Kowloon Peninsula and the New Territories (see Figure 18.20).

Hong Kong's future is somewhat uncertain, since it is due to be taken back into Chinese control when Britain's 99-year lease expires in 1997. There are fears that the Chinese government will impose restrictions on what has been until now a very successful, western-style capitalist economy. Over the last 100 years, Hong Kong has developed into one of the most vibrant of all Far East countries and a major world trading nation. As well as being a successful leisure travel destination, it is also a major business travel destination, with seating for more than 15,000 conference delegates alone.

Hong Kong's appeal to business travellers

Hong Kong's location is one of its greatest assets. It is at the heart of arguably the fastest growing economy of any region in the world, the Pacific Rim. Easy access to the so called 'tiger' economies of such places as Singapore, Taiwan and Malaysia, gives Hong Kong a unique business advantage. It is also an ideal base from which UK businesses can exploit the many opportunities presented by the growth of mainland China and its economy. The concentration of banking, legal, manufacturing and service sector enterprises in such a small space, makes Hong Kong an ideal business travel location. Hong Kong's social, shopping and entertainment facilities are also important factors in its success as a major business travel destination, as is its subtropical climate.

Fig. 18.20 Hong Kong

Transport links to Hong Kong

Hong Kong International Airport is some 5 miles from the city centre, with regular bus links to all parts of the city. The flight time from London to Hong Kong is approximately 14 hours. There are hovercraft and jetfoil services linking Hong Kong with China and Macau, plus regular ferry services across the harbour. The metro also offers a cross-harbour link, as well as serving all parts of the city. Bus services operate throughout the territory.

Assignment 18.3

Overseas destinations for UK business travellers

Performance criteria satisfied: 18.3.1, 18.3.2, 18.3.3, 18.3.4

Core skills opportunities at level 3:	Communication	3.1, 3.2, 3.3, 3.4
	Information technology	3.1, 3.2, 3.3
	Application of number	3.1, 3.2, 3.3

Situation

You have recently taken up the post of Marketing Executive with a major business house travel agency with branches throughout the north of England. Your line manager, Tracy Dodds, wants you to contribute to a new marketing strategy for the company.

Tasks

So that Tracy can begin to consider future options, she needs you to carry out some background research. You are to write a report entitled 'Overseas destinations for UK business travellers'. In the report you should:

- Locate and assess the importance of major overseas destinations for UK business travellers.
- Explain the main features of major overseas destinations that determine their appeal to UK business travellers.
- Identify and locate major gateways and transport routes used by UK business travellers on trips to major overseas destinations.
- Assess the suitability of transport routes and modes of transport for two different categories of business travellers.

Your report should be word processed and include relevant charts, maps, diagrams and statistics.

Unit 19

TOUR OPERATIONS

Element 19.1
   Investigate UK-based tour operators

Element 19.2
   Investigate UK-based tour operators' products

Element 19.3
   Investigate UK and overseas operational practices in tour operating

Element 19.1 Investigate UK-based tour operators

Performance criteria

1. Describe the size and structure of the UK tour operating market.
2. Identify, with examples, types of tour operators within the UK tour operating market.
3. Explain, with examples, the factors affecting the market share of tour operators within the UK tour operating market.
4. Describe the legal and regulatory requirements affecting UK-based tour operators.
5. Explain, with examples, the effects of unforeseen and uncontrollable events on the UK tour operating market.
6. Assess current trends in the UK tour operating market and give examples.

The role of tour operators

Unlike travel agents, who sell holidays and a range of other travel products, tour operators actually assemble the component parts of a holiday, i.e. the means of travel, accommodation, facilities, transfers, excursions and other services. If we consider that travel agents are the retail arm of the travel business, then tour operators can be likened to wholesalers, since they buy in 'bulk' from the providers of travel services, such as the hoteliers and airlines, break the bulk into manageable packages and offer the finished product, the inclusive tour (IT), for sale via a travel agent or direct to the consumer. The package is sold for an all-inclusive price, which is generally lower than if the component parts of the holiday been booked individually by the holidaymaker. Figure 19.1 shows the role of tour operators and their position as intermediaries between the suppliers of travel products and travel agents.

Figure 19.1 also shows that some tour operators deal direct with their customers rather than selling through travel agents. In the case of foreign package holidays booked by British people, 75 per cent of customers use the services of a travel agent rather than booking direct with the operator. There are, however, a number of high-volume 'direct sell' operators, such as Portland Holidays, and many smaller, specialist tour operators who prefer to deal directly with their clients, advertising their holidays through newspapers and other media. Direct sell operators stress that, since they do not have to pay a commission to a travel agent, they are able to pass this saving on to the client who should benefit with a cheaper holiday. The more specialist the product on offer, the more likely it is that the customer will deal direct with the operator, for example, skiing holidays and mountain exploration tours.

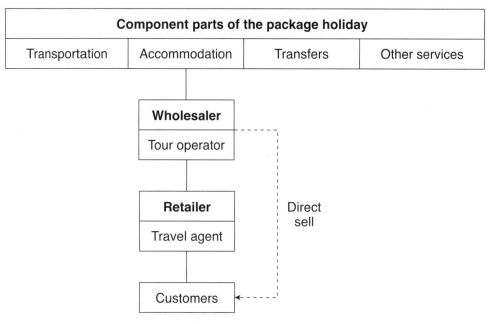

Fig. 19.1 The role of tour operators

The size and structure of the UK tour-operating market

Data from the Central Statistical Office (CSO) shows that UK residents made more than 41 million visits abroad in 1995, over 80 per cent to destinations in western Europe (see Table 19.1). This compares with a total number of 40 million visits in 1994, indicating a 4 per cent growth between 1994 and 1995.

Table 19.1 Visits abroad by UK residents in 1995

Area visited	Number of visits (000s)
Western Europe	33,950
North America	3,240
Other	4,420
Total	**41,610**

Source: Central Statistical Office

The figures in Table 19.1 are not, however, the number of package holidays (inclusive tours) taken by British people, since the statistics include travel for a number of different purposes, including:

● Independent holidays
● Inclusive tours

- Business travel
- Visiting friends and relatives (VFRs)
- Excursionists
- Miscellaneous travel

Statistics from Stats MR, an independent market research organisation, show the percentage breakdown of these categories of travel for 1994 (see Table 19.2).

Table 19.2 Categories of overseas travel by UK residents in 1994

Category of travel	Share (%)
Inclusive tours	38
Independent holidays	23
Business travel	14
VFR	12
Excursionists	8
Miscellaneous	5

Source: Stats MR

From a total figure for visits abroad in 1994 of 40 million, we can calculate the volumes in each travel category to be as follows:

- Inclusive tours   15.2 million
- Independent holidays 9.2 million
- Business travel   5.6 million
- VFR   4.8 million
- Excursionists   3.2 million
- Miscellaneous   2.0 million

The total market for inclusive tours in 1994 was, therefore, 15.2 million packages. The bulk of this market is made up of air inclusive tours (AITs), including scheduled and charter-based packages and seat-only travel on charter flights, but it does also include package holidays offering other transport arrangements, e.g. cruising, ferry inclusive tours, self-drive packages and rail inclusive tours.

Tour operators' market share

One of the most accurate ways of estimating a tour operator's share of the air inclusive tour (AIT) market is to study the figures released by the Civil Aviation Authority (CAA) on the number of passengers carried under their ATOL (Air Travel Organisers' Licence) scheme (see page 147 for an explanation of ATOLs). CAA figures for the 12 months to September 1995 are shown in Table 19.3. It shows that Thomson Tour Operations was the market leader with 4.2 million passengers carried.

Thomson Travel's own estimates for the relative market share of the top tour operators is shown in Table 19.4, which indicates that the top three operators,

Table 19.3 Passengers carried under the top ten ATOL licences in the 12 months to September 1995

Tour operator	Number of ATOLS
Thomson Tour Operations	4,207,668
Airtours	2,720,588
First Choice Holidays and Flights	1,928,533
Iberotravel	705,256
Unijet Travel	652,091
Avro	574,968
Cosmosair	515,854
Inspirations East	435,769
Sunset Holidays	361,238
Thomas Cook Group	258,240

Source: Central Statistical Office

Table 19.4 Relative market shares of the top UK tour operators 1995 (Thomson estimates to nearest 0.5%)

Tour operator	Share of total market (%)	Share of through agents market (%)
Thomson Tour Operations	24	29.5
Airtours	15.5	18
First Choice	11.5	12.5
Cosmos/Avro	6.5	5.5
Iberotravel	4.0	4.5
Top five	61.5	70
Other operators	38.5	30
Total	**100**	**100**

Thomson, Airtours and First Choice, account for 60 per cent of the total air inclusive tour market.

There are many factors that affect the size of market share held by UK tour operators, such as:

- Product range and variety
- Pricing levels
- Promotional techniques
- Market appeal
- Branding
- Reputation
- Standards of customer service

- Management and staffing structure
- Financial management

Activity

Select a UK-based tour operator that offers packages to long-haul destinations and list the factors that will influence its market share.

Integration in tour operating

As competition in the outbound travel industry has intensified, tour operators have sought alliances and mergers with other businesses as a way of maintaining or increasing market share and maximising profitability. This is most noticeable in the tour operator/travel agent relationship, where:

- Thomson owns the Lunn Poly travel agency chain
- Airtours owns Going Places
- First Choice Holidays has a strategic alliance with Thomas Cook travel agencies
- Inspirations owns the AT Mays travel agency chain

These are all examples of vertical integration in the travel industry, when a company has control over other companies that are at different levels in the chain of distribution. Some of the largest tour operators also own their own airlines, giving even greater control over the component parts of package holidays, e.g. Airtours PLC owns Airtours International (see Figure 19.2).

Horizontal integration occurs when companies at the same level in the distribution chain, or in the same industry sector, merge voluntarily or are the subject of a takeover bid. In the airline sector, for example, British Airways is seeking to achieve its

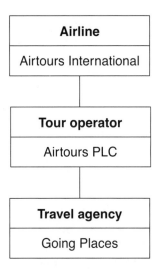

Fig. 19.2 *Vertical integration in the travel and tourism industry*

ambition of becoming the world's biggest airline by mergers and takeovers with other operators, including American Airlines, Qantas and TAT, a French domestic airline. It has also taken over the former British charter airline Dan Air and has interests in Germany with Deutsche BA. Horizontal integration is also common in the hotels sector, where hotel chains such as Inter Continental and Queens Moat Houses achieve economies of scale by controlling the operation and marketing of large numbers of individual hotels. Thomson Travel's acquisition of Country Holidays in 1994, and their takeover of Blakes Country Cottages and English Country Cottages in 1995, is evidence that the major tour operators are actively engaged in both horizontal and vertical integration within the travel and tourism industry, as a way of securing competitive advantage.

There is growing concern among consumer groups and the public generally that the concentration of ownership through vertical and horizontal integration is against the public interest, since it may limit choice and reduce competition in the industry. It is for this reason that any large-scale merger between travel and tourism companies is often referred to the Monopolies and Mergers Commission (MMC) for investigation.

Types of tour operator

There are approximately 600 UK tour operators, most of which are small companies specialising in a particular destination or type of product. Most operators fall into one of the following four categories:

- Mass market operators
- Specialist operators
- Domestic operators
- Incoming tour operators

Mass market operators

These tour operators include some of the best-known names in the industry, such as Thomson, Airtours and First Choice Holidays. They organise air inclusive tours (AITs), often referred to as package holidays, for around 11 million British people each year, thereby dominating the UK outbound tourism market.

At present, three companies together share 60 per cent of the total package holiday market:

- Thomson   29.5 per cent
- Airtours   18 per cent
- First Choice Holidays   12.5 per cent

As the figures show, Thomson is the market leader in the UK outbound tour operating market, followed by Airtours and First Choice Holidays, which operates such companies as Sovereign and Free Spirit. There has been a great deal of uncertainty in the outbound tour operating industry over the last 4 years, ever since Airtours announced a takeover bid for Owners Abroad (now First Choice Holidays) in January 1993. Had the bid not failed, due mainly to an injection of capital by Thomas Cook, the industry would have been left with two major companies controlling nearly two-thirds of all package holiday sales. The collapse in 1991 of Intasun (together with the rest of the International Leisure Group, ILG), had already strengthened Airtours' position in the market, since it had gained the majority of Intasun's previous clients.

The three top tour operators all have their own airlines:

- Thomson owns Britannia Airways.
- Airtours operates it own airline under the Airtours International name.
- First Choice Holidays owns Air 2000.

This is a further example of vertical integration in the travel industry, which we saw earlier in this Element with the major tour operators owning travel agency chains, e.g. Thomson owns Lunn Poly.

Activity

How do you think that the 'products' offered by mass market tour operators might change in the next 10 years? Is the role of the travel agent likely to change over the same time period?

Specialist operators

Although less well-known than the mass market operators, there are literally hundreds of specialist operators in the travel industry, including:

- Those that offer holidays and other travel arrangements to a particular geographical region or destination, e.g. Paris Travel Service and Magic of Italy.
- Those that cater for a particular segment of the market, e.g. PGL Adventure Holidays for young children and Saga Holidays who specialise in the 'senior' market.
- Those that specialise in a particular type of activity, e.g. walking holidays offered by the Ramblers' Association and Susie Madron's 'Cycling for Softies', which offers all-inclusive packages to France.
- Those that cater for the special interests of their clients, e.g. wine-tasting holidays in the Loire and art history tours to Italy.
- Those that specialise in sporting holidays and breaks, e.g. Roger Taylor's tennis holidays in the Algarve and tours to see the motor racing Grand Prix around the world.
- Those that use a specific type of accommodation or form of transport, e.g. EuroSites, part of the Airtours Group, which organises self-drive camping holidays on the Continent, and operators who offer nostalgic tours using steam railways.

A glance at the *Travel Trade Directory* will show that the range of specialist operators is vast, indicating that the travel industry is not afraid to rise to the challenge of meeting the needs of many different types of customer.

Activity

Select a small number of activities and special interests, and carry out some research to discover if there are any UK tour operators that sell programmes in your chosen areas.

Domestic operators

Although, in general, the British tourism product has not been extensively 'packaged', there are a number of UK operators that put together inclusive tours for the home market. Probably the best known are coach operators, such as Shearings and National Holidays, which offer value-for-money products geared mainly to the older age groups.

The packaging and marketing of UK short breaks has been something of a success story in recent years. Companies such as Superbreak and Rainbow Holidays have led the development of city and country breaks offered for sale through travel agencies. Some local authorities, keen to boost their visitor numbers, have worked with tour operators to feature their particular destinations in brochures and tour programmes.

Special interest groups are well catered for by domestic operators. Activity holidays are growing in popularity and operators, large and small, are emerging to cater for the demand, e.g. YHA Holidays and HF Holidays. Companies offering specialist services and facilities, ranging from sketching holidays to ballooning breaks, are being increasingly sought by a public looking for something unusual to do in its leisure time.

Hotel groups and marketing consortia (for example, Best Western Hotels), have created and marketed domestic tours for some time, often in conjunction with coach companies. The competitive situation which has arisen in the hotels sector in recent years, however, has forced some hotel groups to widen their customer base by developing themed breaks and activity and special interest tours.

CASE STUDY

Hoseasons Holidays

Introduction

Hoseasons Holidays is the leading independent holiday booking agency in the UK, with its headquarters in Lowestoft, Suffolk. Although its name is most often associated in the public's mind with boats, two-thirds of its clients actually book holiday homes. All Hoseasons' holidays are self-catering, with the company's boating clients booking self-drive, live-aboard cabin motor cruisers or yachts, while the remaining customers opt for a self-catering holiday in a range of accommodation, from modern chalets, caravans and bungalows, to detached country cottages and Scandinavian style lodges. Hoseason's staff book around 200,000 holiday-weeks each year; with an average party size of 4.8 persons, this gives a grand total of 960,000 clients per year. The company claims that it is responsible for arranging one in 22 of all paid-for holidays taken in Britain each year.

Company mission and ethos

The company's mission statement is as follows:

> *Hoseasons Holidays continually aims to be the UK's leading company profitably selling quality self-catering holidays in Western Europe and setting the highest standards of customer service.*
>
> *We will develop complementary businesses by using our established skills and resources.*
>
> *We will continue to provide an environment in which staff are encouraged to play a full part in the development of the business and to share in its profitability.*

For more than 25 years, Hoseasons has been run on a formal management by objectives (MBO) regime, with impressive results. The company's commitment to its staff and their personal and professional development, resulted in it becoming one of the first organisations in the UK to be awarded the 'Investors in People' standard in 1991.

Company history

Hoseasons Holidays was founded in 1944 by Wally Hoseason, the father of the present Chairman James Hoseason OBE. When the business began it was a combination of a booking agency for boating holidays and a sales agency for boats. In 1945 the agency booked 200 people for a boating holiday on the Norfolk Broads and, from that point on, the business grew and grew.

In the late 1960s, the purpose and style of the business was totally overhauled to keep in line with the social and demographic changes taking place in the UK, not least the dramatic rise in car ownership. In the 1970s, the whole basis of the business was broadened, when the company focused on booking boat holidays nationwide on all the waterways in Britain and booking holiday homes throughout England, Scotland and Wales. During the 1980s, the range of destinations grew to include holiday boats in France and Holland, and holiday homes in France, Belgium, Holland, Germany, Italy and Spain.

Staffing the organisation

Hoseasons employs just over 90 full-time, permanent staff and around 130 part-time staff who work all the year round. There are also seasonal part-timers who work during the main booking campaign, working either in the mail room, brochure despatch area, the dial-a-brochure operation or in Hoseasons Marketing Systems, an associated business unit of the main company specialising in bureau services as diverse as direct mail and credit card control. The company's organisational structure is shown in Figure 19.3.

Departmental structure

1. *Booking services* – the hub of the operation, with specially trained teams of sales staff using the latest computer technology. The department is divided into the two core product areas, namely holiday homes, with more than 60 members

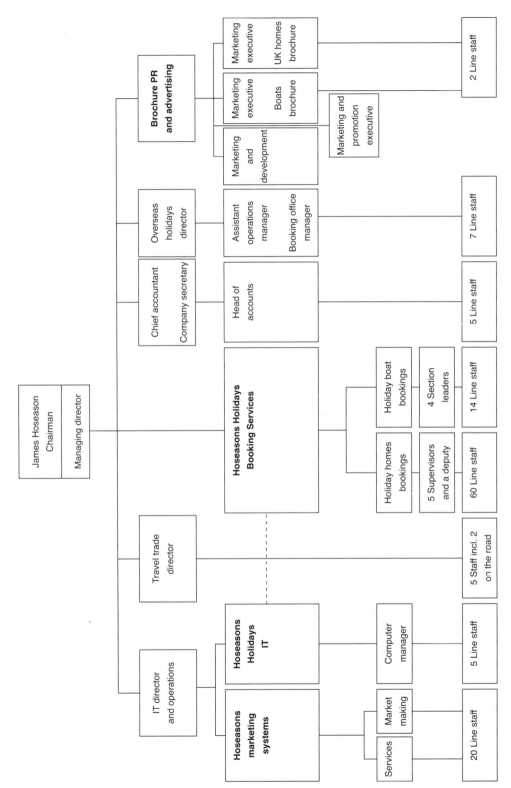

Fig. 19.3 Organisational structure of Hoseasons Holidays

of staff, and holiday boats, with four section leaders controlling the work of 14 sales staff.

2. *Marketing* – the company's marketing team designs and produces the company's brochures, as well as controlling the £9.5 million national advertising and promotional campaign. They also handle the arrangements for exhibition stands and are responsible for liaison with the media and PR companies.
3. *Finance and accounts* – staff in this department pay the wages and ensure that suppliers and principals are paid on time. They also administer the company's insurance and pension schemes. In addition, they prepare monthly management accounts, annual statutory accounts, and budgets, forecasts and financial plans. They also ensure compliance with all current regulations concerning VAT, tax and national insurance.
4. *Travel trade* – the travel trade team is responsible for the day-to-day management of the distribution of Hoseasons' brochures to travel agents nationwide. They also plan and manage their own annual trade marketing campaign, involving the production of a comprehensive marketing information folder, advertising and media relations in the travel trade press, joint sales promotions and agency staff training.

(Information courtesy of Hoseasons Holidays)

Case study discussion questions

1. How does Hoseasons Holidays organise and carry out its marketing function?
2. What are the company's two core products?
3. What techniques does it use to maintain loyalty within its travel trade partners?
4. Who are its main competitors?
5. What internal and external factors are likely to affect the company's performance over the next 10 years?

Incoming tour operators

Incoming, or inbound, UK tourism is concerned with meeting the needs of the increasing numbers of overseas visitors who choose to visit Britain; outbound tourism, on the other hand, deals with UK people taking holidays abroad. Just as we would visit a travel agency to book our annual overseas holiday or business trip abroad, so many overseas visitors do the same in their own country when they want to come to Britain. A travel agent in the USA, for example, who has a client wanting to spend a week in Scotland, has to contact a tour operator to make all the arrangements; this operator, who may be based in the USA or in Scotland, is known as an incoming tour operator, since it is providing a service for overseas visitors to Britain.

There are around 300 incoming tour operators in this country that specialise in dealing with the incoming market. Some are little more than handling agents offering a transfer or 'meet and greet' service on behalf of an agent or operator. Others, such as British Heritage Tours, Frames Rickards and Evan Evans Tours, offer complete package tours of the UK, which are sold through overseas agents. The packages are often themed, including tours based on British heritage, gardens or castles. Approximately 100 incoming tour operators in the UK are members of BITOA (the

British Incoming Tour Operators' Association). Founded in 1977, BITOA is an independent organisation that aims to provide a forum for the exchange of information and ideas, to follow an accepted code of conduct and to act as a pressure group in dealing with other bodies in the UK with a common interest in tourism matters.

Legal and regulatory requirements of tour operators

In addition to carrying out their business within the standard requirements of UK and European legislation, tour operators have a number of specific legal and regulatory requirements to take into consideration. The most important include:

- Premises legislation
- Company law
- Health and safety legislation
- Employment law
- Contract law
- Consumer protection legislation
- EU Package Travel Directive
- Codes of conduct
- Bonding requirements

These are shown diagrammatically in Figure 19.4.

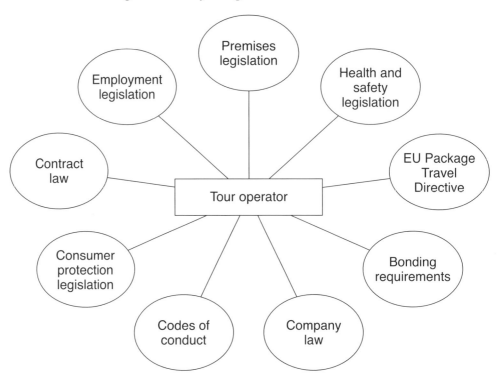

Fig. 19.4 UK tour operators' legal and regulatory framework

Premises legislation

Any tour operator setting up premises for the first time, or making significant alterations to buildings, is likely to come within the scope of UK planning legislation and building regulations. As well as physical alterations to premises, planning regulations also cover 'change of use', when planning permission is needed for any material change to the use of land or buildings. A tour operator converting a house into offices, for example, would fall within the scope of a material change of use.

Under the Occupiers' Liability Acts of 1957 and 1984, the 'occupier' of premises, who will be either the owner or the person in control, owes a legal duty of care to all who use the premises. The duty is to make the visitor, as opposed to the premises, as safe as is practicable. The Acts specifically state that the occupier must be prepared for children to be less careful than adults. Tour operators who invite customers onto their premises to enquire and make bookings must ensure their safety at all times.

Company law

The main form of business organisation in the UK is the limited company and most UK tour operating businesses are run under this type of setup, either as private limited companies or public limited companies (PLCs). The principal piece of UK legislation concerning the formation of companies and their operation is the Companies Act of 1985. The Act stipulates the documentation and records that all companies must keep, including the Memorandum of Association and the Articles of Association. The former is concerned with the company's relationship with the outside world and contains the company name, its address, the purpose for which the company is formed, the liability and voting rights of the shareholders, and the amount of share capital. The Articles of Association are essentially the company's set of rules, outlining details regarding the frequency of meetings, types of shares, voting procedures, the names of directors and their powers, and other company matters. Parts of the 1985 Act were amended in 1989 to bring it into line with European legislation.

Health and safety legislation

There is a wide variety of legislation that imposes certain duties on the management and staff of tour operators in relation to health and safety issues in the workplace. To begin with, there is a common law duty of care, under which each citizen owes a duty to all others who may be affected by his or her activities. If a person takes insufficient care in relation to another citizen, and that person suffers damage as a result, the injured party may begin an action in the civil court to reclaim damages. However, this civil law only comes into action after damage has been suffered. Although the outcomes of civil cases have given the courts many opportunities to create precedents that guide the conduct of similar occurrences in the future, the civil law has always been considered an inappropriate instrument in the area of accident prevention. The advent of the Health and Safety at Work, etc. Act 1974 changed all this.

The Health and Safety at Work, etc. Act (HSW Act) was introduced to provide the legislative framework to promote, stimulate and encourage high standards of health and safety at work. It is an enabling measure superimposed over existing health and safety legislation. In addition to placing duties of a general nature on employers, manufacturers, employees, the self-employed and others, the Act provides wide powers for the making of regulations. Part I of the Act, the part that is of most concern to travel and tourism organisations, aims to:

- Secure the health, safety and welfare of people at work.
- Protect other people against risks to health or safety arising from the activities of people at work.
- Control the storage and use of dangerous substances, e.g. chemicals, and preventing their unlawful use.
- Control the emission into the atmosphere of noxious or offensive substances from premises.

Under the requirements of the Act, it is the duty of every employer to safeguard, so far as is reasonably practicable, the health, safety and welfare of all those in his or her employment. This duty is extended to others who may be affected by the operation of the facility, e.g. contractors, visitors and members of the general public. In practice the employer must have specific regard for the following:

- To provide plant and equipment that is not a risk to health.
- To ensure that work systems and practices are safe.
- To ensure that the work environment is regularly monitored in respect of health and safety requirements.
- To provide safe storage for substances that could pose a threat to safety, and to ensure their safe use.
- To provide a written statement of safety policy and bring it to the notice of employees (applies only to those employing five or more staff).
- To provide adequate information and training for all staff in matters relating to health and safety.

Employees also have a duty under the HSW Act:

- To take reasonable care to avoid injury to themselves or to others by their work activities.
- To co-operate with their employers and other agencies to ensure that the requirements of the Act are carried out.
- Not to interfere with or misuse anything provided to protect their health, safety and welfare under the Act.

European Union Directives on health and safety

Six new sets of health and safety at work regulations came into force on 1 January 1993. They apply to almost all kinds of work activity, including travel and tourism, and, like the health and safety laws we already have, they place duties on employers to protect:

- Their employees.
- Other people, including members of the public, who may be affected by the work being carried out.

These new UK regulations are needed to implement six European Union (EU) directives on health and safety at work. They are also part of a continuing modernisation of existing UK law. The new regulations cover:

- Health and safety management
- Work equipment safety
- Manual handling of loads
- Workplace conditions
- Personal protective equipment
- Display screen equipment

The regulation that is particularly relevant to tour operators is that concerning display screen equipment. Nowadays it is very common for tour operating staff to use computers and visual display units (VDUs) in their work. Under the new regulations, employers have a duty to:

- Assess display screen equipment workstations and reduce risks that are discovered.
- Make sure that workstations satisfy minimum requirements.
- Plan display screen equipment work so that there are breaks or changes of activity.
- Provide information and training for display screen equipment users.

Staff using display screen equipment are also entitled to appropriate eye and eyesight tests by an optician or doctor, and to special spectacles if they are needed and normal glasses cannot be used. It is the employer's responsibility to provide tests and special spectacles if needed.

Employment law

Tour operators, like all business enterprises, are bound by the many regulations concerning employment that exist in Britain today. The most important are considered below.

Contracts of employment

A contract of employment, like all other contracts, is formed when there is an offer and an acceptance, i.e. the personnel director of SunSky Tours offers John West a permanent post as a reservations clerk with the company and John accepts the job. Employment contracts do not have to be in writing, but if a written contract is not given, employees must be provided with a statement of the most important terms of the employment. Under the Trade Union Reform and Employment Rights Act of 1993, employees who are eligible to be given a contract of employment must receive it within two months of starting their job. The contract will contain details of a number of conditions of employment, including the names of both parties to the contract, the job title, the date when employment began, details of remuneration, hours of work, holiday entitlement, termination arrangements and grievance procedures.

Discrimination

In Great Britain the principal Acts of Parliament that prohibit discrimination are the Sex Discrimination Act 1975 and the Race Relations Act 1976. The Sex Discrimination Act states that employers must not treat people of a particular gender any less favourably for recruitment and selection, training and promotion. The Race Relations Act makes it illegal for an employer to discriminate against employees on the grounds of race, colour, national or ethnic origin, or nationality.

Activity

Carry out some further research into the scope of the Sex Discrimination Act and investigate if there are circumstances in which a person of a particular gender can be specified in a job advertisement.

Redundancy

Redundancy is defined as dismissal of an employee wholly or partly due to:

1. The fact that an employer has ceased, or intends to cease, to carry on the business for the purposes of which the employee was employed, or has ceased, or intends to cease, to carry on that business in the place where the employee was so employed.
2. The fact that the requirements of that business for employees to carry out work of a particular kind, or to carry out work of a particular kind in the place where they were so employed, have ceased or diminished, or are expected to cease or diminish.

These rather lengthy definitions mask a process that can be very painful for both employers and employees. For the employers, it can be seen as the ultimate sign of failure, after what is often a long struggle for survival. For employees, it means the loss of a job that they may have held for many years, with all the financial and emotional repercussions that this entails. In simple terms, redundancies occur when an organisation ceases to trade entirely, or is forced to reduce its workforce. In travel and tourism, one of the biggest collapses in recent times was that of the International Leisure Group (ILG), best known for its Intasun tour operating brand, with the loss of many thousands of jobs. Less publicised, although no less tragic, are the daily redundancies of employees working in all sectors of travel and tourism, as their employers cut back on staffing levels in order to survive the difficult economic climate in Britain today.

Dismissal

There are occasions in all industry sectors, and tour operating is no exception, when the dismissal of an employee can cause problems that may end up being resolved by way of an arbitration scheme or an industrial tribunal. Dismissal is defined as:

- The termination of an employee's contract by his or her employer either with or without notice.
- Where a fixed term contract comes to an end and is not renewed.

- Where the employee is entitled to terminate the contract without notice by reason of the employer's conduct (constructive dismissal).

There are provisions in the Employment Protection Act 1978, as amended by the Employment Act 1989, concerning the protection of employees who feel that they have been unfairly dismissed. Under present law, not all workers can claim for unfair dismissal. Those excluded are:

- Employees over the age of 65, or the normal retirement age of their organisation if this is lower.
- Those who work for less than 16 hours per week.
- Staff who have been with their employer for less than two years.

Contract law

The principles of contract law are of concern to all UK tour operators, since, in the normal course of business trading, they make contracts with a wide range of individuals and organisations, including:

- Suppliers – e.g. hoteliers, airlines, coach companies, handling agents, etc.
- Intermediaries – e.g. travel agents selling the tour operator's products to the public
- Customers
- Staff

Contrary to popular belief, most contracts do not need to be in writing. From a lawyer's standpoint, a contract is any agreement that the law will enforce, whether in writing, verbal or implied, i.e. assumed from the conduct of the parties. Contracts range from the very simple, e.g. buying a drink at a resort complex, to the very complex, e.g. building the Channel Tunnel. The law of contract is principally concerned with promises which constitute part of an agreed exchange. It governs such questions as which agreements the law will enforce, what obligations are imposed by the agreement and what will happen if the obligations are not carried out.

The following conditions must be satisfied if a contract is to be legally enforceable:

- There must have been agreement between the parties on all material aspects of the contract.
- The parties must have intended to create a legally binding contract.
- There must be at least two parties to the contract.

It is an essential requirement of English law that, for a contract to be legally binding, each party must have agreed to provide something of value to the other. For example, when a customer books a package holiday, but the booking has yet to be confirmed, the contract between the customer and the tour operator may still be legally binding even where he or she has not yet paid for it. The important point is that the customer has promised to pay the price for the holiday when required to do so. The tour operator, on the other hand, promises that the holiday is available.

It is important to remember that when a holidaymaker books a package holiday through a travel agent, the contract is between the customer and the tour operator, with the travel agent merely acting as an intermediary. It is against the tour operator that the customer must seek legal redress in the event of a breach of contract.

Activity

Study a current brochure from a mass market tour operator and list the commitments that the operator undertakes to make to the customer and what is expected in return from the customer.

Consumer protection legislation

The last 25 years has seen a dramatic growth in the power of the consumer in the UK. Driven often by consumer groups and media pressure, today's consumers are far more sophisticated in their purchasing habits and much less likely to put up with shoddy goods and services. The government has responded to this consumer revolution by introducing a wide range of consumer protection legislation of relevance to the tour operating sector, the most important of which are considered below (the EU Package Travel Directive also provides protection for the travelling public and is discussed below).

Consumer Protection Act 1987

The Consumer Protection Act makes it a criminal offence for an organisation or individual to give misleading price information about goods, services, accommodation or facilities being offered for sale. The Act defines a 'misleading' price as one which:

● Is greater than the price given.
● Is described as being generally available, but in reality is only available in certain circumstances.
● Does not fully state what facilities are included in the price and the fact that surcharges will be payable after booking.

The Act has special significance for tour operators who must ensure the accuracy of any price information in their brochures and other publicity material. This is because it is an offence to include incorrect price information even if the inclusion was innocently undertaken, but is later shown to be misleading.

Trade Descriptions Act 1968

This Act protects customers against false descriptions made knowingly or recklessly by those who are selling or providing services, including tour operators' products and services. Any description of, for example, a hotel or resort, must be truthful at the time it was written (if circumstances subsequently change, then the operator must inform the customer of the nature of the changes). This places a duty on owners and operators of travel and tourism facilities to produce brochures and other promotional materials that are not intended to deceive the customer.

EU Package Travel Directive

The Package Travel, Package Holidays and Package Tours Directive was adopted in June 1990 and came into operation on 1 January 1993 in the then 12 Member States of the European Union (the number of countries in the EU rose to 15 in 1995). Its main aim is to give people buying package holidays more protection and access to compensation when things go wrong, while at the same time harmonising the rules covering packages operated throughout European Union countries. The provisions of the Directive did not replace national laws and, in the case of the UK, simply consolidated existing legislation and industry codes of conduct. The Package Travel Directive has, nonetheless, caused something of a stir in the UK travel and tourism industry, given its wide-ranging powers and scope. Up to the introduction of the Directive, tour operators had been able to disclaim responsibility when holiday arrangements went wrong – for example, overbooking at a hotel or the failure of a coach transfer to arrive – on the grounds that they had no control over these unfortunate events. Under the terms of the Package Travel Directive, tour organisers must accept legal responsibility for all the services they offer to travellers. Exceptions would be made in circumstances which could neither have been foreseen nor overcome, although in such circumstances, organisers must give all necessary assistance to consumers.

What is a 'package'?

This may seem a relatively easy question, but the precise interpretation of the word 'package' has caused problems in some cases where the organiser of a trip has questioned whether his or her activity falls within the scope of the Directive. The Directive does not define a package as, for example, a two-week holiday to Spain with a major tour operator booked through a high street travel agency. For the purposes of the Directive, a 'package' is defined as:

> . . . the pre-arranged combination of not fewer than two of the following when sold or offered for sale at an inclusive price and when the service covers a period of more than 24 hours or includes overnight accommodation –
> transport;
> accommodation;
> other tourist services not ancillary to transport or accommodation, and accounting for a significant proportion of the package.

This would mean, for example, that:

- A hotel with a golf course next door, where rounds can be booked for guests on request, is not a package.
- A hotel with a golf course next door, with a guaranteed minimum number of rounds included in the holiday price, is a package.
- A hotel with a golf course next door, with golfing instruction included in the holiday price, is not a package.
- A hotel with a golf course next door, with golfing instruction and transport to the hotel included in the price, is a package.

These examples indicate the difficult task of Trading Standards Officers, the people given the job of policing the Directive in the UK, when deciding exactly what constitutes a 'package'. Recent cases have shown that their interpretation of the Directive can be different, depending on where in the country they operate.

Other definitions included in the Directive are as follows:

1. *'Organiser'* – the person who, other than occasionally, organises packages and sells them directly or through a retailer.
2. *'Retailer'* – the person who sells or offers for sale the package put together by the organiser.
3. *'Consumer'* – the person who takes the package (the 'principal contractor'), or any person on whose behalf the principal contractor agrees to purchase the package or any person to whom the package is transferred.
4. *'Contract'* – the agreement linking the consumer to the organiser and/or the retailer.

The scope of the Package Travel Directive

While it is easy to see that the Directive would apply to foreign holidays taken by UK residents, an important feature of the regulations is that they also apply to domestic operators, including tourist information centres, resorts, conference and event organisers, school trip leaders and voluntary groups, although there are allowances for non-profit-making voluntary organisations operating less than four excursions in any one year. Organisers cannot escape the requirements of the Directive by billing separately for the various components of the same package.

Where do the package travel regulations apply?

The regulations apply to packages sold or offered for sale in the UK, regardless of the operator's place of establishment. They do not apply to packages sold in other countries by operators established in the UK, although similar provisions apply in other member states of the European Union and in those countries that are part of the European Economic Area (EEA). The Directive does not apply to packages sold in the Channel Islands or the Isle of Man, although the regulations do apply to organisers based in these areas, or anywhere else in the world, who sell their packages within the UK.

What does the Directive cover?

The Package Travel Directive places a number of duties and responsibilities on the organisers of packages, namely:

- Providing information to customers on the organiser responsible for the package they have booked. That person or organisation is then liable in the event of failure to deliver any elements of the package.
- Providing clear contract terms.
- Giving emergency telephone numbers.
- Providing proof of the organiser's security against insolvency and information on any available insurance policies.
- Giving immediate notification with explanation of any increase in prices permitted within the terms of the contract.
- Providing a variety of compensation options if agreed services are not supplied.
- Producing accurate promotional material including brochures.

The EU Package Travel Directive has been something of a shock to the UK tourist industry since, as we have seen, the Directive covers domestic as well as outbound packages. The travel and tourism industry generally fears that the extra insurance and bonding requirements needed by tour organisers to cover against claims under the Directive is bound to put up the cost of holidays to the consumer.

Codes of conduct

Codes of conduct are, in essence, the minimum standards and rules under which members of trade organisations are expected to conduct their everyday operations, governing such matters as their trading relationships with customers, promotional practices and financial security. ABTA is the principal trade organisation concerned with UK-based tour operators and travel agents. It has developed two Codes of Conduct, the Travel Agents' Code of Conduct and the Tour Operators' Code of Conduct, which were drawn up by ABTA in association with the Office of Fair Trading. The Tour Operators' Code of Conduct lays down the minimum standards of operators' brochures, requiring that they contain clear, comprehensive and accurate descriptions of facilities and services offered. It details rules which govern booking conditions in brochures as they relate, for example, to the cancellation or alteration of tours, holidays or other travel arrangements by the tour operator. The Code also contains strict rules concerning the prompt handling of complaints and regulations relating to the conduct between tour operators and travel agents.

Other trade associations working in the travel and tourism industry have also developed codes of conduct, including the Association of Independent Tour Operators (AITO), the Confederation of Passenger Transport UK (CPT), the former Bus and Coach Council, and the Passenger Shipping Association.

Bonding requirements

All tour operator members of ABTA must provide a bond securing their liability in respect of all forms of transportation, accommodation, travel and holiday arrangements, whether outside or within the UK. The bond is a formal undertaking from an approved bank or insurance company to pay a sum of money to ABTA or the Civil Aviation Authority (CAA) in the event of the company's financial failure. The bond moneys are used primarily for the purpose of reimbursing customers who would otherwise lose money that they had already paid, so that:

- Clients whose holidays are actually taking place when a tour operator ceases trading can continue with their holiday as planned or be brought back to the UK.
- Clients who have yet to travel on holidays already paid for can get their money back when an operator fails.
- Alternative holiday arrangements can be made for clients who have paid for trips which have yet to take place when a tour operator ceases trading.

For bonding purposes, tour operators are classed as either 'licensable' or 'non-licensable'. Licensable activities are those that require the operator to hold an Air Travel Organiser's Licence (ATOL); all other tour operations are classed as non-licensable. The CAA bonds provided by ATOL holders provide the first line of defence for licensable activities when things go wrong, whereas ABTA bonds provided by members fulfil the same function in respect of non-licensable activities.

The Association of Independent Tour Operators (AITO) also operates a bonding scheme for its 150 member companies, under the AITO Trust banner. It is responsible for monitoring the financial performance of AITO members within the scheme, setting bonding levels and collecting premiums. AITO Trust has approved status under the regulations developed out of the 1992 Package Travel Directive, offering full financial security to the customers of companies bonded via the system, including repatriation to the UK if necessary. The arrangement is designed to bond non-licensable turnover, i.e. holidays including surface transport options such as self-drive, coach or train-based trips.

Current and future trends in the tour operating market

Over the last five years, the trading situation for tour operators has been very difficult. The inclusive tour market grew rapidly during the first half of the 1980s, when the economy as a whole was buoyant and bookings were growing at about 8 per cent annually. The package holiday market in the UK relies heavily on volume sales to offset small profit margins and the recession of the late 1980s and early 1990s has put pressure on the tour operators, which in turn has been reflected in the low profitability of many travel agents. In recent years, tour operators have tended to cut back on the supply of holidays made available to the public, rather than trim their already perilous margins even further.

Industry experts suggest that the outbound (ex-UK) tour operating market is set to remain highly price competitive for the foreseeable future. Intense competition between the leading mass market operators is likely to lead to reduced industry profitability, with inevitable casualties along the way, and a continuation of the trend for large operators to acquire other travel companies to enlarge their product portfolio. Specialist operators will continue to fill important market niches and capitalise on the growing public interest in 'unpackaged packages', offering a greater degree of choice and flexibility.

 ## Activity

With reference to one market sector, e.g. families, young single couples or 'empty nesters', consider the main factors that will affect your chosen tourists' demand for overseas package holidays in the future.

Future developments in the tour operating sector

The continuing recession in the UK economy will mean that the market for outbound and domestic leisure and business travel products and services is likely to show little growth over the next 2–4 years. Profit margins of tour operators and travel agents will be further squeezed and all companies will be constantly monitoring their costs of operation, making cuts in staffing and premises whenever the need arises. Within this rather gloomy overall picture, however, there will be successes and opportunities for expansion. Some of the most likely future developments include:

1. *Continued growth in the long-haul market* – helped by new aircraft technology and the consequent availability of charter flights, destinations such as the USA, Australia, the Caribbean and the Far East will continue to be popular with both package and independent tourists.
2. *Growth in independent travel* – the trend away from inclusive tours towards more independent travel is likely to continue. In order to retain market share, tour operators will need to offer more flexibility in the design of their holidays, while some travel agents will seize the opportunity and offer a more customised service to their clients.
3. *Growth in short holidays and breaks* – both domestic and outbound operators will continue to provide short breaks to meet growing demand. Developments in transportation, such as the Channel Tunnel and the deregulation of European air fares, will stimulate increases in this sector.
4. *Demand for activity and health-related holidays* – growing interest in health and fitness will offer an opportunity for travel organisers to develop greater variety in their activity programmes.
5. *Continuation of the trend towards late bookings* – changes in lifestyle and work patterns will mean a shorter lead time for travel purchases.
6. *Greater concern for quality* – concern over indifferent standards of package holidays have dogged the tour operators in recent years, making it crucial for tour operators to put quality at the top of their agenda when planning new products.
7. *Heightened concern for the environment* – customers will expect their travel organisers to operate in a manner that is respectful of the long-term well-being of the environment when choosing the elements of their packages.

Assignment 19.1

UK-based tour operators

Performance criteria satisfied: 19.1.1, 19.1.2, 19.1.3, 19.1.4, 19.1.5, 19.1.6

Core skills opportunities at level 3:   Communication   3.1, 3.2, 3.3, 3.4
Information technology   3.1, 3.2, 3.3
Application of number   3.1, 3.2, 3.3

Tasks

Working with a partner, you are to prepare a detailed report on the UK tour operating market. In particular, your report should:

● Describe the size and structure of the UK tour operating market.
● Identify the main types of UK tour operators, giving examples of one major operator, one specialist operator, one domestic operator and one incoming tour operator.
● Explain the factors affecting the market share of tour operators.

- Describe the legal and regulatory requirements influencing UK-based tour operators.
- Explain, with examples, the effects of unforeseen and uncontrollable events on the UK tour operating market.
- Assess the current trends in the UK tour operating market.

Your report should be word processed and include relevant charts, diagrams and statistics relating to the UK tour operating market.

Element 19.2   Investigate UK-based tour operators' products

Performance criteria

1. Describe, with examples, the component parts of tour operators' products.
2. Explain, with examples, the relationship between cost of components and pricing and profit.
3. Describe, with examples, how tour operators' products relate to market needs.
4. Explain the importance of brochures for tour operators' products.
5. Explain, with examples, how tour operators sell products to customers.

Tour operators' products

The nature of a particular tour operator's products will be determined by the market in which it operates, since all tour operators are in the business of providing products that satisfy their clients' needs. We saw in Element 19.1 that there are four main types of UK-based tour operators, namely:

- Mass market operators
- Specialist operators
- Domestic operators
- Incoming tour operators

Figure 19.5 gives an indication of the many products offered by the various tour operators.

The principal product of the mass market operators, such as Thomson, Airtours and First Choice Holidays, is the package holiday, which combines accommodation, transportation and other services for an all-inclusive price. Figure 19.5 shows us that these can be classified according to the destination chosen (long haul or short haul) and/or the season of travel (summer or winter). Seat-only sales have become a major growth area for mass market tour operators, as more travellers choose to put together their own foreign holidays or take advantage of cheap flights to visit friends and relatives abroad. Specialist operators focus on specific market niches by providing products based on particular themes, destinations or activities – e.g. Eurocamp specialises in self-drive camping holidays in Europe, Saga provide holidays for older travellers and The Paris Travel Service specialises in holidays to the French capital. Domestic tour operators provide a range of products using a variety of accommodation and transportation arrangements – e.g. coach tours, short breaks in city centre hotels, boating holidays on England's waterways and farm holidays. Incoming tour operators specialise in products for overseas visitors to the UK, such as coach tours of England,

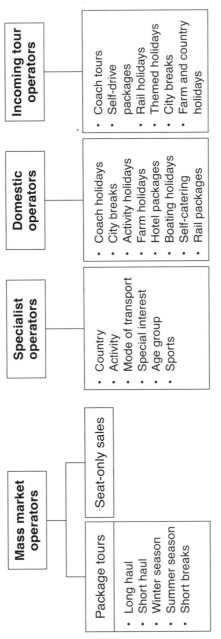

Fig. 19.5 The wide range of tour operators' products

Mass market operators

Seat-only sales

Package tours
- Long haul
- Short haul
- Winter season
- Summer season
- Short breaks

Specialist operators
- Country
- Activity
- Mode of transport
- Special interest
- Age group
- Sports

Domestic operators
- Coach holidays
- City breaks
- Activity holidays
- Farm holidays
- Hotel packages
- Boating holidays
- Self-catering
- Rail packages

Incoming tour operators
- Coach tours
- Self-drive packages
- Rail holidays
- Themed holidays
- City breaks
- Farm and country holidays

Scotland, Northern Ireland and Wales, often based on themes, such as castles, historic houses, gardens and industrial heritage.

Short-haul destinations

Early package holidays were developed using popular short-haul destinations such as Spain, Greece and Italy. Today, tour operators offer packages to a wide range of short-haul destinations (considered to be those within 5 hours' flying time of the UK), although Spain still retains its popularity as the number one package holiday destination for UK travellers, with France second and Greece third (see Table 19.5). It is important to remember that the statistics shown in Table 19.5 relate to travel based on package holidays only; International Passenger Survey (IPS) data shows that, when *all* visits by British people are taken into consideration, France was ahead of Spain in the popularity stakes in 1994.

Table 19.5 Top 10 short-haul package holiday destinations 1994

Country	Number of package holidays (000s)
1. Spain	4,911
2. France	2,111
3. Greece	1,829
4. Italy	716
5 Cyprus	704
6. Portugal	618
7. Turkey	553
8. North Africa	376
9. Austria	375
10. Malta	338

Source: ABTA

The principal product offered by tour operators who sell packages to short-haul destinations is the 'summer sun' holiday. Typically, this product comprises self-catering or serviced accommodation, return flight, transfers and the services of a holiday representative, and takes place during the peak summer period of May to October each year. There is, however, a wide range of other short-haul products offered by UK-based tour operators, including:

- Ski-ing trips, e.g. to the French Alps, Austria, Switzerland, Bulgaria, etc.
- Winter sun packages, e.g. to the Balearic Islands, North Africa, Malta, etc.
- Short breaks to cities such as Amsterdam, Paris and Berlin
- Fly-drive and fly-cruise packages
- Camping and mobile home holidays
- Rail packages
- Coach-based holidays

- Self-drive packages using a variety of accommodation, e.g. gîtes in France, hotels in Italy, etc.
- Attraction-based packages, e.g. to Disneyland Paris, Legoland in Denmark, etc.
- Activity holidays, e.g. bird watching in Majorca, walking in the Alps, cycling in France, etc.
- Sports packages, e.g. motor racing grand prix, golfing packages in Portugal, etc.

Products to short-haul destinations will continue to dominate the UK outbound tour-operating market, although the growth in the popularity of destinations further afield will provide UK-based tour operators with increasing sales opportunities.

Long-haul destinations

Advances in aircraft technology, coupled with low aircraft charter prices from the major tour operators, have led to a steep rise in the demand for holiday packages to long-haul destinations. The USA is the number one long-haul destination for UK holidaymakers, due in no small part to the popularity of Florida as an all-year-round holiday destination (see Table 19.6). The Caribbean is also growing in popularity, with new destinations such as Cuba and the Dominican Republic attracting many British tourists for the first time. Statistics from the International Passenger Survey (IPS) show that the number of UK packages to the Caribbean rose from 32,000 in 1985 to 202,000 in 1994. The Far East is an increasingly popular long-haul destination, not only with package holidaymakers but also for those travelling independently; Thailand, Malaysia and Singapore are particularly popular with British tourists. Goa, on India's west coast, has long been a favourite destination for independent travellers, but its popularity with package holidaymakers looking for winter sunshine is growing steadily. On the African continent, Kenya and the Gambia are following suit, while the change in political climate in South Africa has meant that many UK holidaymakers are eager to explore the country for the first time. The USA and Canada are both emerging as attractive ski-ing alternatives to the pistes of Europe. As for cruising, the Caribbean remains a firm favourite with UK tourists and the west coast of America is the third most popular fly-cruise destination with the British. ABTA estimates that around 300,000 UK travellers are likely to book a cruise package in 1996, while the Lunn Poly chain puts the forecast as high as 400,000, on the back of a 24 per cent rise in the cruise market between 1994 and 1995.

Short breaks

Short breaks taken by British people both in the UK and abroad, have been a resounding success story, particularly since the beginning of the 1980s. Although the traditional British two-week holiday is in something of a decline, innovative tour operators and accommodation providers have joined forces to develop a wide variety of short-break programmes, often utilising unfilled bedspaces in hotels at weekends and during other slack periods. Short breaks based on themes as diverse as sculpture, archery and murder-mystery weekends are now commonplace throughout the UK.

Table 19.6 Top 10 long haul package holiday destinations 1994

Country	Number of package holidays (000s)
USA	519
Commonwealth Caribbean	202
Africa (excluding North and South Africa)	154
Latin America	62
Canada	60
Middle East	53
Australia	16
New Zealand	9
South Africa	4
Japan	1

Source: ABTA

Short breaks are also an important part of the short-haul outbound market from the UK. ABTA estimates that there will be in the region of 2.5 million British people taking short breaks to European countries in 1996, travelling with companies such as British Airways Holidays, Time Off and many of the large, mass market operators, including Thomson with its own Citybreaks product. Although Paris, Amsterdam and Rome are the three most popular short-break cities, new destinations such as Prague, Berlin, Budapest, St Petersburg and Istanbul are finding favour with those wishing to travel further afield. Long-haul short breaks are also increasing in popularity and, of these, New York is the most popular with the British, followed by Toronto.

The dramatic growth in short breaks lies in the changing leisure habits of much of the population, linked to changes in working practices, making the traditional two-week break unpopular with a growing section of the UK travelling public, many of whom have a number of short periods off work and sufficient disposable income to be able to enjoy more than one holiday each year.

Activity

Select a European city or region and find out which operators offer short breaks to your chosen area. Investigate if there are any similarities or differences in the way that the operators present the destination in their promotional materials.

Seat-only sales

Since the restrictions on the sale of airline seats without pre-booked accommodation were relaxed in 1992, following the introduction of the Single European Market, seat-only sales from the UK to overseas destinations have grown dramatically. Indeed the growth in seat-only sales has been so rapid that Lunn Poly, in its annual holiday market report, estimates that more UK travellers bought seat-only packages than inclusive tours in 1995 – a total of 12 million seat-only sales that the company expects to rise to 12.3 million in 1996. Historically, the seat-only market has been seen as a way of disposing of unsold charter airline seats at discounted rates. Today, however, it is regarded as a holiday product in its own right, with companies such as Vivair, Flightbookers and Connexions specialising in this industry sector. All the major mass market tour operators also sell seat-only packages in addition to their inclusive tours. Demand for seat-only packages has come from the growth in second home owner-ship, including timeshare accommodation, plus the desire on the part of an increasing number of travellers to create their own 'DIY packages'.

Component parts of tour operators' products

We have seen so far in this Unit that the role of the tour operator is to assemble the individual parts of a holiday and offer the final product to the customer at an all-inclu-sive price. This involves negotiation with the providers of accommodation, trans-portation and other travel services to put the packages together, and distribution to travel agents for those operators who do not sell direct to the public. Although the range and variety of tour operators' products is vast, they all have a similar structure, with three distinct components, namely:

1. *Accommodation* – serviced or self-catering.
2. *Transportation* – to, from and within the destination.
3. *Other travel services* – including transfers, excursions, guiding, equipment hire, etc.

Element 17.2 looked in greater detail at the component parts of package holidays, the principal product offered by UK tour operators (see page 59).

Costing and pricing tour operators' products

A tour operator's main source of income is the revenue it receives from its main holiday product, the package holiday or inclusive tour (IT). This revenue may come direct from the customer if it is a 'direct sell' company, or, more usually, through a travel agent who will sell the holiday on behalf of the operator. A large tour operator such as Airtours may have a number of separate operating divisions, each of which will contribute to overall group profits; Airtours owns its own airline, runs camping holidays under the EuroSites brand and operates a chain of travel agencies under the Going Places banner. Mass market tour operators offer a wide range of holiday prod-ucts catering for different sectors of the market. Although this range will vary from time to time in response to fluctuating demand, there is likely to be a series of prod-ucts, which may include:

● A main summer programme
● A winter programme
● City breaks
● Flight-only

- Programmes featuring particular countries or regions, e.g. the Caribbean
- Holidays geared to the youth market
- Programmes for 'seniors'
- Budget holidays
- Specialist programmes, e.g. golf or sailing

Other sources of income to tour operators include:

1. *Interest on money held in account* – deposits for holidays are sometimes paid up to 12 months before departure and balances settled 6–8 weeks before the start of the holiday. This money accumulates for the tour operator who receives interest on its balances.
2. *Commission on 'extras'* – commission for items such as car hire, insurance, flight-only and excursions is generally paid direct to the tour operator. Most operators will offer their own insurance and car hire in their brochures, hoping to benefit from the higher commission levels that these two products attract.
3. *Currency dealing* – large operators may buy foreign currency in advance if rates are favourable to use later for payments to suppliers. Surplus funds can be invested to provide a return.
4. *Vertical integration* – tour operators who have financial interests at more than one level of the distribution chain, can generate income from a greater number of sources, e.g. duty-free sales on aircraft and hotel bar sales.
5. *Charges* – tour operators levy charges for cancellations and amendments to holiday arrangements, which are another source of income.

Costs

Having considered the sources of income available to tour operators, we now have to look at the costs they must bear in order to generate revenue. Like any commercial concern, a tour operator's costs can be categorised as either fixed or variable.

Fixed costs

These are the costs of running a business that do not alter with changes in the level of activity. For example, the rent or rates for a tour operator's premises will be fixed over a period of time, regardless of the number of holidays it sells. Similarly, the insurance and cleaning costs will be the same whether it has a successful or poor season. Fixed costs for tour operators include:

- Rates
- Rent or mortgage
- Interest on loans
- Bonding
- Essential maintenance
- Cleaning
- Insurance
- Permanent staff salaries
- Lighting and heating
- Market research

Variable costs

Variable costs alter in direct proportion to the volume of business generated by tour operators and include:

- Postage
- Telephone, fax and telex charges
- Computer time and equipment hire
- Printing and stationery
- Advertising and publicity
- Part-time staff
- Professional fees and charges
- Bank charges
- Transaction charges, e.g. credit cards

Determining tour prices

In the same way that it is important for tour operators to control costs, pricing their products is crucial to overall profitability. Pricing is a very risky business; a mass market tour operator that sets the prices of its main summer programme holidays too high in relation to the competition, will not achieve optimum levels of sales. On the other hand, if its prices are too low it will find it difficult to produce an adequate profit.

There are two basic methods that can be adopted to arrive at the cost of an inclusive tour:

- Cost-based pricing
- Market-based pricing

Cost-based pricing involves calculating all the fixed and variable costs of a tour product, including any commission payments to agents, and setting the price at a level which covers all these costs and allows a profit margin. This is the method adopted by small, specialist operators who are unlikely to be operating in such a competitive environment as the mass market holiday companies and whose products will have a degree of uniqueness. In large tour companies, apportioning all costs to particular cost centres may be a very difficult task; while it will be relatively easy to determine the variable costs of a tour programme, calculating the proportion of fixed operating costs to be allocated to that programme is a much more difficult task.

Sometimes referred to as 'what the market will bear', market-based pricing sets pricing in a wider context by taking account of what competitors are charging when determining prices. Re-issuing brochures with revised prices is now commonplace among tour operators that are constantly checking competitor activity and making adjustments to maintain their market share. Following the market leader's pricing is a risky business, if a company has not fully taken into account its own costs of operation; the collapse of Intasun in 1991 is a good example of this type of 'overtrading'. The hope is that the economies of scale involved in tour operating will enable the larger operators to reduce their costs, but still allow a profit margin at the end of the day.

To show that pricing is often a combination of market- and cost-based approaches, we will look at a simplified example of how the pricing policy for a typical overseas package holiday is worked out.

EXAMPLE

Costing an inclusive tour to the Costa Blanca

14 nights half-board

	£	£
Flight costs		
26 return flights during the season @ £12,000 per flight	312,000	
Empty leg at beginning and end of the season	12,000	
Total flight costs	324,000	
Cost per occupied flight (£324,000 divided by 26)	12,461	
Cost per seat based on 90% load factor using Boeing 737 with a capacity of 130 passengers		106.50
Hotel costs per person for 14 days		90.00
Transfers and handling fees		7.50
Total costs of tour per person		204.00

Having calculated that £204 is needed to cover the direct costs of the holiday, the tour operator will now determine a price which covers these costs plus a mark-up to cover a proportion of fixed costs, the commission payment to travel agents and leaves a profit margin for the operator. The exact amount of the mark-up, and hence the final price of the holiday, will be determined by:

● Prices of similar holidays offered by competitors
● The cost of the holiday last year
● The season in which the holiday is being taken

Assuming a mark-up of 25 per cent, the final brochure price of this holiday to the Costa Blanca will be:

$$£204 \times 25\% = £255$$

This figure is known as the break-even point. The operator will sell the holiday at above break-even when demand is high and below £255 when demand is low, out of season.

We have seen that tour operators rely on obtaining the elements of their inclusive tours at discounted rates, from suppliers such as hoteliers and airlines, which are happy to negotiate a discount in return for releasing an agreed amount of stock. Discounting is also prevalent at the other end of the distribution chain, namely discounted holidays offered for sale in travel agencies. In the past, tour operators have frowned on travel agents that have offered cut-price holidays, but in today's very competitive holiday industry, discounts are a common way for a travel agent to attract custom. At the time of writing, high street travel agents are offering up to 10 per cent off the brochure prices of most major tour operators, in return for the clients taking out the agents' or operators' holiday insurance.

Meeting market needs

We saw in Element 17.2 that tour operators use market segmentation as a way of developing products and services to meet the needs of a wide range of customers. By dividing its market into identifiable segments, each with similar characteristics, a tour operator can concentrate on providing packages that holidaymakers will want to buy. If we take the example of the number one UK tour operator, Thomson, it produces a variety of package holiday products, each aimed at a particular market segment, including:

- Main summer sun programme
- Main winter sun programme
- Specialist programmes to particular regions – e.g. Greece, Cyprus, Turkey, USA/Florida
- Cruises programme
- Citybreaks programme
- Faraway Shores – long-haul programme
- Niche market programmes – e.g. Young at Heart, Small and Friendly, À la Carte, Lakes and Mountains
- Main winter ski programme – Ski Thomson

Developing programmes involves a great deal of planning and market research, focusing on changes in tastes and habits, consumer-buying behaviour and competitor activity. In order to maintain a successful portfolio of holiday products, tour operators must constantly monitor sales performance and customer satisfaction levels. This internal company information will allow the operator to make alterations to programmes from one year to another, in order to continue to meet the needs of the travelling public.

The importance of brochures

Element 22.2 looks in detail at the role of brochures and the key stages in the brochure production process. For tour operators, the brochure is their most crucial promotional tool, providing detailed information, images and prices to potential clients, designed to persuade them to make a booking. In particular, brochures aim to:

- Accurately present products and services to the reader.
- Supply product information to travel agents.
- Convey an image of the company.
- Offer a means of booking a holiday.
- Explain booking and contractual conditions.
- Present the information within the bounds of current UK and European Union legislation.

Above all, brochures should be designed in such a way that they have the best chance of converting enquiries into sales.

ABTA's standards on brochures

The ABTA Tour Operators' Code of Conduct states that:

> *Every brochure published by or in the name of any ABTA member shall contain clear, legible, comprehensive and accurate information to enable the client to exercise an informed judgement in making his choice.*

The Code goes on to say that, as a minimum, brochures produced by ABTA members must contain the following information:

1. *Government/statutory licensing authority* – all information necessary to comply with the regulations for the time being of the Civil Aviation Authority or any other governmental or statutory licensing authority.
2. *Legal identity* – the legal identity of the member responsible for publishing the brochure containing the tour, holiday or travel arrangement offered, including their registered company number where applicable.
3. *Financial protection* – the means of financial protection attached to the tour, holiday or travel arrangement offered within the brochure, including the ABTA number and ATOL number where applicable.
4. *Means of travel* – the means of travel, e.g. ship, train, coach, motor vehicle, aircraft; the characteristics of the transport, e.g. charter, scheduled; the category of transport used, e.g. economy, business class, first class or class of cabin.
5. *Destinations and/or itinerary* – as appropriate.
6. *Date, place and time of departure and return* – the date, place and approximate time of departure and return. Where any or all of these items are subject to alteration by a regulatory body, e.g. Airport Scheduling Committee, reference must be made to same.
7. *Nature of accommodation* – including its location, category or degree of comfort, its main features and, where the accommodation is to be provided in an EC member state, its approval or tourist classification under the rules of that member state, where such rules exist.
8. *Meal facilities* – the meals that are included in the price, if any.
9. *Additional facilities* – any additional facilities or special arrangements included in the price.
10. *Changes to brochure details* – the Package Travel Directive 1993 (see page 144) makes the particulars contained within a brochure binding upon the tour operator, unless the brochure contains a clear, express statement that changes may be made to the particulars within the brochure at any time after publication.
11. *Booking conditions* – the procedures for booking and the contractual conditions under which the booking is made must comply with all relevant provisions of the Tour Operators' Code of Conduct and should include details of, for example, payment of deposits and balance due dates, confirmation of the booking, any alteration to a confirmed booking made by the client, cancellation procedures and charges, the tour operator's liability to the client, etc.
12. *Insurance details* – if a tour operator offers holiday insurance, an accurate and sufficiently detailed summary of the cover provided and the associated premiums must be shown in the brochure. Where the purchase of the tour operator's own insurance is compulsory, the relevant premium must be included in the basic price.

13. *Price policy* – the total price, or a means of arriving at the total price, together with a precise statement of the services included therein, must be shown in the brochure. If a tour operator reserves the right to levy a surcharge, a statement to that effect must appear close to the basic price, with an indication of where further information may be found in the brochure. If a price indication becomes misleading while the brochure is still current, the tour operator shall inform all travel agents to whom the brochure has been distributed.

14. *Health matters* – the brochure must contain adequate information relating to both recommended and compulsory health requirements of countries featured or a reference to the Depart of Health leaflet *Advice on Health for Travellers*, available from their ABTA travel agent or direct from the Department of Health. Clients should also be advised to check with their own doctor before their departure as to which inoculations are available and necessary for specific areas.

15. *Arbitration* – it is recommended that a statement to the effect that any disputes arising may be referred to arbitration under a special scheme, which, although devised by arrangement with ABTA, is administered independently by the Chartered Institute of Arbitrators.

16. *Noise* – brochures which feature resort-based holidays shall contain adequate information relating to all known sources of noise which exist or might be expected to exist at resorts, and which may reasonably be considered to cause offence to clients. Such sources of noise include, but are not limited to, nightclubs, bars, discos, amusement parks and airports.

17. *Building works* – where it is known, or can reasonably be expected, that building works which are likely to adversely affect the enjoyment of a holiday will take place during the period covered by the brochure, all specific information must be published on the relevant page in the brochure.

18. *Publication date* – the month and year of publication must be printed in the brochure.

19. *Delays at points of departure* – brochures must state clearly and unambiguously the tour operator's policy on the handling of clients who are delayed at the outward and/or homeward points of departure. Tour operators are encouraged, but not obliged, to provide refreshments/meals appropriate to the time of day and overnight accommodation dependent upon the length of delay and nature of the holiday.

Selling tour operators' products

We have seen that the majority of overseas package holidays are sold through travel agents, some of which are owned by, or have trading relationships with, the major tour operating companies (see Figure 19.6).

Successful selling of holidays in these circumstances hinges on an effective brochure distribution system and the selling skills of the agency staff, backed up with national and local advertising and promotion. Tour operators that sell direct to their customers do not have to pay commission to agents, but instead have to invest in a variety of advertising and other sales promotion activities to generate enquiries and

Fig. 19.6 Travel agencies are the first port of call for the majority of package holidaymakers

sell their products (see Unit 22 for more detailed information on promotional techniques in travel and tourism). In addition to the vertical integration practised by the major tour operating companies in the UK, some smaller, specialist operators have sought formal alliances with travel agents in the expectation of improved business relationships leading ultimately to increased sales. The work of the Association of Independent Tour Operators (AITO) and their alliance with independent travel agents is a good case in point (see the case study below).

Activity

Investigate a variety of specialist tour operators to discover what methods they use to sell their holidays to the public.

AITO and The Campaign for Real Travel Agents

Introduction

AITO is an alliance of over 150 smaller, specialist travel companies dedicated to providing a quality product, personal service and choice to the consumer. It was established in 1976, mainly in response to the problems posed for smaller travel companies by a sudden, sharp increase in bonding requirements following the collapse of a number of major tour operators. In recent years, AITO has come to be recognised increasingly as the official voice of the smaller or specialist tour operator, whose views had seldom been represented or given due consideration by those who regulate the travel industry. The majority of AITO members are small, owner-managed companies, giving high standards of personal service and attention to detail.

Membership of the Association has grown significantly since 1990, when it introduced its own bonding scheme, administered by AITO Trust Ltd. Currently, AITO has over 150 member companies, whose individual passenger carryings range from several hundred to just under 200,000, with the majority of members responsible for between 10,000 and 20,000 passengers per year. AITO members as a whole carried 1.9 million passengers in 1995, which gives the Association a certain degree of credibility in the travel industry. Member companies include Eurocamp, Explore Worldwide, Allez France Holidays and Cox & Kings Travel.

Aims of the Association

AITO's stated aims are:

- To ensure that the public can book AITO members' holidays with every confidence.
- To inform members of the issues of the day and to encourage higher standards and greater professionalism among members.
- To encourage members and their clients to be aware of environmental issues and to promote environmentally sustainable tourism.
- To help members market their wares more effectively to customers.
- To ensure that the views and problems of the smaller, specialist tour operators are understood and that the interests of their clients are protected.

The work of AITO

The Association's work spans a wide variety of travel concerns, including:

1. *A social forum* – AITO acts as a forum for the exchange of ideas and views between its members and the industry in general. It holds regular meetings in the UK and an annual overseas meeting for members, their guests and the travel press.
2. *Lobbying* – AITO has become increasingly important as a political lobbying group over recent years, as a respected body of opinion representing a significant section of the UK tour operating market. Its views have been sought by the Monopolies and Mergers Commission, Office of Fair Trading, Department of Trade and Industry, etc.
3. *Promotion and public relations* – AITO has worked hard to raise the profile of its member companies with the press and the public in general. It organises press functions for member companies, two main brochure launches each year and a series of smaller press lunches throughout the year. The Association's *Directory of Real Holidays*, produced annually with a 1996 print run of 75,000 copies, is a major part of its marketing activity. It lists all member companies and is distributed to the public, the press, retail agencies, Trading Standards Officers, MPs, Members of the European Parliament and a wide cross-section of representatives of the travel and tourism industry. There is also a *Ski Directory* and a *Guide to Real Holidays*, racked in over 400 independent travel agencies.

4. *A regulatory body* – all AITO members agree to comply with the Association's quality charter and code of business practice, laying down basic standards relating to the quality of service to customers, accuracy of brochures, financial security and related matters.
5. *Member services* – AITO ensures that its members are kept up to date on all issues that may affect them by providing information, advice and background notes, where appropriate. This includes material on such matters as health and safety, contracting and insurance.
6. *Green tourism* – AITO was involved, in 1990, in the establishment of Green Flag International, a non-profit-making company set up to encourage tour operators to understand the importance of environmentally sustainable tourism. The principles of 'green tourism' are promoted in AITO's publications and AITO intends to continue backing initiatives relating to tourism and the environment.

The Campaign for Real Travel Agents (CARTA)

In June 1994, AITO launched a new initiative to link independent tour operators with independent travel agents, with the aim of generating new business for both parties. Originally called the AITO 100 Club, the initiative was expanded in June 1995 and renamed the Campaign for Real Travel Agents (CARTA). To date there are 120 tour operator brands (85 companies) and 442 travel agents in the scheme. Each of the holidays in the Association's *Guide to Real Holidays* can be booked through an independent agent, who can offer advice on product and destination selection and availability. The Guide is designed for racking in travel agencies and the Association has developed a range of point-of-sale materials to accompany the CARTA initiative (see Figure 19.7).

Training is an important aspect of the CARTA scheme, as a way of improving links between operators and agents. Public relations activity and local advertising are used to increase awareness among customers, and the campaign has been reported extensively in the consumer and travel trade press.

(Information courtesy of AITO)

Case study discussion questions

1. What were the main reasons behind the formation of AITO in 1976?
2. If you were the owner of a specialist tour operating company, what benefits would you receive from membership of AITO?
3. How can AITO help the drive for more environmentally sustainable tourism?
4. What benefits does the CARTA scheme offer to agents and operators?
5. How does AITO help to raise the profile of its member companies?

Assignment 19.2

UK-based tour operators' products

Performance criteria satisfied: 19.2.1, 19.2.2, 19.2.3, 19.2.4, 19.2.5

Core skills opportunities at level 3:   Communication   3.1, 3.2, 3.3, 3.4
                                         Information technology 3.1, 3.2, 3.3
                                         Application of number   3.1, 3.2, 3.3

Fig. 19.7 *The Campaign for Real Travel Agents' promotional materials (reproduced courtesy of AITO)*

Situation

As part of your induction training for your new role as marketing assistant with a major UK tour operator, you have been asked to produce a detailed report on UK-based tour operators' products for your line manager Jennie Sleight, the company's training services manager.

Tasks

You are to prepare a detailed report entitled 'UK tour operators' products', comparing and contrasting two UK tour operators. In relation to your two chosen companies, your report should:

- Describe the main components of tour operators' products.
- Explain the relationship between cost of components and pricing and profit.
- Describe how tour operators' products relate to market needs.
- Explain the importance of brochures for tour operators' products.
- Explain how tour operators sell products to customers.

Your report should be word processed and include relevant diagrams, charts and statistics.

Element 19.3 Investigate UK and overseas operational practices in tour operating

Performance criteria

1. Explain UK operational practices of UK-based tour operators.
2. Explain overseas operational practices of UK-based tour operators.
3. Match UK personnel and job roles to UK operational practices.
4. Match overseas personnel and job roles to overseas operational practices.

Tour operator organisation

All tour operating companies differ in terms of their strategic and day-to-day organisational structures, although the functions they need to undertake are very similar. Organisational differences usually depend on the scale of operations and the management style adopted by senior staff in the organisation. It is quite possible, for example, for a single person to run a small tour operating concern, using the latest computer and communications technology. This individual will be responsible for all aspects of the operation, from contracting with accommodation and transport providers, producing a brochure and selling the packages to the public. It is more usual, however, for UK outbound tour operators to be medium-sized enterprises, handling the travel requirements of perhaps 15,000 or 20,000 customers per year. The largest operators, Thomson (see case study on page 173), Airtours and First Choice Holidays, between them handle in the region of 8.5 million passengers per year. These mass market operators will have a main UK head office, regional offices in the UK and overseas offices, all employing a wide range of full- and part-time staff. Smaller, specialist operators with fewer staff on the payroll, will focus their work in their UK office and often sub-contract parts of their operation to overseas agents, e.g. ground-handling agents and resort representatives.

UK operations

The UK head office of a major outbound tour operator will be organised on a departmental basis in order to carry out a variety of functions, including:

- Marketing
- Market research
- Contracting

- Flights
- Brochure production
- Brochure distribution
- Sales promotion
- Reservations
- Agency sales support
- Administration
- Customer services
- Personnel
- Finance and legal

Marketing

Staff employed in the marketing department are responsible for planning and developing the different holiday products, which will be aimed at particular segments of the market. Product managers will focus on the selection of resorts, choice of accommodation and selection of regional UK departure airports. Typical segments of the market for whom products are developed include:

- Singles
- Families
- Couples without children
- Disabled travellers
- Groups
- Business travellers
- Youth market
- Elderly travellers

Planning and organising a holiday programme does not happen overnight. Staff in the marketing department will start making plans for a season 12–18 months before the brochures go on sale. The first task is to assess the total number of holidays that will be taken during a season by all UK holidaymakers. Having calculated this total market figure, individual brand managers or product managers decide what share of the market it is realistic to sell (the programme capacity). Having decided on the capacity of the programme, detailed planning on how many holidays should be arranged in each resort and what accommodation and flights are needed can begin. Marketing staff are also responsible for the key activity of pricing the holidays, which can be very risky given the advance planning necessary before the launch of a programme and the potential for fluctuations in currency exchange rates.

Activity

Draw a flow chart of the main tasks involved in developing a package holiday product to a new long-haul destination in South America. Include timescales and staff responsibilities in your chart.

Market research

A great deal of background research is undertaken to ensure that the tour operators' products have the best chance of meeting their sales potential. Sources of research data available to market research personnel include:

- Internal sales data
- External sales data (available from commercial sources)
- Analysis of competitors' programmes
- Analysis of customer comment questionnaires
- Financial analysis

Staff in the market research department work with marketing department personnel to identify potential new market opportunities, as well as assessing the changing needs and tastes of previous customers. This is achieved by studying sales statistics and market research surveys. They particularly look at the feedback collected from existing customers via CSQs (customer satisfaction questionnaires). The staff try to predict what holidaymakers will want, in terms of which resorts, what type and length of holiday, what standard of accommodation, which departure airports, what price they are prepared to pay, etc.

Contracting

Once the structure of the programme is finalised, staff in the contracts department will negotiate with accommodation providers over the number of beds and names of accommodations required. This function is often the responsibility of senior management, under the direction of the overseas regional manager, who may be assisted by specific product managers. The staff involved in contracting the accommodation and related services have to negotiate on price, quantity and quality, within a very competitive environment. It is likely that other mass market operators, for example, will be using the same hotels in their programmes. An operator may try to negotiate exclusive use of particular accommodation, but this will involve a financial commitment on behalf of the operator that it may not be willing to risk.

Flights

At the same time as accommodation contracting is under way, the flight programmes have to be negotiated, either with an in-house airline in the case of the large operators, or with charter or scheduled airlines in the case of smaller operators (see Figure 19.8). In large tour operating companies, teams working on different programmes and products liaise with the flight or aviation department over how many seats they will need, which regional airports are to be used and whether day or night flights are required. The flight department must make optimum use of its resources, which will include selling spare capacity in the seat-only market.

Fig. 19.8 Flight planning is a vital part of the tour operating business (reproduced courtesy of Airtours)

Brochure production and distribution

The brochure is the most visible part of the tour operator's sales and marketing process. Teams working in the marketing department will liaise with brochure production staff to finalise design, copy and photographs. A lot of brochure printing takes place outside the UK to save on costs. Sales staff will make decisions about how many brochures are required and to which travel agents they will be distributed. Element 22.2 looks in detail at the role of brochures and the key stages in the brochure production process.

Sales promotion

Marketing staff will plan and co-ordinate a range of activities including advertising, direct mail, sales promotion and PR, to ensure that the operators' products are given maximum exposure and sales opportunities. This may be long-term brand support or short-term advertising and promotion. It may involve advertising in consumer and trade arenas, or special point-of-sale materials to raise awareness of particular products.

Reservations

Reservations staff are employed to handle bookings from travel agents and direct from the public. All large operators, and many small to medium-sized companies, use computerised systems developed by in-house computer operations personnel or outside consultants. Staff in reservations are fully trained on the operation of the reservation systems and briefed on the features of products included in the operator's brochures. Large tour operators will have separate reservations teams handling group bookings and last-minute bookings.

Agency sales support

Sales representatives will regularly visit travel agencies and offer product training and point-of-sale materials, such as posters and window displays, in order to maximise sales opportunities. The travel agencies that sell the most holidays will receive particular attention, including enhanced incentives for management and staff to continue high-volume sales.

Administration

The administration department is responsible for producing invoices, receiving payments and issuing tickets and other documentation. Staff will also produce passenger lists, known as manifests, for distribution to airlines, hoteliers, ground-handling agents and resort representatives, plus carry out the full range of everyday administrative duties associated with the operation of a commercial concern.

Activity

Working as part of a small group, list the main tasks that would be undertaken by staff in the administration department of a major outbound tour operator. Use your list as the basis for drawing up a job description and person specification for the permanent post of administrative assistant for a mass market operator based in Manchester.

Customer services

This department will be responsible for handling complaints and queries from agents and members of the public. They will try to ensure that all matters are dealt with quickly and efficiently in order to retain goodwill. Often part of a major tour operator's marketing department, the customer services teams are increasingly involved in analysing customer feedback. Relevant information is passed to appropriate UK or overseas personnel to ensure that mistakes are not repeated and that overall quality is enhanced.

Personnel

Staff in personnel are responsible for a wide variety of tasks, including all recruitment for the UK and overseas operations, job evaluation, employee appraisal, training, payments to staff and pensions management, plus all administrative matters related to employees and their welfare.

Finance and legal

Control over finance is crucial for success in tour operating. Staff in the finance department handle the flow of revenue into the business and payments to suppliers in the UK and overseas. Senior staff will be responsible for meeting planned sales and revenue targets and managing budgets. The legal department advises on a range of matters, such as the content of contracts, accuracy of brochure copy and statutory regulations concerning the company and its relationship with customers and suppliers.

Overseas operations

As well as having a general duty to provide a high standard of service to the tour operator's customers while abroad, staff in the overseas office of a major UK tour operator will have a number of specific responsibilities, including:

- Organising transfers to and from the accommodation and airport.
- Selling and arranging excursions and other 'extras' such as car hire.
- Finalising contracts with hoteliers and transport operators.
- The well-being, training and deployment of representatives.
- The handling of complaints and emergencies.
- Feeding back to the UK office any formal or informal research findings.

Smaller, specialist UK operators may have a small number of permanent employees based in overseas resorts, but will also use the services of seasonal and part-time UK staff. They also rely on the services of specialist individuals and companies in the resorts to provide a range of ground-handling services, such as a 'meet and greet' service, coach transfers and welcome meetings for clients.

Thomson Travel Group

Introduction

The Thomson Travel Group is part of the International Thomson Organisation, which has interests not only in travel, but also in publishing and oil. Thomson Travel is one of the world's leading leisure travel and holiday companies, with 4.8 million holidaymakers and a sales revenue of £1.5 billion (1995 figures). Its overall aim is to develop and retain strong leadership positions in all its markets by providing high-quality, competitively priced, leisure air travel and holiday services. Thomson Travel Group companies include:

1. *Thomson Tour Operations (TTO)* – one of the world's largest air inclusive tour operators.
2. *Portland Holidays* – a division of TTO specialising in direct sell inclusive tours.
3. *Britannia Airways* – Europe's leading leisure airline.

Table 19.7 Sales revenue of Thomson Travel Group in 1995

Company	1995 sales revenue (£m)
Thomson Tour Operations	1,277.3
Britannia Airways	605.5
Lunn Poly	118.4
The Holiday Cottages Group	17.6
Corporate and other	5.0
Total	**2023.8**

Source: Thomson Travel Group's *Annual Report and Accounts 1995*

4. *Lunn Poly* – the UK's largest travel retailer of inclusive tours.
5. The Holiday Cottages Group – the UK's largest letting agency for holiday cottages in Britain.

Sales revenues for the component parts of the Group for 1995 are given in Table 19.7.

History

In 1965, Lord Thomson, a Canadian businessman, took the first step towards the creation of the Thomson Travel Group when he acquired Universal Sky Tours, Britannia Airways and Riviera Holidays. In 1974, when the then number one operator Clarksons failed at the height of the holiday season, Thomson Holidays inherited the enviable number one position which it still retains today. The Lunn Poly travel agency chain with 60 retail outlets was acquired in 1972 and the Thomson Travel Group was made even stronger with the founding of Portland Holidays in 1979, now the UK's leading direct-sell operator. In 1988 the Horizon Travel Group was acquired; this brought Orion Airways and Horizon Holidays into the Thomson Group, plus the Horizon brands of HCI, Wings, OSL and Blue Sky, as well as Horizon Travel Centres. In 1989, Thomson Tour Operations was set up as the new company operating all programmes run by Thomson and Horizon. By summer 1991, all brands and products had been realigned to operate separately, but under the Thomson banner. Only Portland continues to operate as a separate company.

Thomson Tour Operations (TTO)

This is the most familiar of the Thomson Travel Group's companies, responsible for the largest share of the UK outbound package holiday market. Its mission is:

> To be the leader in terms of quality, profit and volume of the ex-UK tour operating industry.

TTO's specific aims are:

- To have the best team of people in the industry working for the company.
- To provide all its employees with a challenging, rewarding and secure working environment.

- To ensure that the quality of product and service is better – and is perceived to be better by holidaymakers, suppliers and travel agents – than all major competitors.
- To operate within a lower cost base, quality for quality, than all major competitors.
- To be the clear market leader in terms of size of the ex-UK inclusive tour business.
- To achieve a superior level of profitability compared to all major competitors to ensure the long-term viability of the business.
- To carry out all tasks with due responsibility towards the communities in which they operate and towards the environment.

Thomson Tour Operations' company structure

1. *Marketing department* – the job of TTO's marketing department is to identify and plan to meet holidaymakers' needs; in other words, to provide the right holiday at the right price to the right person. The department has staff involved in creating products, providing a customer service function, producing brochures, undertaking market research and liaising with the press and media.
2. *Overseas department* – is mainly concerned with operations outside the UK and co-ordinates the overseas operation of all holidays. Its responsibilities include the contracting of all types of accommodation, providing a high standard of service to clients while in the resort and maintaining and improving the standards of accommodation and service on offer. The aviation team draws up the initial flight plans from the capacity requirements, i.e. the number of holidays planned to be sold and the number of aircraft needed.
3. *Personnel services* – this section is divided into two departments, one serving UK staff and the other dealing with staff overseas. The main activities of the overseas personnel department include planning staffing levels, recruitment, job evaluation, salary and benefits administration and staff relations. UK personnel has the task of assisting managers to recruit the right calibre of staff in the most effective way. This may be by internal progression, transfer or external recruitment. Staff training and development is also handled by the personnel department.
4. *Sales department* – one of the main objectives of TTO's sales department is to maintain excellent relationships with travel agents in order to create sales opportunities. This is done through the agency salesforce who provide agents with sales and market information and train agency personnel in products and procedures. Another responsibility of this department is co-ordinating a merchandising team that visits the top agents at regular intervals to check on brochure stocks and visibility on shelves.
5. *Systems division* – staff in this section provide computing services for all areas of the company. The viewdata-based reservation system for travel agents (TOP) is recognised as the standard for the UK travel industry. There is also an automated funds transfer system for payments from agents. Thomson's computer systems provide the means to hold, change and update all business and holiday-related information. They handle all reservations on about 28,000 travel agent terminals around the country.
6. *Finance and legal department* – responsibilities of this department include working with marketing on the pricing of each programme, preparing budgets,

reporting actual results against the budgets and analysing any variances. It handles all financial transactions including credit control and payments to accommodation providers and airlines. Company secretarial and legal matters are also dealt with in this department.

The future of Thomson Tour Operations

At the start of 1991, TTO's managing director set out the agenda for Thomson Tour Operations for the 1990s. He stressed the following points as the way to ensure that Thomson remained at number one:

- Diversity
- Reliability
- Quality
- Value for money
- Efficiency
- People
- Environment

Whether TTO can hold on to its number one position throughout the 1990s remains to be seen, in the light of the fiercely competitive environment for outbound tour operations.

(Information courtesy of Thomson Tour Operations)

Case study discussion questions

1. What are the main functions of Thomson Tour Operations' marketing department?
2. Thomson Tour Operations' operating profit fell from £43.2 million in 1994 to £15.7 million in 1995. Why do you think this happened?
3. What are the risks and advantages of having a number of different companies within the Thomson Travel Group?
4. Why do you think the company has entered the UK self-catering holiday sector?
5. What are the main external threats and opportunities facing the Thomson Travel Group in the next five years?

Personnel requirements of tour operators

The division of major, mass market operators into UK and overseas operations, means that there are many job roles at home and abroad. Figure 19.9 gives an indication of the main personnel requirements of a major outbound tour operator. Smaller tour operators will need fewer staff, given their smaller scale of operations.

Figure 19.9 shows us that the majority of staff based in the UK are concerned with developing the package holidays, promoting their sale and controlling the financial and human resources of the organisation. Overseas staff look after holidaymakers once they are in the resort and handle all administrative duties associated with this function. The UK operation will have a core of full-time, permanent employees, backed up with

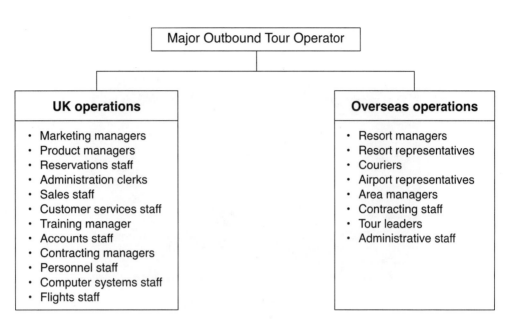

Fig. 19.9 Personal requirements of a major outbound tour operator

part-time and contractual staff at peak periods of the season, for example, when brochures are distributed, reservations are busy and travel documentation is sent to agents and clients. Many of the overseas staff will be on temporary contracts lasting for the duration of the season, although a small number of staff will be offered all-year-round work either on a summer/winter split season or part UK/part overseas. Fluency in one European language other than English is important for those overseas staff liaising with hoteliers, coach companies, handling agents, etc. Resort representatives tend to be the members of staff who come into contact with holidaymakers the most, making their role as an ambassador for the company very important.

The work of the resort representative

Resort representatives ('reps') are, to most holidaymakers, the public face of the tour operating company. Clients going on a Thomson holiday to Benidorm, for example, will not meet the sales manager based in the UK, nor the head of marketing for the company, but they will have daily contact with their rep, expecting him or her to be the fountain of all knowledge about the resort and to be able to help with any problems they may have (see Figure 19.10). How good a rep is at his or her job can have a significant impact on a client's enjoyment of a holiday and the overall image of the company.

From the outside, a rep's job can seem very glamorous, conjuring up images of travel to faraway places, lots of time to explore a resort, endless night life and socialising. This couldn't be further from the truth! Reps work very long hours and are expected to be on call at unsociable hours to answer queries from clients and help in emergencies. Time off in the resort is very limited during the season and the job entails a certain amount of administration and accounting, for example, to do with excursions. Tour operators often consider that the duties of a resort rep cannot be fully

Fig. 19.10 Resort representatives are the public face of the holiday company *(reproduced courtesy of Thomson Tour Operations)*

specified, given the nature of the job with its many aspects. There are, however, a number of principal duties, including:

- Welcoming holidaymakers on arrival at the airport
- Arranging transfers and escorting clients to their accommodation
- Giving welcome talks to new arrivals
- Arranging excursions for holidaymakers
- Preparing files and notice boards with local information
- Handling problems and emergencies
- Regular paperwork and accounting

Tour operators look for people who have a responsible and sensible outlook when recruiting overseas reps. Reps need to be tactful, flexible and patient, with a lot of drive, enthusiasm and stamina.

Activity

Draw up a job description and person specification for the post of overseas representative with a major outbound tour operator. The post will be for the summer season only and will be based in Palma Nova, Majorca.

Tour operators specialising in self-drive camping and mobile home holidays on the continent employ a variety of couriers for the season, ranging from children's couriers, activity couriers to general campsite couriers (see Figure 19.11).

Fig. 19.11 A campsite courier advises holidaymakers (reproduced courtesy of Eurocamp Travel)

The standard duties of a children's courier on a campsite include:

- Providing a variety of activities for children of different age ranges.
- Offering a regular baby-sitting service.
- Visiting newly arrived clients and children to explain the services.
- Maintaining an informative and attractive notice board of events.
- Maintaining basic accounts of expenditure.
- Completing a weekly report form.
- Keeping the tents and surrounding area clean and in good order.
- Exercising care and safe practices when planning and offering activities.
- Liaising with and helping other couriers as required.

Couriers will be employed for the duration of the season and may be required to work in more than one campsite or resort. Large sites will have a senior courier to control the work programme and delegate duties as necessary.

Assignment 19.3

UK and overseas operational practices in tour operating

Performance criteria satisfied: 19.3.1, 19.3.2, 19.3.3, 19.3.4

Core skills opportunities at level 3:   Communication   3.1, 3.2, 3.3, 3.4
Information technology   3.1, 3.2, 3.3
Application of number   3.1, 3.2, 3.3

Tasks

Working with a partner, you are to prepare a detailed report on the UK and overseas operational practices of UK-based tour operators. In particular, your report should:

- Explain the differences between the UK and overseas operational practices of UK-based tour operators.
- Match UK personnel and job roles to UK operational practices.
- Match overseas personnel and job roles to overseas operational practices.

Your report should be word processed and include relevant charts, diagrams and statistics, together with examples from within the UK tour operating industry.

Unit 20

TOURIST ATTRACTIONS

Element 20.1
Investigate tourist attractions within a locality

Element 20.2
Investigate the development of a tourist attraction

Element 20.3
Investigate the operation of a major tourist attraction

Element 20.1 Investigate tourist attractions within a locality

What is a tourist attraction?

This may sound a strange question with which to start an investigation of tourist attractions in a locality. We all have our own ideas of what constitutes an attraction; if you live in Birmingham you might think of Cadbury World as an example of a tourist attraction. Those living in the south of England might mention Thorpe Park or Chessington World of Adventures. People living in Wales may include Rhyl Sun Centre or Caernarvon Castle on their list of attractions, while residents of Scotland are likely to mention the Scott Monument in Edinburgh or the Burrell Collection in Glasgow. The people of Northern Ireland would surely put the Giant's Causeway towards the top of their list of tourist attractions.

While all these well-known examples clearly fall within anybody's definition of a tourist attraction, it is important to remember that the majority of attractions throughout Britain are not household names. Small museums, craft galleries, shops, leisure facilities and farm attractions, to name but a few, are crucial to the economic well-being of many areas of the country. Together, they form the 'critical mass' of attractions in a locality that forms the basis for encouraging tourists to explore and perhaps stay overnight. As the following English Tourist Board definition of a 'visitor attraction' shows, such places should be promoted to local people as well as to tourists:

> *A permanently established excursion destination, a primary purpose of which is to allow public access for entertainment, interest or education; rather than being a primary retail outlet or a venue for sporting, theatrical, or film performances. It must be open to the public, without prior booking, for published periods each year, and should be capable of attracting day visitors or tourists, as well as local residents.*

The importance of tourist attractions

Attractions are one of the key components of the UK travel and tourism industry, along with accommodation, destinations and transportation, as shown in Figure 20.1.

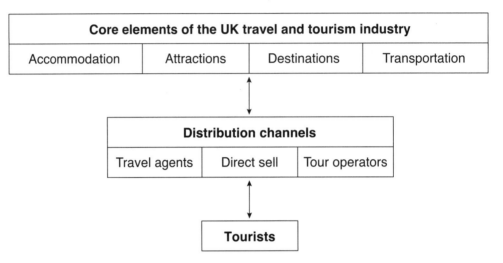

Fig. 20.1 The structure of the UK travel and tourism industry

Indeed, many people would argue it is the drawing power of an attraction that is the prime reason for making a leisure trip at all and that, without an attraction, tourism in an area is unlikely to prosper. The importance of attractions is demonstrated in the following examples:

- Overseas visitors are attracted to London to see its historic buildings and monuments, including the Tower of London, Nelson's Column and Buckingham Palace.
- British holidaymakers are enticed by the natural attractions of a variety of European countries, such as the French Alps and Norway's fjords.
- Day visitors look for fun, education and excitement at major UK attractions, such as Thorpe Park, Chessington World of Adventures and Blackpool Pleasure Beach (see Figure 20.2).

Activity

Working with a partner, draw up a list of 10 UK and 10 world-wide destinations and list the principal attractions of each, e.g. York – Jorvik Viking Centre and York Minster; Paris – the Eiffel Tower and the Louvre. Present your findings as a chart, indicating whether each attraction is man-made or occurs naturally.

Fig. 20.2 The 85 mph Pepsi Max Big One at Blackpool Pleasure Beach (reproduced
courtesy of Blackpool Pleasure Beach)

Attractions and destinations

While it is possible for a single attraction to generate a significant tourism impact on
an area by itself, e.g. Disneyland Paris or Alton Towers, it is more usual for a variety of
attractions to provide the drawing power for a destination. The city of Bristol, for
example, offers day visitors and those staying overnight a wide range of attractions,
including:

- Clifton Suspension Bridge
- Bristol Zoo
- Harvey's Wine Museum
- The Exploratory
- John Wesley Chapel
- SS Great Britain
- Hippodrome Theatre
- Colston Hall

Events are also an important part of the attraction of the city and include, for 1996:

- International Festival of the Sea
- Bristol Flower Show
- International Balloon Fiesta
- St Paul's Carnival
- International Kite Festival

Such a wide diversity of attractions and events offers opportunities for visitors from home and abroad, young and old, active and passive, as well as contributing to the economic, social and cultural life of the area.

It is important to remember that although attractions are very often the reason for visiting a destination, they are only one part of a number of elements, each dependent on the others for its operation and success. This is shown diagrammatically in Figure 20.3.

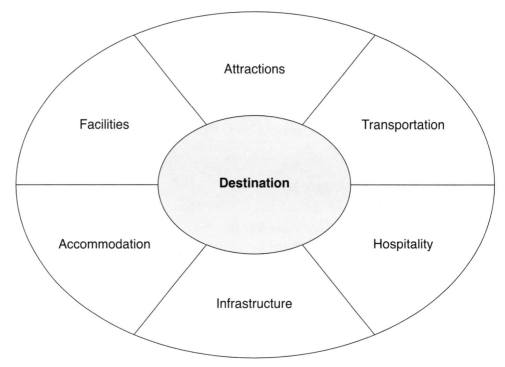

Fig. 20.3 Components of a destination area

Figure 20.3 shows us that visitors' needs are met by a variety of elements, for example:

1. *Attractions* – often the stimulus for a visit.
2. *Transportation* – both to and within a destination, helps ensure accessibility for visitors.
3. *Hospitality* – the way in which tourist services are delivered to visitors.
4. *Infrastructure* – the 'skeleton' of roads, airports, utility services, etc., around which tourist facilities are developed.
5. *Accommodation* – providing visitors with a place to stay.
6. *Facilities* – extra services for visitors, e.g. guiding, shopping, information, etc.

Attractions are part of an overall tourism development and promotion strategy for a destination, involving the private, public and voluntary sectors of the industry, which we shall explore further in Elements 20.2 and 20.3.

Types of tourist attraction

The term 'tourist attraction' generally brings to mind a purpose-built facility, designed to provide a blend of fun, entertainment, activity, stimulation or education. On a national scale, attractions that spring to mind easily include Beamish Open Air Museum, the Tower of London and Edinburgh Castle. Internationally, we can think of the Epcot Center at Disney World in Florida or the Pompidou Centre in Paris. Closer to home, your local area is likely to support a number of attractions, perhaps a museum, heritage centre or leisure park. While these man-made attractions are easily identifiable and provide important facilities for tourists, we must not forget that the natural world also offers visitors a wide variety of sights and experiences. Indeed many of the best-known tourist attractions in the world are not purpose-built, but occur naturally, e.g. the Grand Canyon, Niagara Falls and the Giant's Causeway, to name but a few.

We will now look at some of the different types of tourist attraction in more detail.

Heritage attractions

Today, the word 'heritage' is often used to describe a particular type of tourist attraction that aims to depict what life was like at a particular point in time in the past. Many villages, towns and cities have attached the word 'heritage' to their existing museums as a way of promoting themselves more widely and increasing their visitor numbers. They are part of a trend towards themed attractions, with the Jorvik Centre in York and the Tales of Robin Hood in Nottingham being good cases in point. Certain areas of Britain have established attractions to celebrate their industrial heritage, e.g. Ironbridge Gorge in Shropshire and the Big Pit museum in south Wales.

Cultural attractions

Some destinations attract visitors because of their cultural diversity or associations with music, the arts or famous people. Shakespeare's birthplace in Stratford-upon-Avon is a magnet for UK and overseas visitors alike, while the Cardiff Singer of the World competition attracts visitors from all over the world to Wales. The cultural diversity in cities such as London, Bradford, Leicester and Manchester is used as the springboard for themed events and short breaks, e.g. curry weekends in Bradford and visits to the Chinatown area of Manchester. Cities such as Florence, Leningrad and Vienna attract visitors from around the world to sample their diverse associations with music, the arts and history. Museums and galleries have long been popular places to visit for entertainment and educational purposes. Museums of national importance in Britain are located not only in London, but are also to be found in places as diverse as St Ives in Cornwall (Tate Gallery), Bradford (National Museum of Photography, Film and Television), Glasgow (the Burrell Collection), Cardiff (National Museum of Wales) and Birmingham (National Motorcycle Museum).

Theme parks

A theme park is a visitor attraction offering permanent rides and entertainment in a themed setting or range of settings, providing something for the whole family. Most theme parks charge one price for unlimited access to all rides and attractions in a fun environment. Since the first UK theme park opened at Thorpe Park in 1979, there has been a rapid rise in the number of attractions and volume of visitors; the number of theme parks had risen to 7 by 1984 and increased to 10 in 1993. The number of visitors to UK theme parks rose from 5.4 million to 10.8 million between 1985 and 1994, with revenues up from £29 million to £130 million over the same time period.

Although each UK theme park has its own particular attractions, there are certain common characteristics that theme parks exhibit, for example:

- Parks offer a mix of facilities and activities, e.g. 'white knuckle' rides, live entertainment, animals, gardens, events, children's play areas, education centres, corporate hospitality, retail and catering.
- Most parks operate on a seasonal basis between Easter and the end of October.
- Most visitors are family groups from the C1/C2 social classes.
- Group bookings account for between 10 and 25 per cent of all visitors.
- Typically, parking for 3000–4000 cars is provided.
- Site areas range from as little as 12 acres to 800 acres plus, with 130–140 acres being a typical size.
- Parks are generally close to the motorway network, ensuring very large 2-hour catchment populations (up to 15 million).
- Length of stay on site averages between 6 and 7 hours, presenting park operators with ample opportunities for generating secondary spend, e.g. catering and retail outlets.

(Source: Insights January 1992)

Activity

Carry out some research to discover the principal theme parks and major attractions within a 2-hour drive time of where you live.

Historic monuments

Monuments such as the Westminster Abbey and Warwick Castle, have great appeal to UK residents and overseas visitors to Britain. Most historic monuments are in public ownership, with many London properties under the management of the Historic Royal Palaces Agency, a division of the Department of National Heritage. Many castles and stately homes in Britain are cared for by the National Trust, CADW and English Heritage, who manage the sites and provide facilities and services for visitors. Castles are a particular feature of the attractions scene in Wales, where Caernarvon Castle receives approximately 300,000 visitors per year.

Activity

Find out which historic monuments in your area are open to visitors, what facilities they provide, what they charge for admission and how they promote themselves.

Entertainment

Facilities such as nightclubs, discos, concert halls, theatres, arenas and opera houses, all provide entertainment opportunities for visitors to an area. The bigger the venue, the greater the attraction; arenas such as NYNEX in Manchester and Sheffield Arena, for example, are major venues for concerts, attracting people from wide catchment areas. Part of the appeal of UK resorts is the range of entertainment facilities they can offer the visitor. Tourists at seaside resorts such as Blackpool, Brighton and Scarborough, for instance, will be attracted by live shows, concert halls and a range of 'night life' opportunities. Smaller towns and cities will also attract day visitors from their own locality to enjoy what's on at nearby cinemas, theatres and nightclubs.

Sport and recreation facilities

As well as being popular with local people, sport and recreation facilities can also add to the appeal of towns and cities, helping to attract overnight and day visitors. Many local authorities and private operators have upgraded existing swimming pools or built new leisure centres to cater for their needs. Stark, rectangular municipal baths have been replaced with leisure pools boasting such facilities as wave machines, jacuzzis, saunas, flumes, waterslides and splash pools. Many pools are part of larger leisure complexes offering activities such as squash, badminton, tennis, karate, bowls and hockey. On a national scale, sports facilities can help change the image of an area and attract inward investment, e.g. the National Cycling Centre in Manchester and the Don Valley Stadium in Sheffield. Internationally, cities compete to host major sporting events such as the Olympic Games, Commonwealth Games and motor racing Grand Prix, providing the best in sports entertainment for local people and visitors.

Natural attractions

On a global scale, the range and variety of natural attractions is immense. Everything from the ice caps in Greenland to the Sahara Desert, from the Great Lakes of North America to the foothills of the Himalayas, will appeal to particular types of tourists. Closer to home, Britain itself has an abundance of fine landscapes, with beautiful coastline, rugged mountains and picturesque dales, many of international significance, e.g. Snowdonia, the Lake District and the Highlands of Scotland. Natural attractions are a major factor in motivating people to visit an area and are often the prime reason for travel, around which other tourist facilities, services and amenities are based. For example, tourists may initially be attracted to Devon by the beauty of its beaches and inland scenery, but will also look for other tourist support services, such as accommodation, transportation and man-made attractions to provide a fulfilling experience (see Figure 20.3 on page 186).

Many areas of Britain have been granted special status to help protect their environment and provide facilities for their enjoyment by the public, including National Parks and Areas of Outstanding Natural Beauty (AONBs) (see Figure 20.4).

Fig. 20.4 National Parks and Areas of Outstanding Natural Beauty in England and Wales *(reproduced courtesy of the Countryside Commission)*

Popularity of tourist attractions

All man-made attractions operate within competitive environments, with the need to respond to continual changes in consumers' tastes and fashions. There may be direct competition between rival attractions, perhaps between two stately homes in the same part of the country and offering visitors a broadly similar experience. Competition also exists between different facilities in the leisure and tourism industries, e.g. a heritage centre, ice rink and cinema in the same town, will all be trying to attract customers to their premises, using a variety of promotional techniques. In a wider sense, spending on visits to attractions is in direct competition with other items of household expenditure, such as spending on food, clothing and energy.

It is against this background of competition for visitors that attractions either prosper or fail. Tourist attractions that maintain and even increase their popularity tend to:

- Give customer care a high priority.
- Be responsive to changes in consumers' tastes and fashions.
- Research their markets well.
- Be effectively promoted.
- Have a professional approach to health and safety.
- Have effective management structures.
- Invest in staff training.
- Have effective financial controls.

Attractions that are professionally managed will have a far better chance of retaining their popularity in the face of increasing local and regional competition.

Popularity of national attractions

Figures from the BTA report *Visits to Tourist Attractions 1994* show us that the total number of visits to UK attractions rose by just 1 per cent when compared with 1993 figures, with 84 new attractions opening their doors in 1994. The total estimated number of visits for the year was 387 million and spending rose by 5 per cent to more than £1000 million for the first time; the one billion pound barrier has finally been broken! Outdoor attractions fared better than indoor sites, with farms, gardens, country parks, leisure parks, visitor centres, museums, galleries and workplaces experiencing above-average increases in attendance figures. Visits to historic properties and wildlife attractions showed a small decrease in numbers. Overall, the popularity of national tourist attractions in 1994 remained buoyant.

Figures showing the popularity of major attractions are shown in Table 20.1, which gives details of the 1994 top 10 UK attractions charging for admission, while Table 20.2 lists those giving free entry.

As Tables 20.1 and 20.2 show, Blackpool Pleasure Beach was once again the UK's most popular tourist attraction with 7.2 million visitors, due in part to the opening of the world's tallest rollercoaster, the Pepsi Max Big One (see Figure 20.2). For the third year running, Alton Towers was the most popular attraction charging admission, with a 15 per cent rise in visitor numbers to just over 3 million.

Table 20.1 Top 10 UK attractions charging admission in 1994

Attraction	Number of visits 1994
1. Alton Towers, Staffordshire	3,011,000
2. Madame Tussaud's, London	2,631,538
3. Tower of London	2,407,115
4. St Paul's Cathedral, London	1,900,000
5. Natural History Museum, London	1,625,000
6. Chessington World of Adventures	1,614,000
7. Blackpool Tower	1,305,000
8. Science Museum, London	1,268,839
9. Thorpe Park, Surrey	1,235,000
10. Drayton Manor, Staffordshire	1,104,000

Source: Insights July 1995

Table 20.2 Top 10 free attractions in the UK in 1994

Attraction	Number of visits 1994
1. Blackpool Pleasure Beach	7,200,000*
2. British Museum, London	5,896,692
3. Strathclyde Country Park, Motherwell	4,380,000*
4. National Gallery, London	4,301,656
5. Palace Pier, Brighton	3,500,000*
6. Funland and Laserbowl, Trocadero	2,500,000*
7. Canterbury Cathedral	2,250,000*
8. Tate Gallery, London	2,226,399
9. Westminster Abbey	2,200,000*
10. York Minster	2,000,000*
Pleasure Beach, Great Yarmouth	2,000,000*
Pleasureland, Southport	2,000,000*

*Estimated
Source: Insights July 1995

Popularity of local attractions

The demand for local visitor attractions will tend to mirror national trends and their popularity will often reflect fashions and 'fads' seen across the whole country, for example:

- The growth in visits to cinemas has led to the development of multiplex and multi-screen facilities throughout Britain, often with other leisure and retail services on the same site.
- The general trend towards making museums appeal to a wider range of visitors may also be reflected at local level, with the use of new technology exhibits and artefacts to provide a more 'hands on' experience for the visitor.

- Increasing concern for the environment has led to the development of local attractions focusing on farm life, wildlife conservation, energy, habitat management, etc.
- Many local attractions will have invested in 'all weather' facilities to help extend their use, e.g. indoor arenas, covered leisure pools and 'all weather' sports pitches.
- Many natural attractions, such as waterways, nature reserves and forests, have improved access for visitors and offer a wider range of educational and interpretive facilities, e.g. guided walks, self-guided trails and visitor centres.

No matter how a local attraction has sought to improve its appeal to visitors, its owners or managers will be only too well aware of the fiercely competitive market in which they operate and the problems often associated with funding a tourist attraction. This is a topic that we will return to later in this unit.

Types of visitors to attractions

Tourist attractions appeal to different people for different reasons; one family may enjoy a day out at the Crinkley Bottom Leisure Park at Cricket St Thomas, for example, while another might prefer a trip to the nearby Fleet Air Arm Museum at Yeovilton; yet another family may choose somewhere else entirely. Whatever the reasons behind the choice of an attraction, all sites will have a wide range of types of visitor, each with different characteristics. For a typical tourist attraction, these could be:

- Groups booked in advance
- Individuals who pay at the gate on arrival
- Family groups
- Young couples
- Special interest parties
- People with disabilities
- Overseas visitors
- Local people
- Senior citizens
- School parties

This list gives an indication of the difficult task of satisfying the needs of each of these different types of visitor, often referred to as 'markets', and stresses the importance of precise market research to identify exactly who visits an attraction and whether they are happy with the 'product'.

Activity

Choose a local tourist attraction and find out what particular markets it is trying to attract and whether the types of visitor has changed in the last five years.

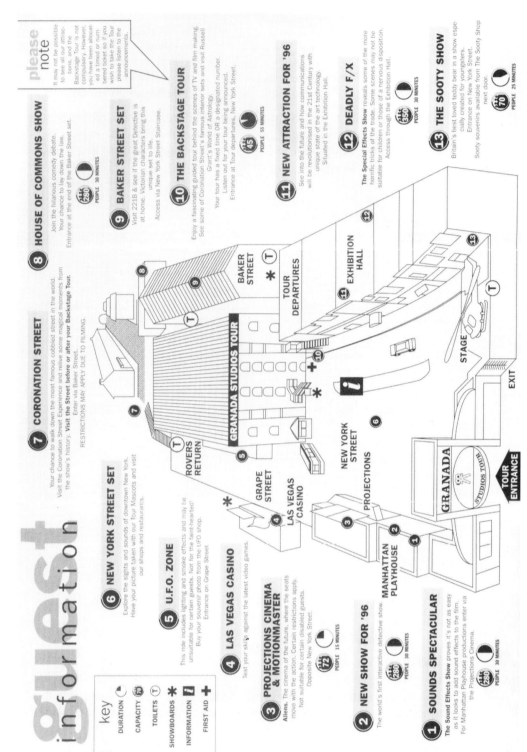

Fig. 20.5 *Facilities at Granada Studios tour (reproduced courtesy of Granada Studios Tour)*

CASE STUDY

Visitor types at Granada Studios Tour

Introduction

Granada Studios Tour was opened in Manchester in 1988 and is best known for housing the set on which the Coronation Street TV programme is filmed. The central theme of the tour is a one-hour backstage guided tour, plus nine other shows and attractions including 'The House of Commons Comedy Debate' and 'The All New Sooty Show'. The tour covers a 3.5 acre site on the outskirts of the city and has welcomed over 4 million visitors since it first opened, including 45,000 coach parties and 9500 school groups. Catering and retail are important revenue earners, with nine catering outlets and five shops on site. Average length of stay is between 5 and 7 hours. For disabled guests, facilities such as ramps, lifts and special toilets are available throughout the site (see Figure 20.5).

Visitor types

Granada Studios Tour has two main markets; individual visitors to the tour during the day and guests at corporate hospitality events staged at the attraction. The individual visitors divide into two distinct categories:

- Groups.
- Individual visitors paying their entrance fee at the gate.

Groups

The prime objective in 1988 when the attraction first opened was to attract group business and in the first full year of operation some 7500 coach parties were welcomed at the attraction, representing 350,000 group customers. On top of the groups, there were around 170,000 members of the public buying tickets at the gate. Groups are an important source of business to large attractions such as Granada Studios Tour, since they can help even out the visitor peaks and troughs. The operators will know in advance when a group is due to arrive and can manage their visitor flows accordingly. Variations in demand can occur in a variety of ways, e.g. at different periods of the year, different times of the week and even peaks and troughs within the same day. Groups are also important since they tend to be cheaper to market to, when compared with individual visitors, and easier to target effectively via coach and tour operators.

Individuals

Individual visitors to Granada Studios Tour, as opposed to groups, tend to come at peak times of the year, usually coinciding with school holidays. They also visit at peak times of the day and peak periods in the week, notably weekends. The individual market breaks down into three distinct types:

1. Families
2. Young couples
3. 'Empty nesters'

Families are a priority for the attraction and much of the advertising and other promotional effort is aimed at the family market. The 'empty nesters' are older adults whose children have left home, leaving the parents with time on their hands. They are important since they have the opportunity to visit outside of the peak times, at the same time taking advantage of any off-peak promotional discounts.

Market research has shown that the visitor profile to the tour is predominantly female, C1, C2, D or E social class as shown by the statistics in Table 20.3. Forty per cent of visitors travel from outside the local region and the majority of visitors live within a two-hour drive time of the attraction.

Table 20.3 Socio-economic grouping of visitors to Granada Studios Tour

Group	National Profile (%)	Granada Studios Tour (%)	Other theme parks (%)
AB	18	16	18
C1	24	41	23.6
C2	28	27	34.4
DE	29	16	23.9

Source: Granada Studios Tour

The age distribution of visitors to the tour is shown in Table 20.4. As the table shows, nearly three-quarters of all visitors are over 25 years of age, perhaps a reflection of the average age of the viewers of Coronation Street, the attraction's best-known feature.

Table 20.4 Age distribution of visitors to Granada Studios Tour

Age range	All Visitors (%)
12–15	13
16–19	7
20–24	6
25–34	22
35–54	38
55+	14

Source: Granada Studios Tour

Corporate hospitality

This is a growing element of the Granada Studios Tour business and represents a major revenue opportunity for the attraction, generating approximately 15 per cent of total turnover. Different parts of the attraction, including the House of Commons set, are used by companies to entertain clients, host events, stage product launches, hold meetings and provide lunches, dinners, etc. Entertaining at Christmas is a particularly busy period for the corporate hospitality staff.

(Information courtesy of Granada Studios Tour)

Case study discussion questions

1. What types of visitor does Granada Studios Tour seek to attract?
2. How do the facilities and attractions it offers meet their needs?
3. Why is the groups market so important to the attraction?
4. How could the attraction market its corporate hospitality facilities?
5. What does the future hold for attractions such as Granada Studios Tour?

Ownership and funding of tourist attractions

The funding of an individual tourist attraction will depend to a large extent on whether it falls within the private, public or voluntary sector of the industry. However, with the privatisation of national and local facilities through measures such as compulsory competitive tendering (CCT) and government agency arrangements, it is not always easy to tell precisely into which sector an attraction falls. Table 20.5 shows some of the major UK tourist attractions and indicates into which sector each falls.

Table 20.5 Ownership of major UK tourist attractions

Private sector	Public sector	Voluntary sector
Alton Towers	Buckingham Palace	York Minster
Drayton Manor	Tower of London	Corfe Castle (NT)
Thorpe Park	Edinburgh Castle	Salisbury Cathedral
American Adventure	Cardiff Castle	Jorvik Viking Centre
Madame Tussaud's	British Museum	Ironbridge Gorge

As Table 20.5 shows, private sector organisations operate the major theme park attractions in the UK, with their primary commercial aim being profit maximisation. Well-known national attractions, such as the Tower of London and the British Museum, are operated and funded through the public purse. Tourist attractions in the voluntary sector, such as York Minster and Salisbury Cathedral, often have charitable status and use part of their revenue for the maintenance of their buildings. The National Trust protects more than 200 historic houses and parks in England, Wales and Northern Ireland, and welcomes some 11 million visitors to its properties each year.

Local ownership of tourist attractions

At a local level, there is likely to be the same split into private, public and voluntary ownership as shown in Table 20.5. A medium-sized market town in a holiday area of the west country, for example, may well have the following range of tourist attractions:

1. *Private sector* – cinema, restaurants, amusements, nature park, health club, discos, etc.
2. *Public sector* – theatre, museum, leisure centre, parks, gardens, etc.
3. *Voluntary sector* – art gallery, bird sanctuary, historic house, church, nature reserve, etc.

Activity

Carry out an investigation of the tourist attractions in your local area and find out which fall into the private, public and voluntary sectors of the industry.
Investigate the funding arrangements of each of the attractions identified.

CASE STUDY

Ownership of tourist attractions – the Tussauds Group

Introduction

The Tussauds Group, a subsidiary of Pearson PLC, the international media group, runs the UK and Europe's top attractions, with combined attendances of nearly 12 million visitors a year. In 1994, the Tussauds Group acquired a 40 per cent equity stake in Port Aventura, near Salou in Spain, and is now managing this new theme park, which opened in Spring 1995. With a total investment of £300 million, Port Aventura is one of the largest leisure developments ever to be built in Europe. This significant expansion in Europe reflects the Group's strategy for developing as a major force in the international entertainment market.

Principal attractions

The Tussauds Group's attractions include:

- Madame Tussaud's, London
- The London Planetarium
- Rock Circus, London
- Chessington World of Adventures (see case study in Element 20.3)
- Warwick Castle
- Alton Towers
- Madame Tussaud Scenerama, Amsterdam
- Port Aventura, Spain

Madame Tussaud's, London

Madame Tussaud's is London's most popular paid attraction, with 2.7 million visitors in 1995 and a history that spans more than 200 years. A recent £21 million investment has created themed areas and a dramatic £10 million 'Spirit of London' dark ride takes visitors back through 400 years of the capital's history in 'time taxis'. A further investment of £1 million in a new Chamber of Horrors, completed in 1996, marks the final stage in the attraction's latest major redevelopment scheme.

The London Planetarium

The London Planetarium offers visitors the chance to see a fascinating star show beneath its well-known green dome and to interact with the latest technology. Following a £4.5 million transformation, the Planetarium re-opened in June 1995 with theatre-style seating, digital surround sound and 3-D images created by the new Digistar II, the most advanced star projector in the world.

Rock Circus, London

The Rock Circus is the world's number one rock attraction with 709,000 visitors in 1995, a record year. The attraction opened in 1989 at the London Pavilion in London's Piccadilly Circus. This high-tech exhibition houses more than 50 figures spanning 40 years of pop music, with a variety of special effects, from lasers to video discs.

Chessington World of Adventures

This major theme park located in Surrey attracted more than 1.7 million visitors in 1995, a record year for the attraction. In recent years, there have been multi-million pound investments in new rides, including Rameses Revenge. (See detailed case study on Chessington World of Adventures on page 225.)

Warwick Castle

Warwick Castle stands on the banks of the River Avon, a few miles from Stratford-on-Avon. The Castle welcomed a record 803,000 visitors in 1995. The attraction was sold to the Tussauds Group in 1978 and is now one of the UK's leading medieval castles open to the public. As well as the grandeur of its architecture, Warwick Castle hosts a range of special events throughout the year, including jousting and falconry.

Alton Towers

Alton Towers was acquired by the Tussauds Group in 1990 and, following a multi-million pound investment, the Staffordshire theme park has become Britain's number one tourist attraction for which a charge is made, welcoming more than 2.7 million visitors in 1995. Alton Towers is set in 500 acres of grounds and gardens, and in 1996 became the first major UK tourist attraction to open a hotel on-site.

Madame Tussaud Scenerama, Amsterdam

Set in the heart of Amsterdam in Dam Square, Scenerama recreates seventeenth-century life in the capital during Holland's Golden Age, as well as more contemporary events such as the first moon landing. The attraction welcomed more than half a million visitors in 1995.

Port Aventura, Spain

This major theme park is situated on Spain's Costa Dorada, near to Salou and one hour's drive from Barcelona. The region receives over 20 million visitors each year and, in its first year of operation, Port Aventura attracted 2.7 million visitors, 8 per cent more than forecast. Like many Tussauds attractions, Port Aventura offers a wide range of themed entertainments and activities.

The Tussauds Group Studios

These studios are the creative resource of the Group, employing up to 100 artists, designers, technicians and engineers. These versatile teams are responsible for creating wax figures, new themed areas and exhibitions, audio-animatronic figures, as well as submitting proposals for new business development projects.

(Information courtesy of the Tussauds Group)

Case study discussion questions

1. What are the benefits to the Tussauds Group of owning attractions with a wide geographical spread?
2. What advantages and disadvantages does each of the Tussauds' attractions have from being part of Pearson PLC, a multinational media corporation?
3. Why do you think Pearson has diversified into the tourist attractions sector?
4. How do you think the Group as a whole, and each individual attraction, is funded?
5. Is the future bright for organisations such as the Tussauds Group which have invested heavily in expansion of their attractions?

Funding of tourist attractions

Most tourist attractions will operate with a mixture of capital and revenue funding. Capital funding is needed for the purchase of assets for the business, such as new equipment, buildings, land, vehicles, etc. Revenue funding becomes available when the attraction has begun trading and is generating income from admissions, retail sales and catering, for example. Element 20.2 looks in more detail at the sources of funding available to develop tourist attractions, which include:

- National government
- Local government
- The European Union
- The National Lottery
- Sponsorship
- Entry fees
- Subscriptions
- Donations and gifts
- Events
- Retail and catering outlets

The element looks at both capital and revenue funding and distinguishes between private, public and voluntary sector funding (see page 211).

Attractions in a locality

Each part of the UK will have its own particular appeal to tourists. Some visitors look for the peace and tranquillity of country areas and quiet market towns, while others will prefer the altogether faster pace of city life and its attractions. The range and variety of tourist attractions in Britain is huge, from world-famous facilities such as Stonehenge and York Minster, to smaller local craft centres and galleries.

To give an indication of the types of attraction that can be found in one locality in England, the following case study focuses on Shrewsbury, one of Britain's finest Tudor towns.

CASE STUDY

Attractions in a locality – Shrewsbury

Introduction

Shrewsbury is located in the heart of the countryside of Shropshire, yet is within easy reach of Birmingham and the West Midlands conurbation. It is a town steeped in history, with its 'black and white' Tudor architecture, annual Flower Show and associations with Brother Cadfael drawing visitors from home and abroad. It is located in the English Marches and commands an imposing position in a horseshoe meander of the River Severn.

Range of attractions

Shrewsbury has a wide range of attractions used both by local people and visitors to the town. The following is a list of some of the most popular attractions, with details of ownership and appeal to different visitor types.

The Shrewsbury Quest

- *Description*: a heritage attraction that re-creates monastic life in early medieval Shrewsbury through mystery, activity and authentic medieval gardens. Illustrates the period and world of Brother Cadfael, the fictional detective monk who features in Ellis Peters' best-selling mystery novels.
- *Ownership*: owned and operated by a private company on a site and buildings owned by, and leased from, Shrewsbury and Atcham Borough Council.
- *Visitor types*: caters for individuals and groups. Particularly attractive to families and readers of the Cadfael books. Has facilities to cater for education groups. Fully accessible for disabled people, with tactile maps, information and games in Braille and large format print. Also facilities for visitors with hearing difficulties.

Rowley's House Museum

- *Description*: sixteenth-century timber-framed warehouse and stone mansion of 1618. Exhibits include information on the Romans in Shropshire, life in medieval Shrewsbury, Shropshire wildlife, geology, costume and prehistory.

- *Ownership*: operated by Shrewsbury Museums Service, Shrewsbury and Atcham Borough Council.
- *Visitor types*: welcomes all visitors to Shrewsbury, individuals and groups. The nature of the building means that there is limited access for visitors with mobility problems.

Clive House Museum

- *Description*: museum that evokes eighteenth and nineteenth century life in Shrewsbury. Taking its name from Clive of India, Mayor and MP for Shrewsbury in the 1760s, the house has exhibits featuring social and domestic life, fine and applied arts and the Victorian kitchen.
- *Ownership*: operated by Shrewsbury Museums Service, Shrewsbury and Atcham Borough Council.
- *Visitor types*: welcomes all visitors to Shrewsbury, individuals and groups. The nature of the attraction means that there is access to the ground floor only for visitors with mobility problems.

Coleham Pumping Station

- *Description*: a steam restoration project in progress. Open days are held during the summer months to view the Victorian sewage pumping house and the two beam engines.
- *Ownership*: owned and managed by Shrewsbury Museums Service, Shrewsbury and Atcham Borough Council, with assistance from the Shrewsbury Steam Trust.
- *Visitor types*: welcomes individuals and groups on the open days. There is ramped access for people with disabilities.

Shrewsbury Castle and Shropshire Regimental Museum

- *Description*: red, sandstone castle guarding the northern approaches to Shrewsbury. Castle grounds include the motte, site of the first Norman castle. Regimental Museum houses collections from the eighteenth century to the present-day campaigns.
- *Ownership*: owned and managed by Shrewsbury Museums Service, Shrewsbury and Atcham Borough Council. Collections displayed and managed by Shropshire Regimental Museum Trust.
- *Visitor types*: welcomes all visitors to Shrewsbury, individuals and groups. Good access to much of the site and buildings for visitors with mobility problems. Coach drop-off point.

Quarry Park

- *Description*: a town park on the banks of the River Severn and the location for the famous Shrewsbury Flower Show every August. Has a wide range of play facilities for children, including boat hire on the river.
- *Ownership*: under the control of Shrewsbury and Atcham Borough Council.
- *Visitor types*: used by local people throughout the year and visitors to the town. Most areas accessible to those with mobility problems. Appeals to all ages.

Meole Brace Golf Course

- *Description*: a 9-hole municipal course on the outskirts of the town.
- *Ownership*: operated by Shrewsbury and Atcham Borough Council.
- *Visitor types*: used by casual visitors to the town, as well as keen, local golfers. No membership required. Used by young and old alike.

Sports and Leisure Centres

- *Description*: a range of purpose-built facilities, including:
  - The Quarry Swimming and Fitness Centre – swimming pool, flume ride, gymnasium, aerobics studio, sauna, steam room, spa bath and solarium suite.
  - London Road Sports Centre – six-court facility, gymnasium and outdoor multi-sport area.
  - The Grange Sports Centre – six-court facility, general hall and outdoor tennis courts.
  - Roman Road Sports Centre – three-court facility and regional standard floodlit synthetic surface.
  - Monkmoor Recreation Centre (Outdoor) – floodlit synthetic surface, tennis courts, multi-sports area, croquet lawn, bowling green, children's play area, football pitches and skateboard park.
- *Ownership*: under the control of the Department of Health, Leisure & Tourism, Shrewsbury and Atcham Borough Council
- *Visitor types*: club and public access is available at all centres, no membership required. Extensive sports development and children's activity programmes available. 'Passport to leisure' discount scheme in operation for all centres.

Guided tours

- *Description*: a range of guided walking and coach tours of the town and surrounding areas, some themed, e.g. based on the Brother Cadfael mysteries.
- *Ownership*: operated by Shrewsbury and Atcham Borough Council using official Green (local) and Blue (regional) Badge Guides.
- *Visitor types*: available to individuals and groups, with foreign language tours available in French, Italian and Welsh. Advice available on guided tours for people in wheelchairs or with impaired mobility.

Shrewsbury Abbey

- *Description*: the heart of the Brother Cadfael stories, the Abbey was founded in 1083 and became a large and powerful Benedictine monastery. The Abbey Church survived the Dissolution and is still a place of worship today.
- *Ownership*: Church of England
- *Visitor types*: open to local people and visitors every day, with interesting displays to illustrate its history.

Gateway Arts Centre

- *Description*: an education and arts centre, with exhibition areas, a book shop and coffee shop. Runs a range of continuing education and leisure day, evening and weekend courses.

- *Ownership*: under the control of Shropshire Education Department, Shropshire County Council.
- *Visitor types*: courses and facilities appeal to both local people and visitors to the town, including those with disabilities.

Events in Shrewsbury

The town hosts a wide variety of events throughout the year. For 1996, this includes:

- Shrewsbury Antique Book Fair
- Shropshire and West Mid Agricultural Show
- Shrewsbury Carnival
- Kite and Boomerang Festival
- International Music Festival
- World Music Day
- Shrewsbury Flower Show
- County of Salop Steam Rally
- Real Ale Festival
- Shrewsbury Abbey Flower Festival

The events are put on by a range of private, public and voluntary sector organisations, and appeal to both local people and visitors to the town.

Access to Shrewsbury's attractions

Shrewsbury's central location in the heart of Britain makes its attractions very accessible by a number of modes of transport.

1. *By car* – the town is a 1-hour drive from Birmingham, 3 hours from London and 2 hours from Holyhead. The recent improvements to the A5 road around Shrewsbury have improved access for visitors, with a direct dual carriageway link to the national motorway network via the M54 (see Figure 20.6).

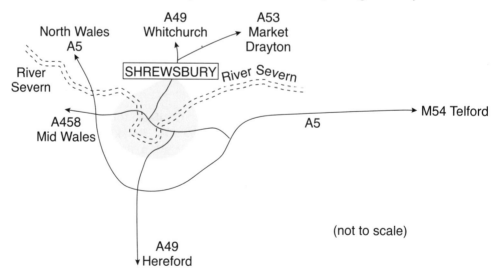

Fig. 20.6 Road access to Shrewsbury

2. *By train* – Shrewsbury's restored Victorian railway station is right in the centre of the town by the Castle. There are hourly train services from London Euston and good connections to Manchester, Crewe, Chester, Cardiff, Aberystwyth and stations enroute.
3. *By coach* – there are direct National Express services daily from London Victoria and connections to other UK towns served by the network.
4. *Buses* – regular buses serve all main parts of the town, as well as the principal Shropshire towns, with most visitor attractions being accessible by bus.
5. *Park and ride* – this service offers an excellent way for local people and tourists to get right to the centre of the town where many of its attractions are situated. Park and ride facilities can be found to the south, west and north of the main town.

(Compiled with the assistance of the Tourism and Marketing Officer, Shrewsbury and Atcham Borough Council)

Case study discussion questions

1. Do you consider that the range of tourist attractions given in the case study meets the needs of the majority of visitors to a town such as Shrewsbury?
2. Are there gaps in the provision of attractions and, if so, what other attractions would you suggest?
3. Why are some of the attractions not wholly suitable for visitors with disabilities?
4. What particular marketing and promotional techniques would you implement to give a town such as Shrewsbury maximum national exposure, given the limited resources available?
5. How could the events listed in the case study be best promoted to attract overnight visitors to the town?

Assignment 20.1

Tourist attractions within a locality

Performance criteria satisfied: 20.1.1, 20.1.2, 20.1.3, 20.1.4, 20.1.5, 20.1.6

Core skills opportunities at level 3: Communication 3.1, 3.2, 3.3, 3.4
Information technology 3.1, 3.2, 3.3
Application of number 3.1, 3.2, 3.3

Situation

In your role as tourism assistant with the local council, you have been given the responsibility of planning and carrying out an investigation into the tourist attractions in your local area.

Tasks

Working with a partner, you are to research and deliver a presentation to the rest of your group on local tourist attractions. In particular, your presentation should:

● Describe the main types of tourist attractions in your locality.

- Explain the appeal of the tourist attractions to different types of visitors.
- Assess the relative popularity of the tourist attractions.
- Describe the ownership and funding of the attractions.
- Describe access to the attractions.

Your presentation should include detailed information gathered from an in-depth investigation of local attractions. You should negotiate specific work tasks with the other members of your group to ensure equality of work load. You will be assessed on the content of the presentation and the quality of delivery.

Element 20.2 Investigate the development of a tourist attraction

Objectives of tourist attractions

The owners and managers of all tourist attractions set themselves objectives or goals in order to provide a framework within which all their resources can be used to best effect and their performance measured. Some objectives may be clearly outlined in a policy document or a mission statement, while other operators prefer an altogether more flexible approach to goal setting, yet still retaining a professional approach to their business activities. Objectives for individual attractions will be very diverse and will reflect the philosophy of the owners or managers, the size of the organisation, its stage of development and whether it is in the commercial or non-commercial sector of the industry. Objectives will be developed and refined by all those who have an interest in the operation of an attraction; sometimes referred to as stakeholders, they may include:

1. *Owners and/or managers* – who will be concerned that the objectives are realistic and achievable, and provide a reward for their effort, skill, investment and management expertise.
2. *Staff* – will want to be sure of safe and secure employment, with no discrimination, and will be concerned about their, and the organisation's, future prospects.
3. *Visitors to the attraction* – who will expect good value for money, high standards of customer care and a safe environment.
4. *Shareholders* – will be looking for a growing return on their capital invested in the attraction.
5. *Local councillors* – these representatives of the local community will be keen to see that any public funds invested in an attraction are used prudently.
6. *Members* (of a charity, club or association) – who will expect to be consulted about changes to the operation or management of an attraction.
7. *The local community* – through the planning process, will expect to be informed of the development of new attractions and alterations to existing premises, so as not to adversely affect their quality of life.

Fig. 20.7 Heirarchy of objective for a large tourist attraction

8. *Society in general* – will expect statutory agencies to investigate the wider social and environmental aspects of any new tourist attraction development.

Objectives of commercial attractions

Many of the largest tourist attractions in the UK are owned and operated by commercial (private sector) organisations. Some of the best-known names in the attractions sector are commercial ventures, such as Alton Towers, Thorpe Park and Madame Tussaud's, to name but a few. The commercial attractions sector is made up of large and small organisations owned by individuals or groups of people whose primary aim is to make a profit. Many individuals rely on the profits generated by commercial organisations for a substantial part of their income. Profit maximisation is an important objective for a number of reasons:

- In order to provide resources for further expansion of the business.
- To reward risk taking.
- To enable the business to respond to the needs of its customers.
- To encourage efficiency and innovation.

Within an overall global objective of seeking to maximise profitability, private sector attractions will identify specific goals for their businesses, which could include:

- Increasing the overall number of admissions.
- Attracting new markets, e.g. more groups.
- Increasing secondary spend, e.g. on catering and merchandise.
- Reducing staff turnover.
- Improving environmental performance.
- Reducing the level of complaints.
- Improving standards of customer care.

In very large attractions, objectives may be set out as a hierarchy, as shown in Figure 20.7.

As Figure 20.7 shows, the overall objective of the organisation is given in its policy or mission statement, at the top of the apex (Figure 20.8 gives an example of the mission statement for a major UK tourist attraction). This is then translated into organisational objectives, which may, depending on the size and structure of the operation, be converted into objectives for particular departments or divisions, e.g. catering, corporate hospitality, merchandising, etc. Targets for individual or team performance will then be developed so that measurement of success or attainment can take place.

Mission Statement

*G*ranada Studios Tour Limited
is committed to retaining its
position as the BEST Leisure attraction in the UK.

Our goal is to achieve complete customer
satisfaction and loyalty by providing a mix of quality,
service and price of which we can be proud.

Our staff will be treated fairly
and will have opportunities to develop their abilities.

We will play our part in the local community in
which we operate. In the long run, these values will
enhance the return to shareholders and they
will not, therefore, be abandoned in response to
short-term pressures.

Fig. 20.8 Mission statement of a major UK tourist attraction (reproduced courtesy of Granada Studios Tour)

Although profit maximisation is the primary aim of most private sector tourist attractions, it is by no means their only objective. Many smaller attractions are run by people who used to work for larger companies, but became frustrated with the high level of bureaucracy they encountered. Operating your own business in leisure or tourism can give a great deal of job satisfaction and the feeling that you have control over the decisions that are made. Some owners will not seek to maximise profits to the full, but may be content with a level of profit that gives them the type of lifestyle they are happy with; after all, why work in a sector concerned with entertainment and recreation, and have no time to enjoy yourself and have fun!

Objectives of non-commercial attractions

Non-commercial tourist attractions, falling within the public or voluntary sectors of the industry, do not have 'profit maximisation' as their primary objective. They have been developed with wider social objectives in mind; a council-run museum, for example, may well have as a primary aim, 'the provision of an educational and recreational facility for the benefit of local people and visitors to the area'. There are many examples of non-commercial organisations in the tourist attractions sector, including:

1. *Central government* – channels funding through the Department of National Heritage and other government departments to operate many attractions of national significance, such as the National Gallery, British Museum and the Tower of London.
2. *Local clubs and societies* – set up by local people with a specific purpose in mind, these organisations will aim to break even on their finances and may apply for some financial help from their local authority. A good example would be a steam railway preservation society that runs excursions in the summer or a wildlife conservation group that opens its nature reserves to the public.
3. *Charitable trusts* – many trusts are established to conserve or preserve our national and local heritage. One of the best known and respected is the National Trust, which today protects more than 600,000 acres of land in England, Wales and Northern Ireland as well as over 200 houses and parks. The Civic Trust, established in 1957, is a registered charity that aims to uphold high standards of environmental quality and management throughout the United Kingdom.
4. *Local authorities* – local councils play a major role in the provision of tourist attractions in Britain. Without their involvement, facilities such as recreation grounds, parks, museums, leisure centres, tourist information centres and visitor centres would not exist. The general move towards privatisation, market testing and compulsory competitive tendering has meant that local authorities are now functioning much more like private sector operators and the distinction between commercial and non-commercial is becoming blurred.
5. *Quangos* – these are quasi-autonomous non-governmental organisations which are primarily financed from the public purse but which have a high degree of autonomy. Examples in leisure and tourism are the Sports Council, Countryside Commission and the Arts Council, which, although not directly responsible for the running of tourist attractions, often provide advice and grant-aid for their establishment.

Although profit maximisation is not the primary objective of non-commercial organisations in travel and tourism, those which are part of local government or are agencies of central government (e.g. the quangos), are expected to offer value for money and meet targets and agreed performance criteria. Many local authorities have recruited staff from the private sector and have implemented private sector management practices in their attractions, in order to help achieve their objectives.

Activity

Choose three local tourist attractions (one private, one public and one from the voluntary sector) and record in detail the objectives of each organisation.

Sources of funding for tourist attractions

The precise funding arrangements of a tourist attraction will depend, to a large extent, on whether it operates in the public, private or voluntary sector of the industry.

Funding of public sector tourist attractions

The funds to run public sector tourist attractions come from a number of sources, including:

1. *National government* – large public sector tourist attractions such as museums and national monuments receive their funding direct from central government via the Department of National Heritage (DNH). The DNH allocates approximately 20 per cent of its budget to museums and galleries (nearly £200 million in 1994). Central government also distributes a proportion of its income from taxation to local authorities, to spend on local facilities and services. Part of this money may be allocated to fund local tourist attractions.
2. *Council Tax* – this is a tax levied by a local authority on people living in its area in order to supplement national government finance for local services. Travel and tourism facilities will be allocated a proportion of Council Tax funds, with some going for the operation and upkeep of local tourist attractions, e.g. museums, theatres, etc.
3. *European Union* – public sector attractions are encouraged to bid for funding from the European Union for specific tourism projects, which may include large-scale visitor attraction projects. Certain parts of the UK have special status when it comes to bidding for funding, e.g. the Highlands and Islands of Scotland, where tourism is seen as a way of injecting extra revenue and employment into the rural economy. The main EU sources for tourism projects include the European Social Fund and the European Regional Development Fund.
4. *National Lottery* – grants from lottery proceeds are a relatively new source of income to public sector tourist attractions. Bids are often formulated jointly with private

and voluntary sector bodies, and are on the basis of matched funding, i.e. every pound granted from the proceeds of the lottery must be met equally from other sources.

5. *Uniform Business Rate (UBR)* – in the same way that local residents pay Council Tax, local businesses have to pay UBR to the local authority for services provided. A proportion of these funds may be channelled into the operation of local tourist attractions.

6. *Sponsorship* – the mixing of private and public sector enterprises in leisure and tourism means that some public sector attractions encourage sponsorship in order to minimise costs and maximise their revenue. This is particularly the case with attractions concerned with the arts and sport, e.g. sports stadia, art galleries and events.

Funding of private sector tourist attractions

The sources of funding for a private sector tourist attraction usually depend on the size of the operation and its legal identity. A very small attraction, for example, whose owner operates as a sole trader or in partnership, may well be able to finance the enterprise from private savings or gifts from friends and relatives. Government grants and loans for small companies may also be available to these businesses. Larger attractions will normally operate as private limited companies, where the investors in the business are only liable for its debts up to the amount that they have actually invested. The first port of call for financing such ventures is often the high street banks, where the attraction may be offered short-, long- and medium-term loans, commercial mortgages and/or an overdraft facility. The directors of the company may also issue shares to their existing investors or seek out new shareholders, as a way of financing expansion of the attraction. Other examples of funding in the private sector include leasing and hire purchase, where capital items such as vehicles, plant and machinery are not purchased outright, but payments are spread over an extended period of time.

Private sector tourist attractions can also apply to a wide range of public sector bodies for grants or low-interest loans to help with expansion or improvements to facilities. These non-commercial sources of finance are offered by a number of agencies, including:

- National tourist boards (although the ETB no longer offers Section 4 grants)
- Department of the Environment
- Countryside Commission
- Rural Development Commission
- English Heritage
- Forestry Commission
- English Nature
- Arts Council
- Development agencies, e.g. Welsh Development Agency, Highlands and Islands Enterprise

As with tourist attractions in the public sector, sponsorship is another important, if uncertain, potential source of finance for private sector tourist attractions. A good example is the Pepsi Max Big One rollercoaster at Blackpool Pleasure Beach (see Figure 20.2 on page 185).

Some of the very largest private sector tourist attractions in the UK are operated as public limited companies (PLCs), although it is interesting to note that the UK's most popular tourist attraction, Blackpool Pleasure Beach, is still run as a private limited company, owned and operated since the early 1900s by one local family. PLCs finance expansion by offering shares to the public, giving their shareholders the same limited liability status that is enjoyed by investors in private limited companies. PLCs sometimes have a parent company acting as the head of a group, with a number of subsidiary enterprises working beneath it. In the tourist attractions sector, a good example of this is the Pearson Corporation, a multinational media organisation which owns a number of attractions operating under the Tussauds Group banner. Included within the group are Alton Towers, Chessington World of Adventures, Madame Tussaud's, Warwick Castle, the London Planetarium and the Rock Circus. Another leisure giant, Granada PLC, has interests in the attractions sector, operating the Camelot and American Adventure theme parks.

Funding of voluntary sector tourist attractions

Many tourist attractions in the voluntary sector have charitable status since they aim to promote a cause, conserve the heritage or help individuals, rather than make a profit. There are benefits to being a charity, such as exemption from certain forms of taxation and reductions in business rates. Whether a voluntary sector attraction is very large, as is the case with many National Trust properties, or very small, such as a local craft centre, the funding opportunities and sources open to them are very similar, including:

1. *Sponsorship* – a local conservation trust attraction, for example, may be sponsored by a local company.
2. *Subscriptions from members* – the RSPB, English Heritage and the National Trust receive funds from this source.
3. *Grants from central and local government* – a local council may make a grant to its local museum, while the Arts Council gives grants to individuals and organisations which it considers are advancing the cause of the arts. The Countryside Commission gives grants towards environmental improvement projects, including interpretation and education centres.
4. *Donations and gifts* – perhaps part of the estate of a deceased person, as is often the case with the National Trust.
5. *Fund-raising events* – anything from a sponsored walk to a jumble sale can help boost funds for voluntary sector tourist attractions.
6. *Fees* – can be levied for certain services, e.g. hiring out of equipment and entrance fees for special events, such as a motor rally in the grounds of a historic house open to the public.
7. *Retail income* – larger voluntary sector attractions have set up shops and mail order subsidiaries as a way of generating income, e.g. National Trust shops and the Science Museum in London.

Revenue funding

The preceding sections of this unit have been primarily concerned with the initial funding to establish a tourist attraction and the identification of sources of funding for capital projects and expansion. Once established, it is vital for tourist attractions to maximise their revenue, while keeping a close check on their expenditure, if they are to survive and prosper. Receipts at the gate are obviously important, but so too is 'secondary spend', i.e. opportunities for visitors to spend more, while in the attraction, on items in retail and catering outlets. Secondary spend is crucial to tourist attractions, hence the number of shops and eating places at major theme parks, for example. Another way of maximising revenue is to diversify into corporate hospitality. We saw in the case study of Granada Studios Tour on page 195 that staging hospitality and catering events can contribute significantly to total turnover, while at the same time utilising a facility to the full.

Access to tourist attractions

In the case of tourist attractions, 'access' is an all-embracing term, with a number of different meanings, including:

- Geographical access to an attraction, e.g. road and rail routes, and parking facilities.
- Physical access to a site, its buildings and facilities, particularly for those with mobility problems.
- Access for all sectors of the community regardless of, for example, their age, gender, race or income level.

Geographical access

All attractions will aim to ensure that it is as easy as possible for visitors to travel to the site either by public transport or in a private car. Promotional leaflets will include travel information, as this example from the Chessington World of Adventures main guide illustrates:

> Chessington is situated 12 miles from London on the A243, just 2 miles from both the A3 and M25 junction 9. Bus/coaches – Bus 71, Flightline 777, West Link 468 and London Country 465, all stop directly at the main entrance. SouthWest Trains – Chessington South station is a 10 minute walk from the main entrance. Regular services run from Waterloo station, also stopping at Clapham Junction and Wimbledon. All coach and car parking is free.

Good signposting, both to the locality of the attraction and within its immediate vicinity, is also necessary to ensure safe and manageable visitor flows for pedestrians and traffic. Larger attractions are eligible to use the tourist board approved 'brown and white' signs on roads close to their sites, while all attractions can make use of the temporary signposting services offered by the AA and RAC. Local planning and high-ways authorities need to be consulted before any signs to tourist attractions are erected, since planning permission may be required.

Physical access to attractions

As well as ensuring good access to a site by both public and private transport, tourist attraction operators will be keen to provide a welcoming, safe and accessible environment on-site for all visitors, including those with impaired mobility or disabilities. It makes good business sense to spend time assessing a site and its facilities from the visitors' point of view, so as to minimise their inconvenience and provide an enjoyable experience for all. Most people's expected 'normal' level of mobility is reduced, temporarily or permanently and to varying degrees at some time in their life, so focusing attention on access to attractions can pay dividends. Injury, illness, pregnancy, ageing or simply walking along with a toddler all present their own mobility problems. Only a small proportion of the population is in the peak-of-fitness age group and nobody stays there long. Back pain sufferers, bifocal wearers and people with slight hearing loss are not uncommon. At any one time, it is estimated that there are 10 million people in the UK in circumstances that affect their mobility. Many would consider themselves 'inconvenienced' rather than 'disabled', but they are nonetheless an important market for tourist attraction operators.

Physical access to an attraction is only one part of the story for those with mobility problems. They will certainly want to feel confident that they will enjoy their visit and not have to struggle to cope, but it is just as important that they should feel accepted as valued customers and not be treated as a nuisance or an inconvenience.

Providing accessible visitor attractions

In 1991 the Visitor Attractions Advisory Committee of the national tourist boards invited a working group, composed of representatives of the UK tourism industry and disability organisations, to propose a system of assessment and accessibility of attractions, supported by relevant design guidance. Its aim was to continue the work of the Tourism for All Campaign (see case study in Element 21.1), but focus particularly on the attractions sector of the industry.

The results of the working group's findings were published in 1994 as an English Tourist Board report entitled 'Providing Accessible Visitor Attractions'. One of the principal assumptions of the report was that attraction operators would want more and happier customers, who would stay longer, spend more on-site, return and recommend the attraction to their friends. The report offered tourist attraction operators an opportunity to:

1. Appraise the market for visitors with impaired mobility or disabilities.
2. Understand the disabled visitor's needs.
3. Examine the best design solutions.
4. Carry out an initial access assessment.

It contained the information needed to assess, plan and put into action an effective access policy, combining physical design with effective marketing and customer care.

The comprehensive report attempted to answer a range of questions concerning access to tourist attractions, such as:

- What are the benefits of catering for visitors with impaired mobility or disabilities?
- What is it like to be a wheelchair user?
- How does information on access help to promote an attraction?
- What signs should be used to welcome and direct visitors?
- How should staff be trained to communicate with disabled visitors and meet their special needs?
- What size should doors and ramps be in order to give unhindered access?
- How can disabled visitors get the best out of exhibitions, rides, play areas, etc.?

The report included a useful checklist for tourist attraction operators who wish to carry out an initial assessment of the existing level of accessibility, including recommended standards and criteria for parking, paths, seating, ramps, steps, lifts, handrails, doors, toilets, telephones, communication and marketing.

Access for all sectors of the community

Attractions and amenities in the non-commercial sector, such as municipal golf courses, leisure centres, museums and sports grounds, will be operated on the basis of providing a service to their local community, as well as welcoming tourists. They will have social and community objectives, often reflected in their pricing and admissions policy. This could involve discounted rates for local Council Tax payers, perhaps via a 'passport' scheme, or cheap rates for senior citizens, single parents and unemployed people at off-peak times. Some facilities will be dual use, where a leisure centre, for example, is used by a school or college between the hours of 9 am and 4 pm and by other local people and visitors at all other times. Private sector attractions will also seek to maintain goodwill with local people by sometimes offering discounted or even free access to facilities at certain times of the year, perhaps the beginning and end of the season. They may also target certain under-privileged sectors of their local community, running special events and promotions for their enjoyment.

Activity

Carry out some research to discover which tourist attractions in your locality have been developed or modified to be able to accept visitors with disabilities.

Marketing and promotion of tourist attractions

The promotion of tourist attractions should follow the guiding principles of all marketing activity in tourism, namely that:

- Marketing is concerned with helping an organisation meet its objectives.
- Identifying customer needs is the starting point for effective marketing.

- All departments and individuals in an organisation contribute to overall marketing success.
- Marketing is a continuous process, not a 'one-off' activity.

The marketing process in tourist attractions can be explained with the help of Figure 20.9, which shows us that:

- Any good marketing strategy (the process by which marketing plans are put into action) should start with the customer as its focus. Knowing who your customers are, where they come from, what they want from your attraction, how much they are willing to pay, whether they are satisfied with the service you offer, and so on, provides an invaluable information base on which to make your marketing deci- sions.
- Once you know the characteristics of your customers, it is much easier to develop products and services which they will want to use. By giving attention to such matters as pricing and location/accessibility of facilities, you will be able to give the customer what he or she wants, at the right time, in the right place and at the right price.
- There are many ways of promoting tourist attractions to existing and potential visi- tors, including advertising, direct mail, sponsorship, sales promotions and public relations activity.
- Marketing is not something that the operators of an attraction do once and then forget about. It is a dynamic activity that reflects the ever-changing tastes and fash- ions of the general public. It is essential, therefore, that all tourist attractions monitor and evaluate what they are doing at each stage of the marketing process, by asking such questions as:
  - Are our customers the same today as they were three years ago?
  - Does our mix of facilities meet their needs today?
  - Is our promotional work reaching its intended target?
  - What are our competitors doing?

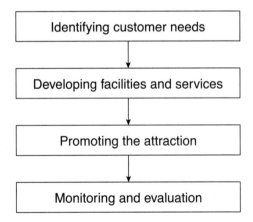

Fig. 20.9 The marketing process in tourist attractions

Element 22.3 looks in greater detail at how marketing and promotion are tackled in some of Britain's major tourist attractions, while the following case study on Longleat demonstrates how one attraction has approached its marketing strategy.

Marketing and promotion – Longleat, Warminster, Wiltshire

Introduction

The Longleat Estate is owned by Lord Bath and comprises some 9000 acres on the Wiltshire/Somerset borders, lying between Warminster and Frome. At the centre of the Estate is Longleat House, which is Lord Bath's home and one of England's finest Elizabethan mansions, surrounded by 900 acres of park land.

Longleat House has been open to the public since 1947 and the Safari Park was opened in 1966 (see Figure 20.10).

Fig. 20.10 Visitors to Longleat enjoying the attractions of the Safari Park (reproduced courtesy of the Estate Office, Longleat)

Visitor admissions to the Estate total some 390,000 per annum, but total visitors are in the region of 500,000 per year. Apart from the House, with its famous murals, other attractions include the 'World's Longest Maze', an Adventure Castle, narrow gauge railway, Postman Pat Village, boat rides, exhibitions, etc. The park is used regularly as a venue for events ranging from balloon festivals to product launches, car rallies, concerts and horse trials.

Marketing objectives

The stated aims of Longleat's marketing strategy are as follows:

● To increase the number of national and international visitors to Longleat.
● To create greater awareness of Longleat in the south-west.

- Conservation – to emphasise the importance of conservation of the House, the Safari Park and the wider estate.
- To increase the number of events, particularly out of peak season.

Summary of 1995 marketing activity

1. *Leaflet distribution* – 1.5 million leaflets distributed within a 2 hours' drive time catchment, covering Bristol, Bournemouth, Reading, Cardiff, Bath, Cheltenham, Weston-super-Mare, Taunton, Southampton and the A303–M3 corridor.
2. *Press advertising* – in over 30 regional and local newspapers covering the same catchment area. Campaigns are timed to coincide with peak holiday periods.
3. *Posters* – a six-week campaign divided into two weeks at Easter and four weeks of the school summer holiday period. Mainly city/town centre sites and railway stations using 4-sheet posters.
4. *Radio advertising and promotion* – campaign ran the week preceding the school summer holidays and during the first week of the holidays, comprising 833 × 30 seconds commercials on the GWR network, including Classic Gold and 210 FM.
5. *Trade advertising* – in *Group Travel Organiser*, *Times Educational Supplement*, *Coaching Tours and Excursions* magazine, as well as annual publications.
6. *Promotions* – competitions on the Family Channel, MGM Cinema Swindon, Purbeck Radio and GWR. Magazine competitions in *Chat*, *Breakout* and *Newbury Out and About*. Newspaper competitions in the *Western Gazette* × 6, *Wiltshire Times* × 2, *Oxford Courier*, *Western Daily Press*, *White Horse News* and others.
7. *Vouchers and on-pack promotions* – in *TV Times*, *Radio Times*, McVitie's biscuits, BT Phonecards, *Daily Star*, *Best* magazine, *Family Circle*, Unigate, *The Daily Telegraph*, Hilton Hotels, local newspapers, *Classic Sights*, *Wessex Top Ten* brochure.
8. *Window displays* – in local tourist information centres (TICs).
9. *Trade fairs and workshops* – World Travel Market, Excursions, Southern Tourist Board and West Country Tourist Board Days Out Fairs.
10. *Market research* – in-house, postage-paid response cards and off-site surveys.
11. *Public relations activity* – mainly themed on animals and events.

The groups market

Longleat has undertaken a major marketing initiative targeted at group organisers, with the aim of increasing the number of visitors from this segment of the market. Research showed that the volume of group business to the attraction had declined over the previous 10 years. This was considered to be a direct result of a number of factors, including:

- No target marketing.
- The increasing expense of private coach hire.

- Increases in car ownership.
- Recession and limited disposable income.
- Low profile of Longleat.
- Failure to provide facilities for coach drivers.
- Perceived expense of Longleat as an attraction.

To address this situation, the marketing team at Longleat undertook a market research exercise that included seeking the views of coach operators, teachers and other group organisers on the current 'product' at Longleat and, in particular, its suitability to the groups market. The research also included an analysis of competitors' printed materials for groups; this led to the redesigning of forms and envelopes to give a more 'fun' image. Prices for groups were reduced in line with competitor attractions and the minimum group size to qualify for discounted rates was lowered to 12, to account for groups arriving in mini-buses. New group packages were also developed in line with the findings of the market research.

Having refined the groups product at Longleat, the marketing team set about implementing a co-ordinated promotional campaign to inform group travel organisers of the new initiative and to persuade them to do business with the attraction. This included:

- Advertising in trade magazines such as *Group Travel Organiser* and annual directories.
- Attendance at trade fairs organised by the tourist boards and local authorities.
- Visits to coach companies to obtain feedback on the new products.
- Public relations activity, including sending press releases featuring the new activities to specialist press outlets.
- Direct mail to group organisers, clubs, societies, etc. on the mailing list.
- Employing an agency to generate new business from group organisers.
- Supporting the initiative within the main advertising campaign, i.e. coach station poster sites now used.

(Information courtesy of Longleat)

Case study discussion questions

1. Which of the promotional techniques undertaken by Longleat will help fulfil its objective of creating greater awareness of Longleat in the south-west?
2. What market research did the attraction carry out to solve the problem of its declining groups market?
3. What types of public relations activity do attractions such as Longleat undertake?
4. In relation to its initiative to increase the number of groups visiting Longleat, what will the attraction need to do to measure whether or not the campaign has been a success?
5. What types of corporate and public events are staged at attractions like Longleat, as a way of generating extra revenue?

Assessing the success of tourist attractions

In determining the success of a tourist attraction, it is necessary to create specific criteria against which to measure its effectiveness. Most attractions will have an overall aim to which staff and management are working, perhaps the provision of an educational service to local children or the conservation of a wildlife habitat. We saw in the section on objectives, at the beginning of Element 20.2, that the specific objectives of tourist attractions will vary depending on whether they operate in the commercial or non-commercial sector of the industry. Whether in the public, private or voluntary sector, all tourist attractions need to establish systems and processes to measure their performance for a number of reasons, including:

- To find out if they are meeting their original aims.
- To establish whether customers are happy with the facilities and services on offer.
- To find out if financial, physical and staff resources are being used to best effect.
- To discover how well they are performing in relation to competitor organisations.
- To identify weaknesses in management systems, including communication and decision making.
- To highlight staff training needs.

In devising systems and processes to measure the success or otherwise of an attraction, it will be necessary for the operators and managers to take into account a number of factors, including:

1. *Financial performance* – a prime concern for commercial operators, but also significant in the running of non-commercial attractions, which have to show value-for-money and the wise use of resources.
2. *Operational performance* – such as the total throughput of visitors and their length of stay.
3. *Customer satisfaction* – frequent customer surveys and other methods of feedback will enable operators to make improvements to their facilities and services.
4. *Health and safety management* – legislation and codes of practice covering health and safety at work, food hygiene, the control of hazardous substances, workplace conditions and electrical safety, to name but a few, all place a duty on the owners and operators of attractions to provide a safe environment for staff and visitors.
5. *Environmental impacts* – large-scale developments may be required to carry out an environmental impact assessment (EIA) before permission to proceed with the development is granted.
6. *Economic, cultural and social impacts* – operators may be asked to quantify the costs and benefits of their activity in relation to the local community. Planning authorities will be keen to see that attractions do not detract from the amenity of an area or reduce the local residents' quality of life through, for example, excessive noise, dangerous vehicle activity or unnecessary financial burdens on local Council Tax payers.

In an effort to ensure that visitors to attractions enjoy a consistently high level of service and facilities, the national tourist boards in the UK have developed 'visitors' charters'. These written documents identify the standards that attractions must comply with in order to become registered organisations. By signing up to a visitors' charter, an attraction immediately demonstrates that it is keen to provide a safe and enjoyable experience for visitors. It also signals that it is a professional operation that strives to be successful in all that it undertakes.

Standards at tourist attractions – the Visitors' Charter

Introduction

In 1991 the English Tourist Board (ETB) accepted a recommendation from its Visitor Attractions Advisory Committee to introduce a National Code of Practice for Visitor Attractions. The Code, which was drawn up by the committee, applies to all visitor attractions that meet the definition given at the beginning of Unit 20.1 (see page 183). The Code, which has now been revised and renamed the 'Visitors' Charter', was introduced as a result of consultations with the proprietors of attractions over several years. Its purpose is to establish standards for this sector of the industry, both to safeguard the interests of the public and to enable the tourist boards to identify those attractions they can promote with confidence. The Visitors' Charter has been accepted by the 11 regional tourist boards in England; a similar Charter is in use in Wales and Scotland. All known visitor attractions that meet the ETB definition are invited to register their undertaking to observe the revised Charter; registration is free.

Tourist attractions that have registered their undertaking to observe the Charter are provided with a certificate to this effect, which they are required to display prominently. A logo is available for use on promotional material and letter-headings, and is also available both in the form of a display sign and as a sticker for display on premises (see Figure 20.11). It is intended that proprietors should demonstrate their observance of the Charter by using the logo. Observance of the Charter is a condition of regional tourist board membership and promotion. The English Tourist Board also makes registration a condition of eligibility for inclusion in its own promotions and publications.

Fig. 20.11 The logo used in the Visitor's Charter (reproduced courtesy of the English Tourist Board)

The content of the Charter

The Charter is a written document that details the conditions with which visitor attractions must comply in order to retain their registered status. Where the ETB considers that an attraction is in breach of one or more elements of the Charter, it has the power, as a last resort, to withdraw its registered status. The Charter states that the owners and management of an attraction have undertaken:

1. To display this Visitors' Charter prominently, and to include the symbol wherever possible in promotional material, to signify compliance.
2. To describe accurately in any advertisement, brochure or other printed means, the amenities, facilities and services provided and to indicate on all such promotional material any significant restrictions on entry.
3. To display clearly at public entry points (a) any charges for entry (including service charges and taxes where applicable) and whether there are additional charges for individual attractions, and (b) hours of operation (opening and closing).
4. To manage and, where appropriate, staff the attraction in such a way as to ensure visitor safety, comfort and service by maintaining a high standard of customer care, cleanliness, courtesy and maintenance. All staff who meet visitors should be distinguishable as employees or volunteer staff.
5. Where appropriate to the nature, scale and location of the attraction, to provide adequate toilet facilities, coach and car parking, and catering arrangements.
6. To give due consideration to the requirements of disabled people and people with special needs, and to make suitable provision where practicable.
7. To deal promptly and courteously with all enquiries, requests, reservations, correspondence and complaints from visitors. To advise visitors of the method of recording comments and to whom comments should be addressed.
8. To provide public liability insurance or comparable arrangement and to comply with all applicable planning, safety and other statutory requirements.

(Information courtesy of ETB)

Case study discussion questions

1. What benefits are visitors likely to experience when visiting an attraction that is registered under the Charter?
2. Do you consider that a voluntary scheme such as the Visitors' Charter is preferable to compulsory registration scheme to improve standards at tourist attractions?
3. Would there be any advantages to the staff working at an attraction that was registered under the Visitors' Charter, as opposed to one that was not?
4. Is a tourist attraction that is registered under the Charter scheme likely to experience a competitive advantage in its operation?
5. Do you feel that the Charter goes far enough in the conditions that it places on registered attractions?

Assignment 20.2

The development of a tourist attraction

Performance criteria satisfied: 20.2.1, 20.2.2, 20.2.3, 20.2.4, 20.2.5, 20.2.6

Core skills opportunities at level 3:   Communication   3.1, 3.2, 3.3, 3.4
                                       Information technology   3.1, 3.2, 3.3
                                       Application of number   3.1, 3.2, 3.3

Situation

While on work experience with a tourist attraction, you are asked by its new owner, Jason Riddick, to carry out a complete review of the past development of the attraction in order to provide him with useful information on which to base future management decisions.

Tasks

You are to prepare a written report on the development of the tourist attraction. In particular, your report should:

- Describe the main objectives of the development of the attraction.
- Explain how the features of the development match the objectives.
- Describe the sources of funding used by the attraction.
- Explain how access to the attraction was developed.
- Explain how the attraction is marketed and promoted.
- Assess the success of the attraction in meeting its objectives.

Your report should be word processed and include relevant diagrams and statistics.

Introduction

We have seen in Elements 20.1 and 20.2 that tourist attractions in the UK come in all shapes and sizes, with their own particular features, aims, funding and markets. There are, however, a number of similarities when it comes to the operation and management of the attractions, such as health and safety requirements, marketing and visitor flows.

This element looks in detail at the operation of two major attractions in the UK: Alton Towers and Chessington World of Adventures, both part of the Tussauds Group. These two case study examples will demonstrate the common operational and management systems found in all major attractions, and will provide details of a number of factors, including:

- Layout
- Visitor flows
- Accessibility
- Attraction features
- Types of visitor
- Marketing
- Safety and security
- Types of job role

CASE STUDY

Chessington World of Adventures

Introduction

Chessington World of Adventures is a major UK theme park situated in a Green Belt area of Surrey to the south of London. It started life as Chessington Zoo, which was opened in 1931, and today combines animal conservation with a variety of 'white knuckle' rides and family attractions. Chessington has long been well known to the people of London and south-east England for the range of entertainment it has offered, e.g. a circus, funfair and miniature railway. But despite this, during the early 1970s, the annual attendance figures of over 800,000 began to decline. The multinational Pearson Group decided to buy Chessington and inject new capital into the attraction. In 1978, they also acquired Madame Tussaud's and put all their leisure interests under one umbrella to form the Tussauds Group. July 1987 saw the opening of Chessington World of Adventures by HRH Prince Edward. The transformation of the park took 6 years of planning and cost a total of £18 million, the opening being linked with the development of the M25 motorway around London. (The Chessington World of Adventures logo can be seen in Figure 20.12)

Fig. 20.12 Chessington World of Adventures' logo (reproduced courtesy of Chessington World of Adventures)

Development of the attraction

The first 6-month opening season in 1987 attracted 840,000 visitors, putting Chessington World of Adventures at No. 15 in the league of the UK's top tourist attractions. In 1988, the park welcomed over 1 million visitors for the first time (see Figure 20.13). Phase II of the park development opened in 1990, with two new, unique rides helping to attract a total of 1.5 million visitors. 1995 was the park's most successful season ever, with 1.77 million visitors.

Layout of the attraction

Chessington World of Adventures is made up of a number of different themed areas, including:

1. *Forbidden Kingdom* – home of the Terror Tomb and Rameses Revenge rides (see Figure 20.14).
2. *Transylvania* – a themed Bavarian-style village.
3. *Calamity Canyon* – a town with a western theme based on the Californian Gold Rush (see Figure 20.15).
4. *Mystic East* – Oriental palaces provide the setting for the Dragon River water ride.
5. *English Market Square* – the starting point of the Safari Skyway for a trip to the zoo.
6. *Toytown* – entertainment for younger children.
7. *Smuggler's Cove* – a themed area housing the Smuggler's Galleon ride.

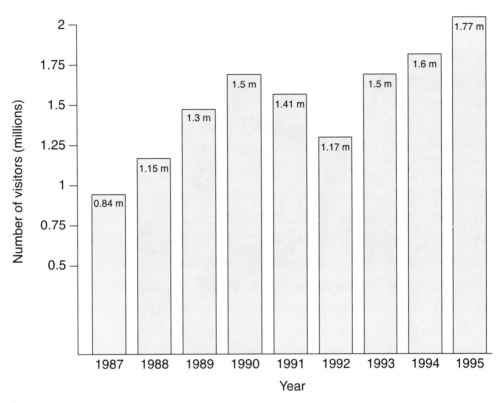

Fig. 20.13 Visitor numbers at Chessington World of Adventures *(source: Chessington World of Adventures)*

8. *Animal Lands* – made up of various areas including Birdland, Monkey Walk and Sealion Bay.
9. *The Big Top* – home to the Mobster Magic show.

The 10 most popular rides at Chessington World of Adventures are shown below in rank order:

1. The Vampire
2. Dragon River
3. Rameses Revenge
4. Bubbleworks
5. Magic Carpet
6. Smuggler's Galleon
7. Runaway Minetrain
8. Seastorm
9. Skyway
10. Rodeo

Pricing

Like most theme parks, Chessington charges visitors an all-inclusive price, giving unlimited access to the attraction's facilities. For the 1996 season (23 March–3 November) the prices are as follows:

Fig. 20.14 Rameses Revenge in the Forbidden Kingdom *(reproduced courtesy of Chessington World of Adventures)*

Fig. 20.15 Calamity Canyon *(reproduced courtesy of Chessington World of Adventures)*

Adults	£16.50
Children (4–14 inclusive)	£13.00
Children (under 4)	Free
Senior Citizens	£7.25

As well as these standard prices, Chessington offers special group rates for parties of 15 or more. Also, as a way of maximising revenue, the park remains open until 9.30 pm on summer nights (normal closing time is 5 pm or 6 pm) and offers special evening entry prices of:

Adults	£9.50
Children	£7.00
Senior Citizens	£5.00

These prices are also available for end of season 'fright nights' in October and November, when the normal rides and entertainments are supplemented with lasers, lights and special effects.

Accessibility

Chessington is situated 12 miles from London, close to junction 9 of the M25 motorway, giving a catchment of 18 million people living within a 2-hour drive of the attraction. It has free parking for cars and coaches and is served by frequent bus, coach and train services. Some rides and areas at the park are accessible to those in wheelchairs. Toilet facilities at the park include special provision for the disabled and wheelchair hire is available on request.

Staffing at the attraction

Chessington employs around 1000 staff throughout the year, offering permanent employment or seasonal contracts of 1–11 months (see Table 20.6). The park employs:

1. *Ride operators* – assisting with the safe loading and unloading of visitors.
2. *Catering assistants* – working in one of the many catering outlets in the park, serving food, cleaning and kitchen portering.
3. *Site cleaners* – helping to keep the park grounds litter-free and tidy.
4. *Security operatives* – ensuring that all visitors and company property are protected.
5. *Admissions assistants* – working as till operators and welcoming visitors as well as controlling car parking.
6. *Games assistants* – helping in the arcades and with side shows.
7. *Shop assistants* – working in the many retail outlets in the park.
8. *Laundry assistants* – carrying out minor repairs to staff clothing, as well as washing and ironing.
9. *Cashiers* – handling cash and operating computerised accounting systems.

Detailed job descriptions and person specifications for two posts at Chessington World of Adventures, namely a seasonal shop supervisor and ride area supervisor are shown in Figures 20.16 and 20.17 respectively.

(Information courtesy of Chessington World of Adventures)

Table 20.6 Break-down of staffing at Chessington World of Adventures

Temporary		Permanent	
Visitor catering	260	Visitor catering	35
Rides	155	Zoo	22
Merchandising	80	Rides	20
Admissions	60	Estates	20
Estates	70	Contracts	20
Games	50	Maintenance	18
Functions	25	Merchandising	6
Other	50	Games	5
		Admissions	4
		Accounts	16
		Administration	25
Total	**750**	**Total**	**191**

Source: Chessington World of Adventures

Case study discussion questions

1. Why do you think visitor numbers began dropping at Chessington Zoo in the early 1970s?
2. What did the owners of the attraction do to stem the drop in numbers?
3. What type of visitor does the park aim to attract and how do its facilities match up to visitor needs?
4. What are the key points that will affect the popularity of theme parks such as Chessington up to and beyond the year 2000?
5. What skills are likely to be needed by the employees highlighted in the case study?

CASE STUDY

Alton Towers

Introduction

Alton Towers (see Figure 20.18) welcomed around 3 million visitors in 1995, making it Britain's most popular paying attraction. Set in more than 500 acres of Staffordshire countryside, it currently has more than 125 rides and attractions. The public were first invited to visit the gardens as long ago as 1860, but it wasn't until the end of the 1970s that the present theme park began to take shape. In 1990 it was purchased by Pearson PLC, an international media corporation, which established the Tussauds Group of attractions (see case study in Element 20.1 on page 198). The Group spent 1991 evaluating the park and investing heavily in refurbishing the existing rides, attractions and facilities, as well as researching into the future development of Alton Towers. On completion of its research, the Group started work on developing three new sites, representing a total investment of nearly £10 million.

Job description

Job title:	**Seasonal Shop Supervisor**
Responsible to:	Merchandise Senior Supervisor Assistant Merchandise Manager Merchandise Manager
Responsible for:	(a) Maintaining stock levels. (b) Stock ordering. (c) Ensuring unit is kept in a clean and tidy state at all times. (d) Ensuring staff in their unit are suitably dressed. (e) Cashing up.
Position in company:	General Manager Business Retail Manager Merchandise Manager Assistant Merchandise Manager Merchandise Senior Supervisor Shop Senior Supervisor
Job purpose:	To ensure smooth running of unit.
Job description:	(a) Stock ordering. (b) Maintaining a clean and tidy unit. (c) Organising breaks. (d) General organisation of unit of responsibilty. (e) Cashing up.
Authority:	(a) To authorise customer refunds and voids.
Hours of work:	40 hrs, as and when required, i.e. Bank Holidays.

Personal specification

Job title:	**Seasonal Shop Supervisor**	
	Essential	**Desirable**
Training:	–	Induction ⎫ Health and safety ⎬ house Health and hygiene ⎭
Experience:	Previous retail experience	Till experience. Cash handling.
Skills and knowledge:	–	Ability to display merchandise. Cashing up. Stock ordering.
Personality:	–	Outgoing Approachable Polite Presentable Organisational skills.
Circumstances:	Fit and active Flexible to work hours	–

Fig. 20.16 Job Description and Personal Specification for the post of Seasonal Shop Supervisor at a major UK theme park (reproduced courtesy of Chessington World of Adventures)

JOB DESCRIPTION

Job title: Ride Area Supervisor

Responsible to: Ride Operations Co-ordinators
                              Assistant Rides Manager
                              Rides Manager

Responsible for: Temporary staff and allocated ride areas

Training received: Customer service   (Internal)
                              On-ride training   (Internal)
                              In-house emergency procedures (Internal)
                              Computer skills   (Internal)

Position in company: General Manager
                              Deputy General Manager (Operations)
                              Ride Operations Manager
                              Assistant Rides Manager
                              Rides Co-ordinators
                              Ride Area Supervisor

Job purpose: To assist the Ride Operations Manager in the smooth
                              running of all the rides and to maintain high standards
                              of presentation and customer relations with special
                              attention to the safety of the employees and visitors.

Hours: Must be prepared to work weekends and bank holidays.
                              Flexible hours as directed by the Ride Operations Manager.

Authority: Supervision of all ride areas, containing multiple attractions.

MAIN DUTIES

1. To ensure that all statutory requirements are met in respect of ride safety (in conjunction with Health and Safety at Work, etc., Act 1974) and that all safe practices are in operation.

2. Ensure that all staff understand and adhere to emergency procedures/instructions laid down in the operational manual.

3. Responsible for the operation of ride areas, containing a number of attractions, as directed by the Ride Operations Manager, including pre-opening and close down checks.

4. To ensure that subordinates receive experienced assistance and operator training to enable them to perform to the standards set by the department.

5. To maintain motivation, discipline and the development of the temporary staff.

6. Attend to, and where possible, take appropriate action for any customer complaints or compliments.

7. Attend to and report any incidents regarding accidents, fire, loss of property, theft, damage or any other irregularities, ensuring necessary documentation or reports have been completed.

8. At all times maintain the departments high standards of customer care, presentation and endeavour to meet the needs of our visitors as directed by the Ride Operations Manager.

9. Responsible for the correct use and storage of cleaning equipment, including the 'Control of Substances Hazardous to Health', awareness.

10. In low season the job holder may be required to work in other areas and departments within the park. They may also be required to undertake project work during the closed season.

11. To interact and liaise with other departments that may use that particular ride area during situations such as breakdowns and film shoots.

12. To use and understand the department computer systems as required.

13. To maintain correct staffing levels within given budgetary specifications.

14. Attend to any reasonable request by the Ride Operations Manager.

15. To maintain cleaning stock and equipment levels within given budgetary specifications.

16. Responsible for maintaining the cleanliness of the locker rooms and Ride Operations offices.

Fig. 20.17 Job Description for the post of Ride Area Supervisor at a major UK theme park (reproduced courtesy of Chessington World of Adventures)

Figure 20.17 continued

Fig. 20.18 Alton Towers' montage (reproduced courtesy of Alton Towers)

Accessibility

Alton Towers is situated 12 miles east of Stoke-on-Trent, close to the motorway network; for those travelling from the north the route is M1 junction 23A, M6 junction 15, while for those approaching from the south it is M1 junction 28, M6 junction 16. It has free parking for cars and coaches. Some rides and all areas of the park are accessible to those in wheelchairs. Toilet facilities at the park include special provision for the disabled and wheelchair hire is available on request.

Amenities and facilities

As well as its 200 acres of landscaped gardens, Alton Towers also has a number of themed areas and rides. The themed areas include Tower Street, Old MacDonald's Farm, Adventureland, Storybook Land, Fantasy World and Merry England. The five most popular rides in 1995 (with ride figures in millions) were:

Nemesis	2.21
Haunted House	1.93
Congo River Rapids	1.85
Log Flume	1.69
Thunderlooper	1.65

The park has a wide variety of retail outlets, offering everything from traditional souvenirs such as baseball caps, mugs, scarves, etc., to the more exclusive ranges of heritage souvenirs. Catering is an important revenue earner for the attraction, with a wide choice of facilities, from *à la carte* restaurants and family eating to fast food and speciality kiosks. The attraction also has a fully equipped medical centre able to cope with any eventuality, including special needs. It also acts as the lost child centre.

New for 1996 is the 175-room Alton Towers Hotel, located in a 7 acre landscaped site within the bounds of the park itself. The themed hotel is primarily aimed at the 17 per cent of Alton Tower's visitors who already stay overnight in the locality, although it will, unlike the attraction, be open all the year round, thereby offering an additional venue for private parties and business functions in Staffordshire.

Pricing

Like most theme parks, Alton Towers charges visitors an all-inclusive price, giving unlimited access to the attraction's facilities plus free car parking. For the 1996 season (16 March–3 November) the prices are as follows:

Adults	£17
Children (4–14 inclusive)	£13
Children (under 4)	Free
Senior Citizens	£5.75
Disabled plus guest	£5.75

As well as these standard prices, Alton Towers offers special group rates for parties of 12 or more. Also, as a way of maximising revenue, the park remains open until 8 pm during the summer school holidays. Visitors who wish to visit the attraction for a second day can purchase a 'Towers Two' second-day ticket for the discounted price of £7.

Management structure

It is important to remember that Alton Towers is, first and foremost, a commercial venture, with a budget commitment to the Tussauds Group Limited and, ultimately, to Pearson PLC, its parent company. This relationship is shown in Figure 20.19, which also gives a breakdown of the departmental structure of the Alton Towers attraction. The attraction's board of management is responsible for setting objectives and targets, which are implemented through the divisional director. Authority and responsibility are delegated from the divisional director through seven other directors, who are charged with the management of:

- Finance
- Marketing
- Presentation
- Technical services
- Retail
- Security
- Management services

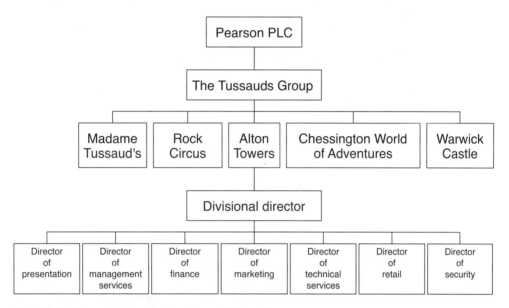

Fig. 20.19 Organisational structure of Alton Towers

The company's finance department exists to provide management with financial information that is accurate, relevant and reliable. Finance staff co-ordinate departmental budgets, ensure that invoices are paid or claimed, that wages get paid and that the attraction's financial matters are always under control.

The marketing department presents the main external images and communications about Alton Towers to a wide range of customer groups, with the aim of stimulating business and brand loyalty. It does this by defining the attraction's markets, committing a seven-figure budget to advertising and promotions, fielding a business development sales team and a press office to ensure wide media coverage. Within the marketing department is the 'front of house' function, whose staff provide accurate information, admission, customer service before, during and after a guest's visit, and a swift, effective response to any customer problems.

Staff in the presentation department operate all 125 rides and attractions at Alton Towers, provide the live shows, costume characters and street entertainers, design and maintain the shows, costumes and uniforms, and keep the park free from litter.

Technical services carry out all park maintenance, including rides, attractions, catering equipment, electricity and water supplies, grounds and gardens. They also co-ordinate all on-site development and construction.

The retail department is one of the largest at Alton Towers and is responsible for food and beverage, games and merchandising at the attraction. Staff offer food and drink to suit all tastes and pockets throughout the park, as well as providing private function facilities for every occasion. Merchandising staff offer a variety of themed novelty and souvenir items across a range of outlets and provide the photograph service on selected rides.

Security department staff ensure a safe, care-free environment and loss pre-vention to the company from fire, theft and wastage. Alton Towers employs its own health and safety adviser, who is responsible for continuously updating the attrac-tion's systems in line with current legislation and operational codes of practice.

Management services include the personnel department, which recruits the 250 permanent staff and 1800 seasonal employees. The park adopts good employ-ment practices in order to recruit and retain the best staff, offering training and staff benefits. The organisational structure of the personnel department is shown in Figure 20.20.

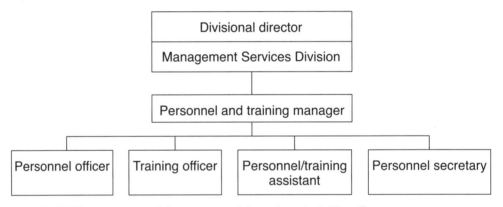

Fig. 20.20 *The structure of the personnel department at Alton Towers*

Marketing at Alton Towers

Alton Towers strives to provide a high-quality service and the ultimate day out. As specified in its mission statement, Alton Towers aims to maintain its market lead-ership by making the park:

> Britain's most magical and unique experience with the highest standards of cleanliness, customer service and safety.

The philosophy of quality is reflected in all marketing undertaken by Alton Towers. All the visitors who pass through the park gates provide the market to which the attraction must cater. However, since these markets are so diverse, each area has been segmented, with each group having its own marketing mix and strategy. The key role of the attraction's advertising and promotions strategy is to communicate strategic brand messages of Alton Towers to the specific target markets. The main objectives that must be met through this communication are to:

- Deliver volume objectives in terms of individual visitors.
- Deliver profit objectives.
- Maintain brand leadership within the UK.
- Continue to position Alton Towers as a destination resort.

The advertising strategy is developed from a thorough review of the competitive environment, the current economic climate, research results, visitor profiles and other internal and external factors affecting the European leisure market.

The principal target markets for Alton Towers are:

1. *General customers* – these are individuals and families that visit the attraction. The promotional plan for this market is designed to deliver high-quality communication of the Alton Towers brand, strong incentives, national coverage, while considering competitor activity and ultimately ensuring that the brand is not devalued. The current promotional plan includes on-pack promotions, retail promotions (in-store), press promotions and video/cinema promotions.
2. *Trade customers* – these are group organisers, coach operators, companies, school parties and hotels. This market is reached via direct mail, direct account handling, exhibitions, advertising in the trade press, PR activity and sales visits.

The corporate market has expanded in recent years and is consequently becoming an increasingly important sector for Alton Towers. It offers various package deals to corporate clients, including:

- Corporate hospitality venue hire
- Company fun days
- Activity day
- Consumer product launches

Like other attractions, Alton Towers holds great appeal to this sector, since it allows a combination of business and pleasure in historical surroundings, with all aspects of organisation handled by professional hospitality co-ordinators.

Security at the attraction

Alton Towers has its own security department that has a wide range of responsibilities, the most important of which is to ensure the safety and well-being of everyone who visits or works at the theme park. Specific areas of responsibility include:

- The movement and control of traffic on and off location.
- The co-ordination of any evacuation from a ride or the theme park.
- Loss prevention of goods/cash from the attraction.
- Lost and found property.
- Assisting the police when requested.

The 30 full- and part-time staff in the department must provide coverage 24 hours a day, 365 days per year to the 500 acres of grounds, 34 catering units, 5 restaurants, 29 shops, 80 rides and 7 arcades.

(Information courtesy of Alton Towers)

Case study discussion questions

1. What are the main factors that go towards making Alton Towers Britain's number one paying tourist attraction?
2. What responsibilities does Alton Towers have towards the Tussauds Group and Pearson PLC?
3. Why does the park carry out market segmentation?
4. Who organises and co-ordinates training throughout the park?
5. What are the main duties of security department staff?

Assignment 20.3

The operation of a major tourist attraction

Performance criteria satisfied: 20.3.1, 20.3.2, 20.3.3, 20.3.4, 20.3.5, 20.3.6

Core skills opportunities at level 3:   Communication   3.1, 3.2, 3.3, 3.4
                                         Information technology   3.1, 3.2, 3.3
                                         Application of number   3.1, 3.2, 3.3

Tasks

Working as part of a small team, you are to prepare a written report on the operation of a major tourist attraction of your choice. In particular, your report should:

- Describe the layout of the attraction and its main visitor flows.
- Explain the factors that determine the types of visitor to the attraction.
- Explain the main types of job role in the attraction.
- Describe how the attraction safeguards the safety and security of its visitors and staff.
- Propose methods to improve visitor use of the attraction.

Your report should be word processed and include a plan of the attraction, plus other relevant diagrams and statistics.

Unit 21

TOURISM DEVELOPMENT

Element 21.1

Investigate the impact of tourism development

Element 21.2

Investigate tourism development in a locality

Element 21.3

Investigate tourism development in a developing country

Element 21.1 Investigate the impact of tourism development

Performance criteria

1. Describe, with examples, the purpose and components of tourism development.
2. Explain the benefits of tourism development.
3. Explain the disadvantages of tourism development.
4. Describe methods which can be used to maximise benefits of tourism development.
5. Describe methods which can be used to minimise disadvantages of tourism development.

What do we mean by tourism development?

Tourism development is the process by which a destination area provides facilities and services for visitors, whether on business or at leisure, as a way of securing economic and social benefits. Tourism development has a number of identifiable characteristics, which can be summarised as follows:

1. *It takes many forms* – everything from the building of a resort complex, construction of an airport, hotel developments to the provision of tourist attractions, are different types of tourism development.
2. *It has associated infrastructure* – tourism development can only take place where there is existing or planned infrastructure, i.e. roads, railways, airports, telecommunications, power supplies and other utilities. Commercial developers often rely on the public sector to provide these facilities and services.
3. *It occurs on differing scales* – tourism development can be as small as a local village hall committee organising an exhibition for day visitors or as big as a major tourist attraction such as Disneyland Paris.
4. *It occurs at different rates* – advances in travel and communications technology mean that some tourism development can take place very quickly, e.g. the growth in the development of long-haul destinations. Other developments occur at a much slower rate, with more planning and a greater concern for the negative impacts of tourism development, e.g. the controlled tourism policies of countries bordering the Himalayas.
5. *It occurs in all countries* – whether a developed, developing or under-developed country, all regions of the world now recognise the important economic benefits that tourism can generate.
6. *It takes place in a variety of environments* – from virgin South American rain forests to the hustle and bustle of cities such as Bangkok, New York and Sydney.

7. *It has both negative and positive impacts* – tourism development can add significantly to the economic well-being of regions, but it can also have detrimental impacts on the environment and culture in destination areas. These points are investigated later in this element.

Who makes tourism development happen?

The individuals and organisations that carry out tourism developments are some-times known as the agents of development. On an international scale, commercial and governmental organisations work together to develop and promote their individual countries, in order to reap economic, social and political benefits. They will be guided, and sometimes helped financially, by global organisations such as the World Bank, World Tourism Organisation and the United Nations. In the case of the UK, the agents of tourism development are shown diagrammatically in Figure 21.1.

Figure 21.1 indicates that the agents of tourism development fall into a number of

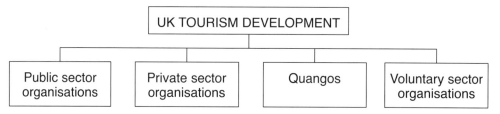

Fig. 21.1 The agents of tourism development in the UK

different categories. Public sector organisations include the English Tourist Board, Wales Tourist Board, Scottish Tourist Board and the Northern Ireland Tourist Board, plus the British Tourist Authority (BTA) and the regional tourist boards in the various countries. Local authority tourism departments are also public sector agents of tourism development. Private sector organisations include the multitude of commer-cial companies that run our tourist attractions, hotels, transport operations, etc., which may be companies in their own right or part of larger groups or multinationals. Quangos (quasi-autonomous non-governmental organisations) are public bodies that are funded from central government, but are not under direct governmental control. Examples in the field of tourism include the Countryside Commission, Forestry Commission and the Arts Council of Great Britain, plus the development agencies located throughout the UK. Voluntary sector organisations include the National Trust and the Youth Hostels Association (YHA).

The agents of tourism development have differing motivations for their involve-ment with tourism. Public sector organisations exist to provide services and facilities, and are often associated with providing the infrastructure within which tourism development takes place. The public sector organisations are also keen to exploit the economic benefits of tourism, particularly the creation of jobs. Private operators are in business to make a profit, while quangos often act as the catalyst for commercial developments, for example, Highlands and Islands Enterprise provides advice, grant-aid and business support to tourism companies relocating or developing in their area. The objectives of voluntary sector organisations include conservation and the preservation of our cultural heritage. The role of the public and private sectors in tourism development is explored further in Element 21.2.

Activity

Carry out some research to discover who are the various agents of tourism development in your own locality.

Benefits of tourism development

The main benefits of tourism development are economic, such as wealth creation, increased national income and the creation of jobs. Tourism is seen by central and local governments, as well as commercial companies, as a way of contributing to the economic prosperity of countries, regions and local areas. Tourism development also has the potential to offer positive social, cultural and environmental impacts, if planned and managed effectively.

Economic benefits of tourism development

Tourism's economic benefits occur on an international, national and local scale. The next section of this element looks at the international and national importance of tourism development, while tourism's contribution to the economy of local areas is investigated in Element 21.2.

Tourism's global economic significance

Estimates from the 1996 Research Report of the World Travel and Tourism Council (WTTC) show that, on a world scale, tourism:

- Employs 255 million people (10.7 per cent of total jobs).
- Generates an output of US$3600 billion (US$3.6 trillion).
- Contributes 10.7 per cent or total world gross domestic product (GDP).
- Represents an investment of US$766 billion.
- Generates US$653 billion in total world taxes.

WTTC forecasts that, by the year 2006, tourism will employ 385.4 million people worldwide, generate an output of US$7.1 trillion and contribute 11.5 per cent of world GDP.

Tourism development also contributes to infrastructure improvements in destination areas, e.g. road and rail improvements, airport developments, improvements in telecommunications and utilities. Member states of the European Union can apply for financial help with infrastructure projects from the European Regional Development Fund (ERDF), while developing countries are often supported with funds from the World Bank, United Nations and multinational corporations.

Tourism and the British economy

Figures for 1994 from the ETB/BTA show that Britain's tourism industry is worth more than £36 billion per year, employs 1.5 million people (6 per cent of all jobs) and accounts for 5 per cent of UK gross domestic product. These figures exclude the estimated 186,000 self-employed people working in UK tourism.

Overseas visitors to Britain in 1994 totalled more than 21 million for the first time, spending a record £9.9 billion. This was divided as follows:

- Accommodation   £3581 million (36.1 per cent)
- Eating out   £2182 million (22.0 per cent)
- Shopping   £2430 million (24.5 per cent)
- Travel within the UK   £794 million (8.0 per cent)
- Travel services   £714 million (7.2 per cent)
- Entertainment   £228 million (2.3 per cent)

Overseas visitors also paid an estimated £2.5 billion in fares to British carriers in 1994, against £2.4 billion in 1993.

Spending by the British on tourism in the UK rose by £2 billion to £14.5 billion in 1994. Britain is still the number one choice for British people on holiday; according to the British National Travel Survey, out of 58 million holidays lasting 4 nights or more taken in 1994 by British adults and accompanying children, 31.5 million were taken in Britain and 26.3 million abroad.

Revenue generated by tourism development is often vital to the economic well-being of an area and is boosted by an important concept known as the multiplier effect. Research has shown that the amount spent by visitors to an area is recirculated in the local economy (by, for example, the wages of somebody working in a tourist attraction being spent on goods and services in local shops) and is actually worth more to the area than its face value. For example, £200 spent by a couple on a short break in a hotel, could be worth £200 × 1.4 (the hotel multiplier effect for that area), i.e. a total of £280.

The actual value of the multiplier (1.4 in the above example is merely an illustration) varies between regions and different sectors of the travel and tourism industry. The multiplier for, say, a farm guesthouse is likely to be greater than for a city centre hotel that is part of a large multinational chain. This is because the farm guesthouse is likely to buy its food and other services locally, while the goods and services for the large hotel may well be brought in from outside the area as part of a national distribution contract; i.e. income is lost to the area (in economic terms this is known as a 'leakage' from the local economy).

Social/cultural benefits of tourism development

Although tourism development is often criticised for its negative social and cultural impacts on destination areas, it can have positive impacts, such as the revitalisation for visitors of neglected regions, the rebirth of local arts and crafts, refurbishment of local architecture and greater understanding between cultures. At a local level, the provision of leisure facilities for the enjoyment of visitors gives local people the opportunity to improve the quality of their lives and to take part in community activities for the benefit of all.

Environmental benefits of tourism development

Rather than being the destroyer of environments, tourism can sometimes be a positive force for environmental change. Tourism to remote areas, such as the rain forests of South America and Papua New Guinea, and hitherto undiscovered Pacific islands, can help expose detrimental environmental activities. Pressure groups, such as Tourism Concern and Friends of the Earth campaign for sensitive tourism development that is respectful of local environments and customs. Closer to home, tourism development can lead to the improvement of derelict land and waterways, the restoration of redundant buildings and environmental improvements linked to schemes such as the Britain in Bloom campaign, co-ordinated by the Tidy Britain Group.

Activity

Gather information about the economic, social/cultural and environmental benefits of tourism development in your local area. How could the beneficial economic impacts of tourism in your locality be improved?

Disadvantages of tourism development

We have seen how tourism development can bring substantial benefits to individuals, companies and governments around the world. With tourism forecast to be the world's biggest industry by the year 2000, there is little doubt that its ability to contribute towards economic growth and social interaction will continue to grow. The very scale and speed of tourism development, however, is giving cause for concern, with host communities, governments and the industry itself all beginning to look at ways of minimising tourism's harmful impacts, whether they be economic, social, cultural or environmental.

Negative economic impacts of tourism development

Although tourism development has the potential to offer significant economic benefits to destination areas, it has a number of associated negative economic effects, including:

- Prices of goods and services in tourist areas are sometimes increased in the peak holiday season in order to maximise tourist revenue. This disadvantages local residents who may have to pay higher prices for food, entertainment, transport services, etc.
- Extra charges levied on the local community to finance facilities and services for visitors. Through their Council Tax, local people may have to pay for such facilities as tourist information centres and promotional literature, which are primarily for

the benefit of tourists. Some sectors of the community will contribute to the costs of running leisure and tourism facilities that they never use.

- The price of land and houses may rise as a result of tourism development, making it difficult for local people to buy their own property. In rural areas of Wales, England, Northern Ireland and Scotland, the purchasing of second homes, which may only be used for a small proportion of the year, can inflate house prices and put them beyond the reach of the local population, particularly young couples looking for their first property.
- Areas of the country that become particularly popular with tourists may lose their local shops in favour of retail outlets geared specifically to the needs of the tourists, such as gift shops and cafés. This means that local people have to travel further to buy their staple foods, thus incurring extra expense. Rural areas are again particularly at risk; the village of Holmfirth, which has become famous as the location where the TV programme 'The Last of the Summer Wine' is filmed, has seen many of its village shops being replaced by facilities for visitors.
- Tourism development can lead to the loss of traditional employment opportunities, when workers move from industries such as farming and fishing into service jobs in tourism. This has been particularly apparent in Mediterranean resorts, including Majorca, the Spanish Costas and Greece.

Negative social/cultural impacts of tourism development

There is a general feeling among those with an interest in tourism development that the negative social and cultural impacts of tourism development are far more harmful in the long run than the environmental problems associated with the industry. This is based on the belief that many of the negative environmental impacts can be easily corrected with the right management and funding. The social and cultural problems, however, can be far more deep-rooted and may take generations to eradicate. Some of these problems are:

- Overcrowding, which may cause a reduction in the quality of life for the 'host community', i.e. those living in the area visited.
- Traditional activities, e.g. farming, may lose labour to the seemingly more attractive jobs in travel and tourism.
- Tourists' behaviour can distort local customs.
- Religious codes may be altered to adapt to the needs of visitors, e.g. Sunday opening of facilities.
- Local languages may be lost through under-use.
- Traditional crafts may be lost in favour of mass-produced souvenirs.
- Loss of communities, when tourists buy second homes in destination areas.
- Increase in crime rates, including public disturbances and burglaries.

Activity

Thinking about your own area, draw up a list of any negative social or cultural impacts of tourism that could be resolved through better planning and management.

Negative environmental impacts of tourism development

Although tourism development can have positive environmental impacts – for example, the Britain in Bloom scheme, the restoration of redundant buildings and improvements to derelict areas – there is much evidence to suggest that the industry could do a lot to improve its negative environmental impacts. On a global scale, tourism can have harmful effects on 'fragile' habitats, such as coral reefs, rain forests and mountain areas. In Britain, the coast, countryside, towns and cities all suffer from the pressures of increasing numbers of visitors and their transportation. Some of the worst problems include:

1. *Physical erosion* – the wearing away of soil and vegetation by walkers, horse-riders, cyclists, cars and motorcycles.
2. *Litter* – both an eyesore and a threat to safety.
3. *Congestion and overcrowding* – in popular holiday areas we all see the effects of too many people and too many cars.
4. *Pollution* – of water and air, not forgetting noise pollution.
5. *Loss of habitats* – for flora and fauna.
6. *Spoiling of the landscape* that people have come to see and enjoy.

Better education, improved visitor and traffic management techniques, use of the price mechanism and better signposting, are some of the possible solutions that are being tried in our towns and countryside to reduce the harmful environmental effects of leisure and tourism (see information on traffic management in Cambridge on page 254).

In the UK, negative environmental impacts of tourism are not confined to country-side areas, but are also to be found in cities and on the coast. Negative impacts in the countryside are most acute in the National Parks, which together accommodate over 100 million visitors per year. Parks close to urban centres come under particular pressure; at summer weekends, some parts of the Peak District and Lake District National Parks reach saturation point, with traffic jams for many miles. The large numbers of people visiting the countryside, most travelling by car, put pressure on the physical environment, resulting in erosion by walkers, cars, cycles, horse-riders and motor-cyclists. Litter and the pollution of fields and waterways are also a constant problem, resulting in harm to the natural flora and fauna.

Tourism's harmful effects on the urban environment affect many historic destinations popular with tourists, such as York, Bath, Chester, Cambridge, Stratford-upon-Avon and Oxford, as well as our capital cities, Cardiff, London, Belfast and Edinburgh. Congestion, pollution and litter are three of the most common problems concerning tourism in the urban environment. Noise pollution, particularly associated with increased traffic flows, can also degrade urban environments.

On the coast, sensitive areas such as sand dunes and estuaries can be harmed by tourist pressure, while the popular seaside resorts, such as Scarborough, Brighton and Newquay in Cornwall, have to deal with the huge influx of visitors for a relatively short period of time, and all that they bring with them. In areas of the country that are prone to drought, water supply can be a problem in the peak tourist season, while sewage disposal is a constant challenge to local authorities.

Activity

Thinking of your own area, list specific examples of negative and positive environmental impacts associated with tourism development.

Maximising the benefits of tourism development

It is in the long-term interest of the travel and tourism industry for public, private and voluntary sector organisations to work together to maximise industry benefits. This can be achieved by careful attention to a number of factors, including:

- Tourism training
- Maximising visitor spending
- Ensuring access for all sections of society
- Investment in tourism projects

Tourism training

Public bodies and commercial operators alike are beginning to realise that one of the most cost-effective ways of maximising tourism potential is to invest in staff training and development. Tourism training brings benefits to a range of parties, as shown in Figure 21.2.

Fig. 21.2 The beneficiaries of tourism training

Staff working in tourism organisations can benefit from structured training in a number of ways, including:

- Enhanced self-esteem
- Greater job satisfaction
- Financial rewards
- Better understanding of the travel and tourism industry
- Higher skill levels

Travel and tourism organisations can also benefit from training by, for example:

- Increased profitability and efficiency
- Reduced staff turnover
- A more motivated workforce
- Reduced costs

- Increased flexibility
- Better identification of business opportunities

The travel and tourism industry as a whole benefits from better manpower planning, an improved image of the profession and better definition of industry sectors. Tourism training brings benefits to customers as well, such as enhanced levels of customer service, better product standards and higher quality facilities.

Activity

Carry out some research to discover what tourism training opportunities exist in your own area. Consider if there are any gaps in provision and how these could best be overcome.

Maximising visitor spending

All tourism operators seek to maximise spending by visitors, although, for public bodies and voluntary sector organisations, it will not be their prime objective. Effective marketing, human resource management and financial control are the key factors contributing to the success of tourism enterprises. In addition to their primary source of revenue, all tourism operators aim to maximise their revenue from secondary sources. Examples of this 'secondary spend' include:

- Catering and retail outlets at tourist attractions.
- Travel agents selling insurance and foreign currency to holidaymakers.
- Tour operators offering car hire and excursions to their clients.
- Hotels promoting leisure breaks to their business guests.
- Airlines and ferry companies selling duty-free goods.

Ensuring access for all sections of society

Making tourism developments open to as wide a variety of potential customers as possible will help all travel and tourism organisations maximise the benefits of tourism. Much has been done in the UK since the late 1980s to improve access to tourist facilities as a result of the pioneering work of the Tourism for All Campaign.

The Tourism for All Campaign

Introduction

Launched in 1989, following the publication of the Baker Report, the Tourism for All Campaign aims to encourage the tourism industry to cater for all people regardless of age or disability, and create a genuinely welcoming and accessible environment in all tourist facilities, including visitor attractions. The Baker Report was commissioned initially by the English Tourist Board, in association with the Holiday Care Service, and was expanded to take in Scotland and Wales, with the participation of the Wales and Scottish Tourist Boards. The Northern Ireland Tourist Board has also joined the other partners in promoting the Tourism for All message. The Campaign believes that by meeting the requirements of people with special needs, such as people with impaired sight, hearing or mobility, operators can make their premises more accessible to many other visitors. Wide ramps and doorways installed for wheelchair users benefit adults with pushchairs and young children; lifts help elderly people and those carrying luggage. The Tourism for All Campaign recommends that the tourism industry should be aware of the statement 'A person is not handicapped by their impairment, but by the environment and the attitudes of the people they encounter'.

Campaign co-ordination

The Campaign is co-ordinated by the national Tourism for All Committee, with a membership drawn from the tourist boards, the tourism industry, the Department of Transport and the voluntary sector. The Committee meets regularly to monitor and to advise on the recommendations in the Baker Report on Tourism for All; to promote the development of the principles in that report and to offer advice on any new initiatives relevant to Tourism for All.

The size of the market

The Campaign argues that an accessible tourism industry should benefit from increased business from this 'last untapped market'. Figures from an OPCS survey in 1988 show that there are some 6.2 million adults in Great Britain with some form of disability, plus an estimated 50 million in Europe and 34 million in the USA. If any one disabled person is turned away, the business of their family, friends, work associates or colleagues may also be lost. With an estimated 6 million carers in the UK, the Campaign suggests it is reasonable to assume a doubling of the effective market size to 12 million people. Furthermore, there is a close relationship between disability and age and in Britain we have an ageing population. By the year 2021 nearly 1 in 5 (20 per cent) of the population will be over 65 years of age, compared with only 1 in 10 in 1951. There is also clear evidence of the increasing aspirations of disabled people in their holiday and travel requirements and expectations.

Access explained

The Tourism for All Campaign considers that true access, in the widest sense, requires attention to three interlinked aspects:

1. *Design or redesign of the physical environment* – for example, the provision of level access, ramps and lifts.
2. *Provision of reliable information based on agreed standards* – e.g. promotional literature should include reference to the level of accessibility.
3. *Staff awareness* – a friendly welcome is essential, as is a knowledge of the facilities on offer, coupled with an understanding of the needs of disabled people. Staff training and development should address this issue and seek to integrate customers with disabilities into mainstream provision.

Industry participation in the Tourism for All Campaign

Many tourist establishments are already accessible and have applied for accreditation under the National Accessible Schemes for Tourism for All run by the tourist boards and the Holiday Care Service. Similar schemes for accessible visitor attractions are in the process of development. Operators are further encouraged to include disability awareness training within their staff training programmes and to consider the adoption of a written policy statement expressing their commitment to Tourism for All in all its aspects.

(Information courtesy of the English Tourist Board)

Case study discussion questions

1. What is the overall aim of the Tourism for All Campaign?
2. Which sectors of the tourist industry does it encompass?
3. How does the Holiday Care Service help people with disabilities?
4. Why is it important for the operators of tourist attractions to provide facilities to meet the needs of customers with disabilities?
5. What can the management and staff working in tourist facilities do to ensure that people with disabilities have an enjoyable visit?

Investment in tourism projects

The growth and development of Britain's tourism industry depends on its ability to generate a return on investment. Returns are generally measured through the financial rewards that the investor receives, in the form of interest or a dividend. Capital growth – for example, the rise in value of a resort complex, hotel or restaurant – is another way of measuring returns on investment in travel and tourism. Public bodies do not always measure the success of tourism investments in purely financial terms, but assess their significance against wider social, political and cultural objectives.

Individuals, private companies and public agencies invest in tourism development for a number of reasons:

- An obvious commercial reason for investing in a tourism development project is that the investor expects to receive a healthy return on his or her investment, in the same way as if the investment was in any other commercial sector of the economy.
- Some governments undertake investment in tourism for non-commercial reasons, such as social and community benefit. Investment in leisure centres, parks, tourist information centres, transport infrastructure and visitor attractions, may be justifiable on social if not always commercial grounds.
- A lot of investment in travel and tourism is property-driven, meaning that entrepreneurs who are essentially property developers, will invest in capital projects such as hotels, resort complexes and theme parks, as alternatives to shops, factories and offices.
- Some investments in tourism are made for 'lifestyle' reasons such as an extension of a hobby or as a tax loss. Investment in tourism may also be needed to subsidise an existing enterprise, such as a stately home or family farm. Travel and tourism

has an appeal to investors outside the industry who consider that it is an easy sector in which to operate and brings with it significant lifestyle benefits.

- Some investments in tourism can be justified on the grounds that they are joint-use. Leisure centres are often joint enterprises between a local authority leisure services department and a school or college. Major out-of-town retail developments often include entertainment facilities such as multi-screen cinemas and bowling complexes.

Activity

Try to find out what plans exist in your area for public and private sector investment in tourism development projects and how they are to be funded.

Minimising the disadvantages of tourism development

The performance of organisations in relation to the impact they have on the environment and on host communities is becoming a major issue for the 1990s. No tourism organisation can operate without having positive and negative effects on its immediate natural environment and, in some cases, on the environment thousands of miles away. Western societies are becoming increasingly concerned about the threats to the environment posed by many tourism developments. The 1980s saw the growth of the 'green consumer' who not only looks for environmentally sound products in the supermarkets, but also for tourism products that are developed in harmony with the environment. Many tourism developments have been criticised for their lack of concern for environmental and socio-cultural impacts, while many argue that the whole of the tourism industry is, by its very nature, environmentally and culturally destructive.

Techniques and practices for minimising the disadvantages of tourism development are many and varied, and include:

- Adoption of the principles of sustainable tourism
- Visitor management initiatives
- Traffic management schemes
- Environmental impact assessments
- Industry initiatives

Sustainable tourism

Sustainable tourism is an emerging concept that has grown out of increased concern about the negative environmental and socio-cultural impacts of unplanned tourism development. An extension of 'green tourism', which has developed out of concern for the environment, sustainable tourism is part of a much wider global debate on sustainable development, highlighted by the Brundtland Report in 1987 and the Earth

Summit in Rio in 1992. Various bodies concerned with travel and tourism have developed policies on sustainable development, including the ETB *Tourism and the Environment Task Force*, whose principles for sustainable tourism developed in 1991 state that:

- The environment has an intrinsic value which outweighs its value as a tourism asset. Its enjoyment by future generations and its long-term survival must not be prejudiced by short-term considerations.
- Tourism should be recognised as a positive activity with the potential to benefit the community and the place as well as the visitor.
- The relationship between tourism and the environment must be managed so that the environment is sustainable in the long term. Tourism must not be allowed to damage the resource, prejudice its future enjoyment or bring unacceptable impacts.
- Tourism activities and developments should respect the scale, nature and character of the place in which they are sited.
- In any location, harmony must be sought between the needs of the visitor, the place and the host community.
- In a dynamic world some change is inevitable and change can often be beneficial. Adaptation to change, however, should not be at the expense of any of these principles.
- The tourism industry, local authorities and environmental agencies all have a duty to respect the above principles and to work together to achieve their practical realisation.

The challenge facing the travel and tourism industry, especially the mass market tour operators, is to implement the principles of sustainable tourism for the benefit of present and future destinations and their host communities.

Activity

In relation to your own area, carry out some research to find out if the local authority has a policy on sustainable tourism development.

Environmental impact assessments

The rise in the awareness of, and concern for, the environment has meant that tourism organisations are becoming more involved in measuring their environmental effects. This is often as a direct result of a national or local government regulation linked to the planning and development process. It is now very common for the developers of large tourism projects to be asked to carry out an appraisal of the costs and benefits of the development from an environmental point of view. The most common technique for carrying out such an evaluation is the environmental impact assessment (EIA), which can be applied to a wide range of planned tourism developments. The EIA is a structured process which aims to:

- Identify the costs and benefits of a particular development.

- Establish who will lose and who will gain if the development goes ahead.
- Examine alternative courses of action and their likely impacts.
- Consider ways of reducing impacts if the project is given the green light.

For tourism enterprises already in existence, the technique of environmental auditing is gaining in popularity. Some pioneering work by the Inter-Continental Hotel Group, which has resulted in a manual of procedures giving consideration to the environmental consequences of all its business activities, has led to many large hotel companies, airlines and tour operators looking at their activities and processes from an environmental standpoint. Some organisations have used their concern for the environment as a marketing tool, hoping to capitalise on the growing market for tourism products and services that are truly respectful of the world in which we live.

Visitor and traffic management

The pressures on many of our most beautiful landscapes and historic cities from the growth in visitor numbers, has led to a range of measures to control the impact of people and their cars on the environment. Initiatives in rural areas, often sponsored by the Countryside Commission, have attempted to persuade visitors to abandon their cars and use public transport instead – for example in the Peak District National Park. Some of the busiest roads in the National Parks are closed to traffic altogether at peak times, encouraging walkers and cyclists to explore areas free from noise and pollution. Historic cities such as Canterbury, Cambridge and York have developed integrated transport policies aimed at reducing cars in the city centres and encouraging cycling and the use of public transport, including park-and-ride schemes. Cambridge City Council in its draft Local Plan proposes a transport strategy with the following elements:

- Increasing the role played by public transport, particularly buses, including bus-based park-and-ride schemes and bus priorities.
- Supporting increased investment in local rail services.
- Limiting car use, particularly in the city centre and at the busiest times, by traffic management, parking controls and the investigation of road pricing.
- Providing improved facilities for people with disabilities, pedestrians and cyclists.
- Considering new road building only where this gives clear and sustainable benefits, particularly in terms of environmental protection and improvement.

Industry initiatives

The mainstream travel and tourism industry is slowly waking up to the fact that it needs to give consideration to the potentially damaging effect that its operations can have on the environment and host communities. Pressure from a travelling public that is more environmentally and culturally aware is forcing airlines, tour operators, destination planners and accommodation providers to implement the principles of sustainable tourism. It is no longer uncommon to find statements of environmental policy in the holiday brochures of the mass market tour operators, giving advice to holidaymakers on how to protect local environments and respect local cultures and traditions. One of the most recent initiatives is 'Green Globe', a world-wide environmental management and awareness programme for the travel and tourism industry. Green Globe was developed by the World Travel and Tourism Council (WTTC) in 1994 with the following aims:

- To increase systematically environmental responsiveness throughout the travel and tourism industry, its suppliers and customers.
- To encourage the widest possible environmental participation from companies of all sizes and sectors.
- To promote and emphasise the synergy between good environmental practice and good business.
- To identify and demonstrate, through the Green Globe logo, the commitment of travel and tourism companies to environmental improvement.
- To highlight leading examples of best practice and outstanding progress through Achievement Awards.

As part of its programme of work to advance the cause of environmentally friendly and culturally sensitive tourism, Green Globe produces a leaflet for travellers, with a list of practical tips on holiday preparation and planning, including:

- Look at the environmental content of brochures and ask companies about their environmental policy.
- Take time to think about your holiday plans.
- Take time to learn in advance about the place you intend to visit.
- Consider what you really need to take with you.
- Only take environmentally friendly detergents and shampoos.
- Choose natural oils.
- Take a camera to record any wildlife you see.
- Take a few small gifts from your home country.

While on holiday, the Green Globe 'Tips for travellers' leaflet suggests:

- Look at personal travel options – choose public transport, cycling and walking, where appropriate.
- Ask your hosts where they go in their off-duty hours to enjoy their leisure.
- In rural areas, try to use small, locally owned accommodation.
- If beaches are dirty, let your travel representative know.
- Try out local food dishes and specialities.
- Buy locally made crafts.
- Ask your holiday representative about local environmental issues.
- Try to get to and from the airport by public transport.
- If travelling by car, ensure that your vehicle is well maintained and energy efficient.

Many major travel and tourism companies, including Thomson Holidays, British Airways and Inter-Continental Hotels, have developed environmental policies and train staff in their implementation. The British Airways 'Tourism for Tomorrow Awards' recognise environmentally responsible tourism developments on a world-wide basis. Recent global winners have included Whale Watch Kaikoura, New Zealand, and the Sea to Sea Cycle Route across the north of England.

Assignment 21.1

The impact of tourism development

Performance criteria satisfied: 21.1.1, 21.1.2, 21.1.3, 21.1.4, 21.1.5

Core skills opportunities at level 3:
Communication	3.1, 3.2, 3.3, 3.4
Information technology	3.1, 3.2, 3.3
Application of number	3.1, 3.2, 3.3

Situation

You are working for the newly formed tourist association in your local area. Before going ahead with future developments in tourism, the members of the association are keen to learn more about the impact of tourism development.

Tasks

You have been asked to prepare a written report on the impact of tourism development, to be studied by the members of the association. Your report should:

● Describe the general purpose and components of tourism development.
● Explain the benefits of tourism development.
● Explain the disadvantages of tourism development.
● Describe methods that can be used to maximise the benefits of tourism development.
● Describe methods that can be used to minimise the disadvantages of tourism development.

Your report should be word processed and include examples of tourism development from the UK, Europe and a developing country. It should be supported by relevant charts, diagrams and statistics.

Element 21.2 Investigate tourism development in a locality

Performance criteria

1. Define the scope of tourism development in a locality.
2. Describe the role of public and private sector organisations in tourism development in a locality.
3. Explain the appeal to tourists of the tourism development in a locality.
4. Describe how tourism development in a locality is promoted to tourists.
5. Assess the benefits and disadvantages which have resulted from the tourism development in a locality.

The scope of tourism development in a locality

Element 21.1 investigated the role and purpose of tourism development at international, regional and national levels. Closer to home, it is clear that tourism, if planned and managed effectively, has considerable development potential at the local scale, offering:

- The provision of facilities for local communities.
- Financial returns for the commercial sector.
- Injections of income into rural and urban areas.
- The creation of jobs and new business enterprises.
- The ability to help promote a positive image of an area.
- A contribution towards the regeneration of derelict industrial areas.
- The ability to stimulate environmental improvements in an area.
- A contribution towards the retention of local customs and languages.

The role of the public and private sectors in tourism development

Historically, tourism development in the UK has been championed by private sector entrepreneurs, with little direct public sector involvement or support from either central or local government. It is the private sector that has been responsible for developing attractions, hotels, transport companies, car hire firms, tour operators and travel agencies, to name but a few. It is only in the last 30 years or so that the public sector has begun to play a significant part in UK tourism development, usually at the strategic level in a co-ordinating role.

It is becoming increasingly apparent to the UK tourism industry that the most effective way forward is for public and private sectors to work together in partnership arrangements, so as to make best use of scarce resources and to pool expertise (see case study on tourism development in York on page 266). By so doing, central and local government can help provide the infrastructure and development funding within which private sector operators can develop facilities for visitors.

Activity

Find out if there are any tourism development initiatives in your local area that aim to encourage the public and private sectors to work in partnership.

Public sector tourism development

Public sector involvement in UK tourism can be traced back to before Victorian Times when many 'resorts', both inland and on the coast, benefited from investment in tourist facilities by their local councils. Central government recognition of the economic significance of tourism was not forthcoming until as late as 1969, with the passing of the Development of Tourism Act. This first piece of tourism legislation, now more than 25 years old, still applies today, although the nature and scale of the industry has changed dramatically. The principal outcomes of the Act were:

- The establishment of the British Tourist Authority (BTA), English Tourist Board (ETB), Wales Tourist Board (WTB) and Scottish Tourist Board (STB).
- The introduction of 'section 4' grants for tourist developments.
- The establishment of a hotel development grants scheme.
- Legislation to introduce a compulsory registration scheme for accommodation.

The Northern Ireland Tourist Board was not included in the Act since it had already been established in 1948.

The structure of public sector tourism

Figure 21.3 shows the relationships between the various public sector organisations with an interest in tourism in the UK.

While the Department of National Heritage (DNH) can be regarded as the 'lead' government department in tourism matters, other departments, including the Department of the Environment and the Ministry of Agriculture, all undertake activities that can impinge on tourism development. Quangos (quasi-autonomous nongovernmental organisations) include bodies such as Highlands and Islands Enterprise and the Welsh Development Agency, which have interests in tourism development in their respective regions.

The role of the tourist boards

Tourist boards in Britain exist at two distinct levels:

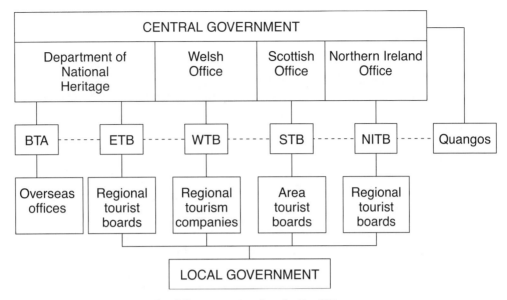

Fig. 21.3 The structure of public sector tourism in the UK

1. National tourist boards
2. Regional tourist boards (RTBs)

National tourist boards

The national tourist boards aim to set the framework and policy for their particular country, within which the private and public sectors can undertake tourism development. The English Tourist Board, for example, has the following objectives:

- To stimulate the development of English tourism by encouraging the British to take holidays in England and by the provision and improvement of facilities for tourists to England.
- To develop and market tourism in close co-operation with regional and national tourist boards, the BTA, local authorities and public sector organisations, and the private sector.
- To advise government and public bodies on all matters concerning tourism in England.
- To maximise tourism's contribution to the economy through the creation of wealth and jobs.
- To enhance the image of England as a tourism destination by all appropriate means, including undertaking and encouraging innovative marketing.
- To encourage and stimulate the successful development of tourism products of a high standard, which offer good value for money.
- To bring greater recognition of tourism as an industry for investment, employment and economic development, by providing information and, where appropriate, advice and financial support.
- To produce and disseminate information on tourism to the trade and the consumer.
- To research trends in tourism and consumer requirements to show marketing and

development needs and opportunities and evaluate past performance, future prospects and the impact of tourism.

- To improve the industry's status and performance by encouraging and stimulating the adoption of up-to-date business methods and appropriate technology and the provision of education and training programmes.
- To ensure that England's unique character and heritage is recognised and protected through the sensitive management of tourism.

In order to achieve these objectives, the ETB is engaged in a wide-ranging programme of work with public bodies and commercial companies, including:

1. *Marketing* – direct to the consumer and via the travel trade, through the production of publicity materials and development of new products.
2. *Information services* – the co-ordination of the network of Tourist Information Centres (TICs) and a research function.
3. *Development* – co-ordinating national and regional development policies on tourism and advising on local tourism initiatives.

Unlike the Wales and Scottish Tourist Boards, ETB no longer has powers to fund tourism projects under 'section 4' of the 1969 Development of Tourism Act, meaning that its ability to stimulate new investment and development is severely limited. ETB suffered another funding blow in 1992, when the 1993/94 allocation of funds to the Tourist Boards was announced by the government; ETB's grant had been cut from £15.6m in 1992/93 to £14.2m in 1993/94, with further planned reductions to £10.8m in 1994/95 and £9.1m in 1995/96.

Regional tourist boards

The work of tourist boards at regional level is altogether more commercial, with close liaison between public and private sector concerns. In order to manage its three designated regions, the Wales Tourist Board has established associated companies, namely 'North Wales Tourism', 'Mid Wales Tourism' and 'Tourism South Wales'. The number of English regional tourist boards is now 11, following the recent demise of the Thames and Chilterns Tourist Board, which ran into financial difficulties in the early 1990s (see Figure 21.4). Discussions about the future of the East Midlands Board are currently in progress.

The commercial nature of regional tourist organisations is shown by the ways in which they generate revenue, which include:

- Grants from central government sources via the DNH, Welsh Office, Northern Ireland Office or Scottish Office.
- Subscriptions from local authorities.
- Subscriptions from commercial members.
- Revenue from sales, e.g. selling advertising space in regional publications and letting space on exhibition stands.

A typical English regional tourist board has a diverse range of members, including:

- Hoteliers and other providers of accommodation
- Operators of tourist attractions
- Local district councils
- County councils

Fig. 21.4 The regional tourist boards in England *(reproduced courtesy of the English Tourist Board)*

- Restaurateurs and owners of pubs
- Coach companies
- Local tourist guides
- Providers of tourism training

The main responsibilities of the English regional tourist boards are to:

- Have a thorough knowledge of tourism within the region, as well as the facilities and organisations involved in the tourism industry.

- Advise the English Tourist Board on the regional aspects of major policy issues and to supply management information.
- Service enquiries attributable to nationally developed promotions and to provide literature.
- Co-ordinate regional tourist information services as part of the national TIC network.
- Maintain close liaison with planning authorities on policies affecting tourism.
- Carry out a continuing domestic public relations campaign with the local authorities, the travel trade and the public within the region, with a view to ensuring that issues are understood and the regional and national objectives are known; to create awareness of the need for tourism to be managed for the benefits of residents as well as tourists.
- To promote tourism to the region both from other parts of the country and from overseas.

Activity

Find out which regional tourist board your area falls into and what plans it has for future tourism development.

Local authorities and tourism

At the local level, district, city and county councils in the UK are keen to develop tourism in their areas as a way of injecting income into the local economy and creating much needed employment. Many will support the establishment of local tourism groups and associations which will bring together the private and public sector. The Local Government Act of 1948 gave local authorities the powers to set up information and publicity services for tourists. This was reinforced by the Local Government Act 1972 which empowered them to publicise their areas for tourism and provide facilities for visitors.

Today, there are few local authorities in the UK that are not actively involved in some way with promoting their areas to tourists; places as diverse as Brighton and Berwick, Newcastle and Nottingham, Scarborough and Shrewsbury, are all competing for a slice of the 'tourism pound'. The scale of involvement is very variable, ranging from authorities with a single person given the responsibility for tourism development and promotion, to councils with separate tourism departments under a Director of Tourism. Some local authorities see tourism as a natural extension of their planning function and house their tourism officer and staff in this department. The more proactive authorities consider that tourism is an integral part of economic development and so assign individuals into this section. Still others view tourism, and particularly the marketing and promotion of tourism, as a PR activity which lends itself very well to their press and PR department.

Local authorities use their resources to provide as wide a range of tourism facilities and services that finances will allow. In a typical area, this might include:

- Promotional leaflets and brochures
- Parks and gardens
- Theatres

- Museums
- Tourist Information Centres (TICs)
- Accommodation booking services
- Sports and leisure centres
- Outdoor activity centres
- Art and craft galleries

Regardless of how tourism development is organised within a particular local council, it is clear that it will remain a vital and increasing part of the work of local authorities in the future.

Private sector tourism development

Tourism development in the private (commercial) sector involves business units, both large and small, owned by individuals or groups of people whose principal aim is to maximise their profits. Revenue from the sales of their services or goods will hopefully be greater than the costs of operating the business so as to leave a surplus which can be either taken as profit or reinvested in the business in order to build a solid foundation for future success for owners, directors, employees and any shareholders who may have bought a stake in the business.

The commercial sector provides the majority of the tourism facilities, services and products on offer in the UK, including:

- Theatres
- Cinemas
- Hotels and other forms of accommodation
- Restaurants, cafés, pubs and bars
- Discotheques and nightclubs
- Travel agencies and tour operators
- Airlines
- Tourist attractions
- Health and fitness clubs and studios
- Mixed retail and leisure complexes
- Transport operations

Most of the household names in the travel and tourism industry operate in the private sector, e.g. British Airways, Thomson Holidays, Virgin, Thomas Cook, Legoland Windsor, Cadbury World, British Midland Airways, Budget Rent-a-Car and Queens Moat Houses Hotels, to name but a few. The biggest tourism enterprises operate as private and public limited companies (PLCs), while many providers of support services in tourism are organised as partnerships or sole traders, e.g. hoteliers, restaurateurs, guides, marketing consultants, travel writers, chauffeurs and ground handlers.

Activity

Collect information about the main private sector tourism operators in your area. Make a list of the range of activities each provides.

How tourism development is promoted

The various private, public and voluntary sector organisations concerned with tourism development in a locality will employ a wide range of techniques to promote their services and facilities. Unit 22, which looks at promotional techniques in travel and tourism, indicates that the most important include:

- Pricing
- Advertising
- Public relations
- Sales promotion
- Direct marketing
- Personal selling

It is important to remember that promotion will be aimed at both the customer and the travel trade. If we consider the example of a historic city in the south of England, the range of travel and tourism services and facilities it offers and the promotional techniques each uses, may include:

1. *Tourist attractions* – operated by the private, public and voluntary sectors, attractions will produce a range of leaflets, advertise in local and regional media, undertake public relations activities including sending press releases, promote their facilities to coach companies and group organisers, take part in competitions and voucher schemes in conjunction with various media, and offer a variety of pricing discounts aimed at different market sectors.
2. *Travel agencies* – will stock a wide variety of tour operators' brochures, undertake face-to-face selling to potential customers, advertise in the local media, mail out newsletters and special offers direct to previous clients, use a range of point-of-sale materials, including window displays, and organise promotional evenings in conjunction with tour operators and airlines.
3. *Coach companies* – will produce brochures, leaflets and price lists, advertise in the local and regional media, sometimes in conjunction with local attractions, run holiday roadshows and direct mail to previous customers.
4. *Hotels and other accommodation* – will produce brochures and leaflets for leisure and business tourists, advertise locally and nationally, take part in holiday exhibitions, undertake PR work and work jointly with coach and tour operators to develop packages.
5. *Local authority tourism department* – will produce an image-building brochure on the area to be mailed out in response to national, regional and local advertising, direct mail to previous enquirers, attendance at trade and public travel fairs, public relations work, e.g. familiarisation visits for journalists, joint promotions with local accommodation providers and promotions to conference organisers.

Promotion of tourism development – Yorkshire and Humberside Tourist Board

Introduction

Yorkshire and Humberside Tourist Board (YHTB) is the official English regional tourist board covering the counties of Humberside, South Yorkshire, West Yorkshire and North Yorkshire. At its headquarters in York, YHTB employs around 45 full- and part-time staff, who concentrate on marketing and development issues concerning the tourist board's 2000-plus members, who include hoteliers, caravan park operators, local authorities, educational establishments and tourist associations. Statistics produced by YHTB indicate that total tourism spending in the region totalled more than £1.6 billion in 1993.

Tourism promotion

YHTB offers its members a 'shopping list' of promotional opportunities. For 1995–96, these included:

- Advertising in YHTB publications – e.g. the *1996 Official Holiday Guide*, *Bed & Breakfast Touring Map*, *Farm Holidays Brochure*, *Events Guides*, *Pub Guide*, *Overseas Brochure*, *Attractions Map*.
- Exhibitions/workshops – including domestic holiday exhibitions, e.g. Holiday '96 at G-Mex, Manchester, Great Yorkshire Show at Harrogate, British Travel Centre, London, etc., overseas exhibitions, trade exhibitions and workshops, e.g. World Travel Market, British Travel Trade Fair at the NEC, etc.
- Database marketing – using YHTB's extensive mailing lists.
- Brochure deliveries to TICs.
- PR activities – including travel trade familiarisation visits, media familiarisation visits, competitions, Yorkshire and Humberside video, etc.

(Information courtesy of Yorkshire and Humberside Tourist Board)

Activity

Undertake some research to find out how your local area is promoted to visitors. Which organisations are involved in tourism promotion locally?

Advantages and disadvantages of tourism development in a locality

We saw in Element 21.1 that tourism development offers a wide range of positive and negative impacts on a global and national scale. These can be categorised into:

- Economic impacts
- Social and cultural impacts
- Environmental impacts

Locally, tourism development can bring significant economic benefits to destination areas, helping to create and sustain jobs, and inject revenue into rural and urban areas. On the down side, local people may be required, through local taxes, to help pay for visitor facilities and tourism promotion. If not planned and managed effectively, tourism can have serious social and cultural impacts on local communities. Increased traffic, the loss of cultural identity and increased visitor numbers for periods of the year, can all contribute to a reduction in the 'quality of life' for local residents. Environmentally, local tourism development can cause damage to wildlife habitats and landscape features. On the positive side, tourism development can sometimes act as a catalyst for the conservation of local amenities. The following case studies of York and the North Pennines provide good examples of tourism development issues in urban and rural areas.

CASE STUDY

Tourism development in a locality – York

Introduction

The City of York is one of the leading tourism destinations in Britain, offering UK and overseas visitors a wide variety of museums and other attractions, the historic architecture of the city itself, plus a wide range of shopping and accommodation facilities. Tourism is vitally important to the economy of York, as shown by research from Touche Ross consultants carried out in 1994, which indicated that some 4 million visitors each year are attracted to the city, spending more than £250 million and supporting over 10,000 jobs. Of the 4 million visitors, 600,000 were overnight stay visitors who accounted for more than 1.5 million visitor nights in the city's accommodation. A significant proportion of the tourism revenue is accounted for by visitors' shopping spend, contributing substantially to the continued prosperity of city centre shops in the face of out-of-town retail competition. Other important data from the Touche Ross research showed that, of the 4 million visitors to York in 1993:

- 199,000 stayed in the main hotels.
- 379,000 stayed in other accommodation.
- 1,125,000 were on day visits primarily for leisure purposes.
- 2,250,000 were on day visits primarily for shopping purposes.
- Average length of stay of overnight visitors was 2.7 nights.
- Of all visitors to York, 67 per cent were day visitors and 33 per cent stayed.

Although the research highlighted the positive aspects of the York 'product' and the significant economic benefits of tourism to the city, there was also a note of caution, with the comment that 'there is no room for complacency'. There was evidence that some of the attractions in York were experiencing reductions in their number of visitors (see Table 21.1). Moreover, York faces increasing competition as a regional tourist and shopping destination from places such as Leeds, with the new Royal Armouries attraction, Halifax, with its Eureka! Museum for Children, and Bradford, the home of the National Museum of Photography, Film and Television.

SWOT analysis

As part of their research, the consultants analysed a number of factors that affect the competitiveness of York as a tourist destination. These were set out as a SWOT analysis, as follows:

Table 21.1 Visitor numbers to selected attractions in York, 1993–94

Attraction	Number of visitors
York Minster	2,000,000*
Jorvik Viking Centre	676,935
Castle Museum	428,587
National Railway Museum	399,120
Cliffords Tower	136,289
York City Art Gallery	126,304
Yorkshire Museum	120,000
Archaeological Resource Centre	53,852
Treasurer's House	50,744

*Estimated
Source: York City Council

1. *Strengths*
   - strong national and international identity
   - superb built heritage
2. *Weaknesses*
   - poor market intelligence
   - difficulty in identifying growth markets
   - lack of reinvestment by leading attractions
   - limited exploitation of synergies between attractions
3. *Opportunities*
   - development of Castle Museum
   - potential for further developing inbound markets
4. *Threats*
   - lack of monitoring methods to assess performance and make adjustments
   - environmental damage/capacity constraints
   - shopping tourism may 'suffocate' leisure tourism
   - fading appeal of Jorvik

The consultants' implications arising from the SWOT analysis for York fell into three distinct areas, as follows:

- There is little need for broad-based destination marketing of York since there is already a strong positive image of the city.
- There is need for comprehensive and continuous market research, given the increasingly competitive and fast-moving market for tourist destinations.
- York will need to develop a flagship tourist attraction in order to maintain its position as a popular leisure destination.

A tourism strategy for York

At the beginning of 1995, representatives of the tourism industry in York met as the York Tourism Forum to discuss the report of the research by Touche Ross. A small strategy group was established and asked to translate the consultants' findings into a strategy and action plan for the city, which would be recommended to the whole of the tourism industry in York. The strategy group included representatives from the following organisations:

- York City Council
- Yorkshire and Humberside Tourist Board
- York Visitor and Conference Bureau
- York and North Yorkshire Chamber of Commerce
- North Yorkshire Training and Enterprise Council
- York Attractions Group
- York Archaeological Trust
- GMB trade union

The strategy group reported back to the Forum in July 1995 and the 'First Stop York' tourism initiative was born (see Figure 21.5).

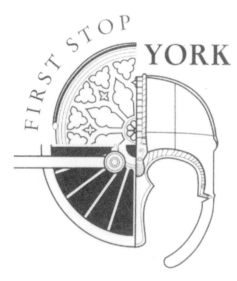

Fig. 21.5 The logo of the First Stop York tourism initiative

The strategic goals of the initiative were to create, through partnership between the public and private sectors, a tourism industry in York where:

- Economic and employment benefits are maximised.
- The city is recognised as a high-quality tourism destination that is continually being enhanced, both in terms of product and customer service.
- A wide range of quality jobs is available, with training and career opportunities.
- The potentially negative environmental and social impacts of the tourism industry are managed so that both the quality of life for residents and the enjoyment of York by visitors are enhanced.
- Local citizens can appreciate the benefits of tourism in York and therefore give it their support.
- Those engaged in the industry in York possess the means to understand and respond to national and international trends in their business.

Based on the outcomes of the Touche Ross research, the strategy group identified a number of core principles and objectives of the 'First Stop York' initiative, including:

1. *Intelligence gathering* – the monitoring of local, regional, national and international trends as an aid to informed planning and management.
2. *Product development* – including the continuation of a clear image for the city, encouraging reinvestment in attractions and facilities, and improving evening facilities in the city.
3. *Product marketing and packaging* – e.g. to adopt a highly targeted and co-ordinated approach to marketing the city, particularly the short-break opportunities, and adopt a single, clear, high-quality brand for the York product. To market York as a year-round destination.
4. *Bookability and management* – including the introduction of booking systems that will facilitate easy access to the York product for potential visitors, improving facilities for the arrival of visitors to the city and ensuring equal access to all sections of the community.
5. *Centre of excellence* – to improve job quality, training and career prospects for those working in the tourism industry and to develop a high-quality and consistent approach to providing services to the visitor.
6. *Citizens' support* – increasing understanding of the tourism industry among local people and developing a greater understanding of residents' concerns about the development of tourism in the city.
7. *Partnership* – to develop a co-ordinated, partnership framework for the management, implementation and monitoring of all activities resulting from the strategic plan for tourism in York.

Action points

Building on the initiative's strategic goals, core principles and objectives, members of the strategy group have devised a series of specific action points, published as an action plan, with detailed timing, leadership and cost implications. The action points concerned with the objective of improving product marketing and packaging, for example, include the establishment of the 'First Stop York' brand, with its associated logo, artwork and displays and a commitment by all partners to corporate, trade-related marketing activities, to include trade fairs, liaison with tour operators, trade advertising, etc. Further product marketing action points include a year-round campaign led by the York Visitor and Conference Bureau aimed at UK and overseas visitors, an enhanced rail campaign with Regional Railways, targeting of incoming visitors through the exploitation of Yorkshire and Humberside Tourist Board's links with the British Tourist Authority (BTA), linkages with Eurotunnel and Eurostar, liaison with air operators and development of the incentive travel market.

(Information courtesy of York City Council)

Case study discussion questions

1. Why is it important for tourist destinations such as York to have accurate intelligence-gathering capabilities?
2. What impacts can tourism development have on local people in destinations

such as York and why is it important to involve local residents in future tourism development plans?

3. How might a city such as York devise and implement a year-round short-breaks programme aimed at UK and overseas tourists?
4. What particular roles do private sector operators, and the different public sector organisations involved with tourism in York, play in the implementation of the strategy?
5. How will the members of the initiative know if it has been a success?

Tourism development in a locality – the North Pennines Tourism Partnership

Introduction to the North Pennines

Lying across the boundaries of Cumbria, Northumberland and Durham, with the market town of Alston at its heart, the North Pennines is known as 'England's last wilderness'. The natural combination of high, uninhabited moorlands and fertile farming valleys embraces an area that is a haven to plants and wildlife, and provides visitors with a chance to experience life and culture in upland communities. Its conservation is of significant importance to both the local population and the nation as a whole, with its official designation as an Area of Outstanding Natural Beauty (AONB).

The Partnership

The North Pennines Tourism Partnership (NPTP) was established in 1991 under the English Tourist Board's Tourism Development Action Programme (TDAP) initiative, which, in collaboration with a range of local authorities and agencies, provided pump-priming funding for an initial three-year period. The current members of the Partnership include:

- Cumbria and Northumbria Tourist Boards
- The County Councils of Cumbria, Durham and Northumberland
- Tynedale, Eden, Wear Valley and Teesdale District Councils
- The Countryside Commission
- Cumbria and Durham Training and Enterprise Councils (TECs)
- English Tourist Board
- Rural Development Commission
- Parish councils
- Private and voluntary sector individuals and groups

Aims of the Tourism Partnership

The North Pennines Tourism Partnership exists to help strengthen the rural economy and to care for the countryside. Within this overall aim, the Partnership is working towards the achievement of a number of specific objectives, which are to:

- Increase general awareness of the North Pennines as an area and a visitor destination by co-ordinating appropriate marketing opportunities.

- Increase the range of active and informal countryside activities and promote these activities.
- Improve existing attractions and provide quality, small- to medium-scale attractions based on the area's heritage and attributes.
- Improve the quality and standards of existing accommodation and encourage modest expansion in key market sectors.
- Promote the development of rural arts and crafts.
- Help conserve the character of the landscape and heritage, and enhance the appearance of the area's towns and villages.
- Develop community involvement in, and private sector support for, tourism.
- Improve accessibility to business advice and training for the local tourism industry.

Countryside recreation in the North Pennines

In seeking to achieve its objective of increasing the range of active and informal countryside activities in the North Pennines, the NPTP has adopted the following set of principles:

1. Encourage activities which draw upon and respect the particular character and attributes of the North Pennines AONB.
2. Encourage quiet, non-motorised activities which do not adversely affect the ecology of the area, local communities, the enjoyment of other countryside users, or the interests of land managers.
3. In order to minimise damage to the countryside, it will be necessary for some activities to be dispersed to spread the load, while others may need to be focused on adequately robust areas and/or at particular times of the year.
4. Activities which simply use the area as a venue and do not depend upon its particular characteristics for full enjoyment of the activity, should not be encouraged.
5. Ensure that visitors are aware of the opportunities for recreation in the North Pennines and have the confidence, ability and understanding to enjoy it in a considerate way.
6. Ensure that visitors are aware of and respect the ecological importance of the area.
7. Encourage providers and participants in countryside recreation to recognise the human factors which have shaped and are still shaping the area, and highlight the link between conservation and existing management of the countryside, and its enjoyment by the public.
8. Where possible, provision for informal recreation should be linked to public transport and this information highlighted in any promotional literature.
9. Activities should be promoted only where the land and wildlife affected are robust enough to withstand damage and disturbance, and where adequate provision has been made for management and maintenance.
10. Promotion of activities should stress the special nature of the area and the need to respect and conserve the countryside.

Implementation

In line with the above general principles, the Partnership has developed a number of strategies in order to further 'green tourism' in the area, namely:

- To promote as visitor activities walking, cycling, riding and cross-country skiing.
- To promote visitor interests such as photography, painting, crafts, bird watching and practical conservation.
- To encourage the development of low impact themed holidays involving these activities and interests.
- To encourage accommodation providers to hire out or lend bicycles, binoculars, waterproofs, etc.
- To encourage accommodation providers to take an interest in their local footpath network and the overall environment so as to be able to inform and encourage visitors.
- To guide organisers or events to act in accordance with these principles.
- To develop 'green charters' or codes of practice for adoption by outdoor activity centres, riding establishments and all other individuals or organisations who promote the use of the area for any interests.
- To encourage activity centres and establishments to include practical conservation work in their programmes and develop links with countryside management projects.
- To incorporate the above in the Business and Training Initiative.

(Information courtesy of North Pennines Tourism Partnership)

Case study discussion questions

1. What are the aims of the North Pennines Tourism Partnership?
2. How realistic is it to be able to achieve each of its objectives?
3. What benefits are there to private sector travel and tourism organisations from being involved with the Partnership?
4. What types of training is such an initiative likely to offer to its members?
5. What techniques should be used to promote the area to visitors?

Assignment 21.2

Tourism development in a locality

Performance criteria satisfied: 21.2.1, 21.2.2, 21.2.3, 21.2.4, 21.2.5

Core skills opportunities at level 3:
Communication	3.1, 3.2, 3.3, 3.4
Information technology	3.1, 3.2, 3.3
Application of number	3.1, 3.2, 3.3

Situation

In your role as tourism assistant with the local council, you have been given the responsibility of planning and carrying out an investigation into the impact of tourism development in your local area.

Tasks

Working with a partner, you are to research and deliver a presentation to the rest of your group on tourism development in your locality. In particular, your presentation should:

- Define the scope of tourism development in the locality.
- Describe the role of public and private sector organisations in tourism development in the area.
- Explain the appeal to tourists of the tourism development in the locality.
- Describe how the area is promoted to tourists.
- Assess the benefits and disadvantages that have resulted from tourism development in the locality.

Your presentation should include detailed information gathered from an in-depth investigation of local tourism developments. You should negotiate specific work tasks with the other members of your group to ensure equality of work load. You will be assessed on the content of the presentation and the quality of delivery.

Element 21.3 Investigate a tourism development in a developing country

Tourism in developing countries

World tourism is essentially the preserve of developed, western societies, where relatively affluent lifestyles allow people to travel within and between western Europe and North America. Western Europe alone accounts for two-thirds of all international tourist arrivals and, when North American arrivals are added, the figure reaches around 80 per cent. There are, however, two noticeable trends that are beginning to change this situation:

- Residents of western countries are travelling further afield to the so-called 'long-haul' destinations, encouraged by competitively priced charter flights and holiday packages.
- People living in developing countries are themselves experiencing higher standards of living, thereby encouraging more overseas travel.

At the same time as these trends have been growing, developing countries have begun to realise the economic and political benefits that tourism can bring. These include:

- Inflows of foreign exchange
- Creation of employment opportunities
- Improvements to infrastructure
- Diversity of economic activity
- Credibility on the world stage, helping to attract further investment

Multinational hotel groups, airlines and tour operators have been quick to exploit a further market opportunity by working with national governments to expand tourism in developing countries. Some Third World countries, however, have criti-cised these same companies for contributing little to local economies, failing to employ sufficient local people and offering low contract rates for accommodation.

Activity

Carry out some further research to discover which global tourism organisations exist to encourage tourism development in developing countries and the aims of each body.

Negative impacts of tourism development

In addition to the criticisms of multinational corporations in relation to the economics of tourism development highlighted above, the growth in travel to long-haul destina-tions, many of which are developing nations, has led to concern about the social and cultural impacts of unplanned tourism development. The bringing together of people from widely different social backgrounds can lead to a loss of cultural identity and a loss of authenticity on the part of the host communities, e.g. local people are encour-aged to perform ethnic and religious rituals that conform to the tourists' image of an area, but which may bear little relation to the reality of their situation. The affluence of the incoming visitors can also affect young people in the developing countries, who may be tempted to forgo their education in favour of providing services for the tour-ists. In the worst cases, crime and prostitution may flourish as a result of tourism development.

It is for these reasons that the governments in developing nations, and non-govern-mental organisations such as Tourism Concern and Friends of the Earth, are working towards tourism development that is sustainable in the long term, by giving attention to prior planning and responsible management.

The process of tourism development in developing countries

There are no hard and fast rules about tourism development in developing countries. Countries that have little in the way of tourism infrastructure, only limited resources for promotion and little experience of the world travel and tourism industry, tend to lack a planned approach to tourism development, often reacting to initiatives from airlines and other multinational corporations, rather than growing from an indigen-ous base. Typical stages in the process of tourism development in developing coun-tries are shown in Figure 21.6.

As Figure 21.6 shows, tourism is initially encouraged by the national and local governments in the developing country, since it is seen as economically beneficial. Local labour is cheap and the government is likely to offer financial incentives to tourism developers, including tax holidays, grants, waiving of import duties, etc. With the tourism development up and running, there follows a 'honeymoon period' when the hoteliers do well financially, with guaranteed passengers from overseas tour

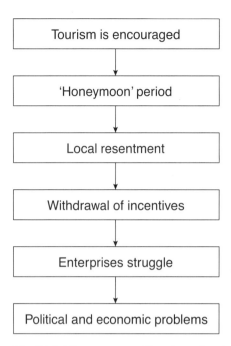

Fig. 21.6 *The process of tourism development in developing countries*

operators and airlines. Once this period comes to an end, resentment begins to grow, a result of the wealth gap between the local people and the affluent visiting tourists. There is also local resentment between those who are benefiting from tourism and those who are not. In the face of this local resentment, the government begins to withdraw financial and other incentives for the developers. Local prices for food and labour begin to rise, while the standards of service and facilities offered to the tourists decline. This results in a fall in repeat visitors, which compounds the problem further. In this business climate, tourist enterprises struggle and some hotels may be taken over by multinational chains. When the process comes to an end, the national government of the developing country is left with a variety of economic and political problems, including loss of revenue and a poor international image.

Although this model of tourism development is by no means universal in all developing nations, it serves to illustrate the importance of a planned approach to tourism development and management, as illustrated in the following case study of tourism development in Botswana.

Tourism development in Botswana

Introduction

Botswana lies in the heart of southern Africa, bordered by South Africa, Namibia, Zimbabwe and Zambia. The tableland of the Kalahari Desert covers the bulk of southern Botswana and nearly one-fifth of the country is designated as National Park. The majority of the population lives in the south-east around the capital Gabarone, Serowe and Kanya along the border with South Africa.

Tourism infrastructure

Sir Seretse is Botswana's principal international airport, located 10 miles to the north of Gabarone. The airport was opened in the mid-1980s and gave the country direct access to the international community, with British Airways and Air France operating regular flights. There is another airport in the north of the country at Kasane, close to the border with Zambia, and a number of smaller airports for internal travel. Work is in progress to upgrade the internal rail system, and the road system boasts over 1200 miles of surfaced highway.

Tourism statistics

Data from the Botswana Department of Tourism show that tourist arrivals more than doubled between 1980 and 1990 (see Table 21.2). The most significant growth in numbers coincided with the opening of Sir Seretse International Airport in the mid-1980s. Table 21.2 also demonstrates that there has been a shift in the proportions of domestic and international tourists over the same time period: domestic tourists accounted for 57 per cent and overseas visitors 43 per cent of all arrivals in 1980, but the figures for 1990 were 40 and 60 per cent respectively. Arrivals from the UK and Ireland jumped from 5824 in 1980 to nearly 36,000 in 1990.

Table 21.3 shows the expenditure of visitors to Botswana between 1981 and 1990. Not surprisingly, expenditure rose sharply from 1985 onwards as a result of the opening of Sir Seretse International Airport. Total expenditure in 1990 amounted to 182 million Pula (approximately £43 million).

Botswana's tourism product

The Botswana government's selling proposition is 'high cost, low volume', i.e. a small number of high-spending tourists. In line with this proposition, the Department of Tourism has increased the entry and camping fees to National Parks in order to discourage mass tourism. They pursue a policy of sustainable tourism, leaving the country's ecosystem in a balanced state. There are wildlife management areas, which are zoned for sustainable wildlife utilisation, protecting one of the country's major tourist assets.

Although there is no grading system, all hotels generally maintain a reasonable standard, particularly those in the main centres in the east of the country. Hotels and motels with the most modern facilities are to be found around Gabarone. There is a wide range of safari lodges and camps, some very basic and some with every luxury, attracting the high-spending tourists from Europe, North America and the Far East.

Tourism promotion

The Department of Tourism produces a variety of brochures and posters in English, French and German. Videos are also available in these languages. Staff from the Department attend major travel trade fairs, such as ITB Berlin and the World Travel Market in London, so as to forge links with tour operators and airlines, thereby further developing their products and promotional outlets. Meetings are also arranged with major tour wholesalers to persuade them to include Botswana in their sales manuals and tour programmes.

(Information courtesy of Botswana Director of Tourism)

Table 21.2 Total arrivals in Botswana by country of residence, 1980–90

Country of residence	1980	1981	1982	1983	1984	1985	1986	1987	1988	1989	1990
Botswana	351,134	330,860	398,173	448,240	434,035	436,779	468,340	449,224	513,313	622,196	561,596
Total excluding Botswana	263,581	226,940	297,678	302,329	338,750	326,950	381,205	432,323	384,335	691,041	844,295
Africa	247,761	213,960	274,475	282,808	297,424	290,602	333,167	382,908	333,783	612,457	759,197
South Africa and Namibia	202,833	149,980	193,570	189,152	226,972	216,263	239,179	247,449	254,241	309,747	363,840
Zimbabwe	30,984	48,960	57,225	75,614	52,071	60,694	55,067	96,933	44,869	249,283	338,264
Zambia	7,269	9,740	16,580	8,637	8,082	3,912	21,402	18,480	15,242	25,241	26,454
Swaziland	1,785	1,360	1,320	2,317	1,146	1,480	2,861	2,618	2,714	2,614	3,997
Lesotho	2,202	1,500	2,200	2,101	2,620	2,531	3,090	4,003	4,771	5,601	5,026
Rest of Africa	2,688	2,420	3,580	4,987	6,533	5,722	11,568	13,425	11,946	19,971	21,616
Asia and the Pacific	1,294	1,180	2,241	1,853	3,804	4,022	4,018	5,303	5,204	7,303	8,771
Asia	704	720	1,301	1,229	2,482	2,693	2,820	3,454	2,976	3,722	4,328
Australia and New Zealand	590	460	940	624	1,322	1,329	1,198	1,849	2,228	3,581	4,443
Europe	11,341	8,940	16,541	13,156	31,708	26,388	37,473	36,918	37,737	60,075	65,473
UK and Ireland	5,824	3,900	8,689	6,160	17,982	13,045	19,074	17,896	18,712	25,735	35,973
Rest of Europe	5,517	5,040	7,852	6,996	13,726	13,343	18,399	19,022	19,025	34,340	29,500
America	3,185	2,860	4,421	4,512	5,814	5,938	6,547	7,194	7,611	11,206	10,854
USA	2,587	2,200	3,681	3,937	4,827	5,248	5,724	5,961	6,162	9,374	8,533
Rest of America	598	660	740	575	987	690	823	1,233	1,449	1,832	2,321
Total	614,715	557,800	695,851	750,569	772,785	763,729	849,545	881,547	897,648	1,313,237	1,405,891

Source: Botswana Director of Tourism

Table 21.3 Expenditure by visitors to Botswana, 1981–90

	Number of visitors	Number of visitors who declared expenditure	Declared expenditure (Pula)*	Average expenditure (Pula)	Average length of stay (Days)	Average daily expenditure per visitor (Pula)	Total expenditure (P'000)
1981	271,060	179,610	12,686,660	70.63	5.4	13.08	19,146
1982	300,413	181,362	19,041,928	104.99	4.8	21.87	31,542
1983	350,453	211,504	24,541,482	116.03	5.9	19.67	40,664
1984	325,204	201,997	28,226,271	139.74	5.9	23.68	45,443
1985	333,871	203,698	27,341,308	134.22	4.9	27.39	44,814
1986	368,499	228,900	47,533,084	207.66	4.3	48.29	76,522
1987	406,008	264,974	49,701,271	187.57	4.9	38.28	76,155
1988	340,436	211,389	38,275,779	181.07	4.9	36.95	61,642
1989	582,871	398,517	73,780,097	185.14	4.5	41.05	107,911
1990	759,867	513,949	126,544,749	246.22	4.8	50.87	182,037

Based on declarations made by departing visitors
* £1 sterling ≃ 4.20 Pula

Source: Botswana Director of Tourism

Case study discussion questions

1. Which other countries in southern Africa are in competition with Botswana for overseas tourists?
2. Why does the country adopt a 'high cost, low volume' approach to tourism development?
3. Are there any dangers in approaching tourism development in this way?
4. What other promotional techniques could Botswana adopt to attract visitors from the UK?
5. Who funds the infrastructure improvements in developing countries such as Botswana?

Activity

Draw an outline map of Botswana indicating the capital, principal tourist areas and internal communication routes.

Tourism development in Bangladesh

Introduction

The People's Republic of Bangladesh is situated in the north-eastern part of south Asia. The Himalayas stand on its northern border, while the southern boundary fronts the Bay of Bengal. West Bengal (India) lies to the west of Bangladesh, while to the east lies the forest of Myanmar (Arakan Province). The landscape is mainly flat with many bamboo, mango and palm-covered plains. Two great rivers, the Ganges and the Brahmaputra, converge in the central plain of the country, giving rise to regular flooding. Much of the country's land area has been built up from alluvial deposits brought down by the major rivers and their many tributaries. The land is mostly flat, except for a range of hills in the south-east of the country. It is mainly characterised by wooded marshlands and jungle, with forest regions in Sylhet, Rangamati, Khagrachari and Bandarban. Dhaka is the capital of the country, famous for its mosques and Hindu temples. Other major cities include Chittagong, Bangladesh's second largest city, and Rajshahi in the west of the country.

Tourism infrastructure

The principal airport is Dhaka International, located 12 miles north of the city. The direct flight time to London is approximately 11 hours. The national airline, Biman Bangladesh Airlines, operates internal flights from Dhaka to a number of main population centres.

Almost all parts of the country are accessible on metalled roads and the rail network is efficient, but sometimes slow given the nature of the terrain. Ferries operate between southern coastal ports and the Ganges river delta, where there are five major ports. There are a small number of western-style hotels, found mainly in Dhaka. Elsewhere, the Bangladesh Parjatan Corporation National Tourism Organisation (NTO) manages several modern hotels throughout the country.

Tourism statistics

Table 21.4 shows total foreign tourist arrivals to Bangladesh between 1981 and 1992.

The statistics show that tourist numbers fell slightly between 1988 and 1992, and that the seasonal spread of tourism is very even throughout the year. The top five countries of origin of foreign tourists in 1992 were as follows:

1. India   35,607
2. Pakistan   14,066
3. UK   10,203
4. USA   7,768
5. Japan   5,937

Bangladesh's tourism product

The country's tourist attractions include archaeological sites, historic mosques and monuments, resorts, beaches, forests, game birds and wildlife. Bangladesh offers opportunities for a variety of active pursuits, including angling, water ski-ing, river cruising, hiking, rowing, surfing, yachting and sea bathing. The Bangladesh Parjatan Corporation (NTO) offers tourists a range of package tours, incorporating the main tourist features, including:

- Tours of Dhaka City and Chittagong.
- The lake district of Rangamati Hill Tracts, known for its scenic beauty and unspoiled tribal life.
- Cox's Bazaar, with its 120 km length of unbroken sandy beach.
- Jungle areas of Khulna and Sundarbans, home of the Royal Bengal tiger.
- Archaeological sites, including the ancient city of Pundrangar, the Buddhist monastery at Paharpur and the old palace of Dighapatiya at Natore.

Tourism promotion

The Bangladesh Parjatan Corporation (NTO) co-ordinates the promotion of Bangladesh as a tourist destination, and produces a range of brochures, leaflets and posters, which are available from its headquarters in Dhaka, and through High Commissions in the UK, USA and Canada. As well as offering its own package tours, the Corporation negotiates with other tour operators world-wide for the inclusion of Bangladesh in their tour programmes. Staff also attend major travel trade exhibitions, including ITB Berlin and the World Travel Market in London to make contacts with airlines and other travel brokers.

(Information courtesy of Bangladesh Parjatan Corporation – National Tourism Organisation)

Case study discussion questions

1. Which other countries in the Indian sub-continent are in competition with Bangladesh for overseas tourists?
2. What type of UK tourists do you think would be attracted to Bangladesh for holidays?
3. Why do you think that its foreign visitor numbers have fallen?

Table 21.4 Bangladesh foreign tourist arrivals by month, 1981–92

Month	1981	1982	1983	1984	1985	1986	1987	1988	1989	1990	1991	1992
January	5,590	4,050	8,963	10,461	9,014	14,688	12,735	11,972	14,521	13,253	11,341	11,179
February	4,254	4,031	6,498	8,856	12,824	11,328	9,600	8,961	12,195	9,458	8,549	8,926
March	5,025	3,975	6,198	8,352	12,432	12,595	10,910	10,091	10,771	10,868	7,791	8,280
April	3,195	3,608	6,067	7,667	11,182	11,707	8,246	9,403	9,949	8,920	12,707	7,671
May	4,165	3,375	6,706	9,258	12,453	9,588	8,623	9,940	11,106	10,802	11,209	7,701
June	3,287	3,249	6,318	9,070	12,574	9,832	9,183	11,125	10,934	9,096	11,083	8,890
July	3,316	3,525	5,895	7,627	10,068	9,479	9,179	9,758	9,655	9,028	10,959	8,815
August	3,851	3,938	6,230	7,076	12,785	10,331	6,996	10,135	7,641	8,752	7,918	10,013
September	3,427	5,017	5,112	7,155	11,887	8,812	9,706	6,429	8,823	8,700	5,872	8,627
October	4,562	4,626	7,477	8,565	13,000	11,378	8,412	9,880	10,210	9,365	8,363	10,971
November	3,911	6,234	6,543	8,065	11,484	8,557	5,841	11,057	10,176	7,593	8,343	9,641
December	4,734	8,077	7,811	10,978	15,931	10,775	7,334	12,031	12,625	9,534	9,115	9,761
Total	49,315	53,705	79,818	103,130	145,634	129,070	106,765	120,782	128,606	115,369	113,242	110,475
Change over previous year (%)	–	+8.90	+48.62	+29.21	+41.21	-11.37	-17.28	+13.12	+6.02	-9.91	-1.84	-2.50
Cumulative total	507,427	561,132	640,950	744,080	889,714	1,018,784	1,125,549	1,246,331	1,374,937	1,490,306	1,603,548	1,714,023

Source: Bangladesh Parjatan Corporation PTS Division (Statistics)

4. What other promotional techniques could Bangladesh adopt to attract visitors from the UK?
5. What improvements or alterations to its tourism product could Bangladesh carry out as a way of improving visitor numbers?

Activity

Draw an outline map of Bangladesh indicating the capital, principal tourist areas and internal communication routes.

Assignment 21.3

Tourism development in a developing country

Performance criteria satisfied: 21.3.1, 21.3.2, 21.3.3, 21.3.4, 21.3.5, 21.3.6

Core skills opportunities at level 3:   Communication   3.1, 3.2, 3.3, 3.4
Information technology   3.1, 3.2, 3.3
Application of number   3.1, 3.2, 3.3

Tasks

Working with a partner, you are to prepare a detailed report on tourism development in a developing country of your choice. In particular, your report should:

- Define the scope of tourism development in the country concerned.
- Describe the roles of national, foreign and international organisations in tourism development.
- Explain the appeal to UK originating tourists of the tourism development.
- Describe how the country is promoted to UK tourists.
- Describe the local, national and international benefits of tourism in the chosen country.
- Describe, with examples, the disadvantages resulting from the tourism development.

Your report should be word processed and include relevant maps, diagrams, charts and statistics.

Unit 22

PROMOTIONAL TECHNIQUES IN TRAVEL AND TOURISM

Element 22.1

Describe the key promotional techniques used for marketing travel and tourism products and services

Element 22.2

Examine and prepare printed material for promoting travel and tourism products and services

Element 22.3

Examine the role of personal selling in relation to travel and tourism products and services

Element 22.4

Examine the role of advertising in promoting travel and tourism products and services

Element 22.1 Describe the key promotional techniques used for marketing travel and tourism products and services

---

Performance criteria

1. Describe the key promotional techniques used for marketing travel and tourism products and services.
2. Describe the benefits of the key promotional techniques to travel and tourism organisations.
3. Explain, with examples, uses of the key promotional techniques in marketing travel and tourism products and services.
4. Select and justify the most appropriate key promotional techniques for travel and tourism products and services.

The importance of promotional techniques

Promotion is one of the key elements of the marketing mix in travel and tourism. Sometimes referred to as the 'four Ps', the marketing mix consists of:

- Product
- Price
- Place
- Promotion

Just as the ingredients must be in the correct quantities to make a successful cake, so the four elements of the marketing mix must be in the right proportions to make an organisation's marketing activities successful. If we take the example of a small specialist tour operator offering villa holidays to Majorca, it must be sure that the product it is offering meets its customers' requirements in terms of quality, availability, features and benefits. It must also be aware of offering the product at a competitive price, giving value for money regardless of the price paid. The place component of the marketing mix refers both to the location of the villas and resorts in the tour operator's programme and how the product is made available to the public, i.e. either sold through a travel agent or direct to the customer. Either way, the customer must have access to reliable information on availability of properties, flights, etc. How the tour operator promotes its products will depend on a number of factors, such as its promotional budget, whether it sells direct or through an agent, the size of its operation and the type of customers it is trying to attract. So we can see that promotional activity is just one element of an integrated approach to successful marketing in travel and tourism.

Key promotional techniques

Promotional techniques are the means by which any travel and tourism organisation aims to sell its products, thereby generating revenue. Specifically, promotional techniques are used to:

1. Inform potential buyers of the existence of products and services.
2. Outline their benefits and advantages to the customers.
3. Create a desire on the part of the customer to purchase.
4. Provide an opportunity for a purchase to be completed to the satisfaction of both parties.
5. Remind customers of the existence of a product or service.

You may see or hear the terms 'above the line' and 'below the line' in connection with marketing and promotional techniques. 'Above the line' generally refers to advertising, while 'below the line' promotional activities include direct mail, sales promotions, public relations, etc. The terms have evolved from advertising agencies, who normally earn a commission from placing advertisements, but charge a fee for 'below the line' activities.

There are a number of promotional techniques that travel and tourism organisations can use to stimulate sales of their products and services, the most important of which are:

- Pricing
- Advertising
- Public relations
- Sales promotion
- Direct marketing
- Personal selling
- Brochures

Pricing

The majority of travel and tourism products and services are sold in highly competitive environments, making pricing a crucial element of any organisation's marketing mix. If we take the example of overseas package holidays to summer sun destinations, competition between mass market tour operators to increase their market share is fierce, often resulting in price discounting and special promotions. Price is just as important as the other three components of the marketing mix, namely product, place and promotion, since, if the price is wrong, no amount of advertising or other promotional activity will make the customer buy the product. Getting the price right in travel and tourism is no easy task, given the highly complex nature of this service industry and the intangibility of the products on offer. In travel and tourism, it is customary to charge different amounts for the same product at different times of the year and even different times of the day. An all-inclusive family French camping holiday with Eurosites, for example, will cost nearly £500 more in August than the same package in late September. Similarly, a round of golf at the local municipal course may well cost more on a Sunday morning when compared to a Tuesday afternoon. Pricing in travel and tourism, therefore, is closely related to the demand for products and services.

Price is also closely allied to value, a concept that is notoriously difficult to define since it varies so much between individuals. Some people put a very high value on a particular leisure pursuit, while others will not be interested at all and it is clearly of little value to them. Value will also fluctuate according to particular circumstances; windsurfing on a local lake in high summer will have a greater value than the same activity taking place in the freezing temperatures of February.

Pricing is clearly a far more complex subject than simply adding up all the costs associated with providing a product or service, then adding a small margin of profit. The idea of what something is worth to the individual comes into play, a feature that will influence the amount he or she is willing to pay.

Before we look at some of the methods used to price travel and tourism products, it is important to understand some of the factors that influence pricing, the most important of which are:

1. *Costs* – it is essential for an organisation to be aware of the costs of providing a particular product or service when deciding on its price. This may, however, only be the starting point of a much more complex pricing policy revolving around many of the concepts discussed above.
2. *Demand* – we have shown that the same product can command a higher price at different times according to customer demand. People will often be expected to pay high prices for accommodation and travel in peak season, for example.
3. *Competition* – in the highly competitive travel and tourism industry, an organisation will need to be aware of what competitors are charging and adjust its own prices accordingly.
4. *The state of the economy* – in times of recession, products may be reduced in price in order to gain revenue, e.g. hotel rooms may be heavily discounted, particularly at weekends when the use by business clients is low, on the assumption that it is better to get a little income for the rooms rather than nothing at all if they are left empty.
5. *Objectives of the organisation* – clearly a private sector company will need to maximise revenue and will try to set prices that help achieve this objective. Public sector and voluntary bodies may be able to offer more concessionary prices to achieve their wider social aims.

Pricing policies in travel and tourism

Travel and tourism organisations need to understand the two different types of pricing that influence their business performance, namely:

- Strategic pricing
- Tactical pricing

Strategic pricing

Strategic pricing is the planned setting of price levels that an organisation undertakes to achieve its business objectives. A tourist attraction, for example, will establish its prices for the season well in advance of opening, based on its financial projections, estimates of attendances and organisational aims. All commercial travel and tourism companies will set their prices so as to maximise revenue for the organisation.

From the many different strategic pricing policies in use in travel and tourism, the following are some of the most common:

1. *Skimming* – when a high price is charged initially for a new product that is unique and that attracts people who are willing to pay the high price for status reasons. The pricing of flights on Concorde is an example of market skimming.
2. *Cost plus pricing* – sometimes known as 'accountant's pricing', this is the rather simplistic approach that totals all fixed costs (buildings, machinery, etc.) and variable costs (wages, energy costs, postage, etc.) and adds a small profit margin to arrive at the price to charge. It assumes that an organisation can calculate its costs accurately, something which a large airline, for example, may find difficult.
3. *Penetration pricing* – this is used by organisations wanting to get into a new market where there are existing suppliers of the same product or service. The price will be set sufficiently low to persuade customers to switch their allegiance (sometimes known as a 'loss leader'). It is important that this pricing method is seen as a long-term strategy since customers will resent an early rise in price.
4. *Competitive pricing* – sometimes referred to as 'the going rate', competitive pricing assumes that where products or services are similar, the organisation will charge the going rate, i.e. will match the price of competitors. This method often leads to very low margins and, in the long run, the collapse of some organisations, e.g. tour operators, who find their profitability is too low.

Tactical pricing

Tactical pricing is any pricing alteration or adjustment made at short notice in response to competitor activity or an unforeseen eventuality. A travel agency chain, for example, that experiences lower than average bookings at a particular time of year may decide to offer a 5 per cent discount on all holidays purchased for a specified period of time. Tactical pricing is now very common in mass market tour operations, with companies cutting prices and issuing new editions of brochures and pricing grids in response to price changes of their competitors. Common tactical pricing techniques used in travel and tourism include:

1. *Quantity discounts* – e.g. one free place per 15 booked on a package holiday.
2. *Party discounts* – tourist attractions will usually offer a family ticket at a discounted rate, while tour operators often advertise reduced prices for children.
3. *Trade discounts* – e.g. discounted hotel rates for travel industry personnel.
4. *Early booking and advance booking discounts* – some tour operators offer a discount for early full payment of a holiday invoice. APEX (advanced purchase excursion) tickets are also a good example of this tactic.
5. *Seasonal discounts* – it is common for most holiday and travel products to be offered for sale at discounted rates at particular times of the year, e.g. short breaks to British cities in the winter months.
6. *'Last minute' discounts* – for travellers who are prepared to wait, airlines, hoteliers, tour operators, coach companies, etc., will usually offer discounted rates to dispose of unsold stocks of airline seats, hotel bedspaces, etc. Tourist attractions also offer discounted entry charges towards the end of their normal opening hours.

Activity

Examine the pricing structure of a local travel and tourism organisation with which you are familiar. Analyse the factors that have influenced the prices charged and what evidence there is of strategic or tactical pricing.

Advertising

Advertising is by far the most visible of all the promotional techniques used by travel and tourism organisations; every day we see advertisements for holidays and travel on our television screens, on buses and taxis, and in newspapers and magazines. These are known as advertising media; the precise choice of media will be dictated partly by cost (a 30-second commercial on TV in peak viewing time can cost as much as £30,000) and partly by the type of product and its intended audience. A new museum aimed at local people is unlikely to use national TV advertising but will rely on advertisements in the local press.

Advertising in leisure and tourism is directed either at the customer (consumer advertising) or at those working in the industry (trade advertising). *Travel Trade Gazette* and *Caterer and Hotelkeeper* are two examples of trade magazines that carry advertisements.

Many people believe that travel and tourism organisations put nearly all of their promotional effort and budget into advertising, over and above other promotional techniques. This is far from the case, since many small and medium-sized organisations find it hard to justify the expense of advertising campaigns. They rely much more on methods such as direct marketing and public relations, which can be just as effective with less investment.

Activity

Study a range of travel advertisements in a variety of newspapers and magazines spread over a seven-day period. Analyse what particular holiday products are being sold and chart the techniques used to attract the reader's attention.

The benefits of effective advertising

Advertising in the various media available has a number of benefits when compared with other promotional techniques, including:

- Access to a large audience.
- The ability to target particular market segments.
- Responsiveness to current events.
- The potential for a high degree of creativity.
- The ability to use sound and visual effects.

Element 22.4 looks in greater detail at the role of advertising in promoting travel and tourism products and services, plus the benefits of using particular media.

Public relations

The Institute of Public Relations (IPR) defines public relations as:

> *. . . the planned and sustained effort to establish and maintain goodwill and mutual understanding between an organisation and its publics.*

The last word of this definition is deliberately used in the plural, since an organisation actually has to deal with many different publics, of which its customers are only one. A travel and tourism organisation, for example, must also maintain goodwill with suppliers, trade unions, the press, councillors (if in the public sector), shareholders (where appropriate), members, distributors, neighbours and voluntary helpers. Public relations is important at all levels and in all departments within an organisation and is not just the concern of the public relations department or public relations officer (PRO).

Public relations, or PR as it is often known, is used a great deal in travel and tourism. Organisations sometimes think of it as 'free publicity', particularly when associated with a newspaper or magazine article that features its products. In reality, there is usually a price to be paid for such editorial coverage, even if it is just the cost of entertaining the journalist who wrote it!

Public relations is more than just keeping the media informed of your organisation, however, although this can undoubtedly pay dividends. PR is also about making sure that all staff and functions of an organisation that come into contact with the public, e.g. staff at reception, promotional literature, telephone technique, uniforms, etc., are well managed so as to gain maximum publicity and goodwill. PR is also about travel and tourism organisations helping in the local community and getting involved in work for local and national charities. As well as providing much-needed cash, sponsorship can also bring PR benefits to travel and tourism organisations. The image of a tourist attraction, for example, can be enhanced by being sponsored by a company regarded as successful in its own particular field.

The benefits of effective public relations

The fact that travel and tourism is a service industry often means that the reputation of an organisation and its products hinges on the attitude of its staff when dealing with customers and users. The highly competitive nature of travel and tourism makes it vital that all organisations make every effort to develop and maintain a friendly and personal image. PR can play an important role in supporting and publicising this image and presenting to its customers the face of a caring and professional organisation.

If used effectively, PR in travel and tourism can:

- Build a favourable image.
- Assist in the launch of new products, services and facilities.
- Help to 'reposition' existing products, services and facilities.
- Generate interest in an organisation.
- Help publicise an event.
- Influence specific target groups.
- Defend an organisation when things go wrong.

As a marketing tool, PR can be far more cost-effective than other promotional techniques, such as advertising or direct mail. This makes it a particularly attractive medium for travel and tourism organisations that have small promotional budgets. In fact, the smaller the promotional budget, the stronger the case for PR.

Press relations

Although public relations can take many forms and is important at all points where an organisation interfaces with its publics, it is most often associated with press or media relations. It is in the interest of every travel and tourism organisation to build a relationship with its relevant media, whether it be personal contact with key reporters on local, regional or national newspapers, feature editors on appropriate trade and consumer magazines, or TV and radio stations. Familiarisation ('fam') trips are frequently used in travel and tourism as a way of giving a journalist first-hand experience of the product or service that is being promoted, e.g. a newly refurbished hotel development in France or a new programme of activity holidays in Scotland. Liaison with the relevant media will not only help the organisation gain publicity for its achievements and success stories, but also improve the chances of putting its side of the story when the news is bad. Good PR can help when a tragedy strikes or unfavourable stories begin to circulate.

The most usual method of informing the media about current news and events is by issuing a press release (see Figure 22.1). They can be sent to local radio and television stations as well as to newspapers and magazines. Editors are inundated with news releases on a whole range of subjects every day, so the chances of gaining some 'free publicity' are limited. If the release is used, however, the information it contains appears far more credible to the reader than the same message conveyed in an advertisement. The disadvantage of press releases, however, is that the organisation has no control over what the editor chooses to include or exclude. Parts of the news release may be printed out of context and give a negative image of the organisation and its activities.

There are some basic guidelines that will increase the chances of a press release being used:

- Keep it crisp, factual and informative.
- Write from the point of view of the journalist.
- Write to suit the style of the publication.
- Answer the basic questions of who?, what?, when?, where?, why?, as early as possible in the release, preferably in the first two paragraphs.
- Get the main newspoint into the first paragraph.
- Don't make it any longer than it needs to be.
- Give a date to the release and indicate clearly if there is an embargo (a date or time before which it cannot be used).
- Respect copy deadlines (the date by which it must be with the editor).
- Include full details of a contact person at the end of the release.
- Use double spacing to allow for editing.
- Include a picture if it will help tell the story (7 in. × 5in. (17.5 cm × 12.5 cm) black and white for preference, captioned on the reverse to explain who is doing what).

It is important to monitor PR coverage by organising the collection of press cuttings either through an agency or in-house. The PR specialist within the organisation

25 MILLION BRICKS

Windsor, 28th March 1996: LEGOLAND® Windsor, which opens to the public tomorrow, is a family theme park with a difference. Dedicated to the imagination and creativity of children and spectacularly located in 150 acres of wooded landscape near Windsor, the Park will surprise, excite, involve and entertain the whole family.

There are five main activity areas in the Park, interspersed with quiet areas. Each activity area relates to a different LEGO® play theme, with interactive rides, shows, playscapes, building workshops, driving schools and 'Miniland' - a series of model towns and scenes from around Europe, recreated in astonishing detail from millions of LEGO bricks.

Miniland

Miniland contains scenes from Europe, including London, Amsterdam, Edinburgh and Paris, all bustling with sounds, traffic, trains and boats. There are some 800 model buildings and another 700 models of trains, cars, ships, cranes, bridges, fountains and people. One hundred model designers have worked for three years and used nearly 20 million bricks to create Miniland.

The DUPLO Gardens

Here, in keeping with the LEGO DUPLO® brand, are delights for the younger members of the family. But its no toddlers ghetto, for older children and parents too will find much to amuse and attract them. There's a helicopter ride, puppet theatre, Fairy Tale Brook boat ride (full of wit and surprises) and perhaps best of all, is an area called The Waterworks.

LEGOLAND Windsor Park Ltd
Windsor Berkshire SL4 4AY

*Fig. 22.1 **An extract from a press release** (reproduced courtesy of LEGOLAND Windsor)*

should be encouraged to organise visits by journalists and VIPs to see facilities first hand. Also, the relevant people within the organisation should go out and speak to local groups, clubs and schools, to let them know what you are doing and why.

Activity

Write a press release for a local tourist attraction or travel company that has something new to publicise.

Sales promotion

Sales promotion describes a range of techniques designed to encourage customers to make a purchase. They usually support advertising, direct mail, personal selling or public relations activity and, in travel and tourism, include activities such as:

1. *Vouchers and on-pack promotions* – travel and tourism companies sometimes join forces with food companies, magazines and newspapers to take part in joint promotions based on collecting vouchers. Longleat House in Wiltshire, for example, worked with McVitie's biscuits and BT phonecards in 1995 to help boost visitor numbers.

2. *Price reductions* – it is common for travel and tourism organisations to offer price discounts to encourage more business, e.g. a 'happy hour' in a bar when all drinks are half-price, a tourist attraction offering discounted rates at off-peak times, tour operators advertising cut-price holidays if bookings are made before a certain date. Sainsbury's joined forces with British Airways in 1993 to run a promotion offering up to 40 per cent off BA flights abroad.

3. *Free gifts* – a travel agent may provide a free holdall or item of clothing to all clients booking a holiday; a tourist attraction may give free badges and hats to all children who visit. In 1993, Hoover offered free flights to anybody who bought one of their vacuum cleaners. Unfortunately, the promotion was too successful and Hoover were unable to completely fulfil their promise to every purchaser.

4. *Exhibitions* – are a good way of showing both the general public and the trade what's new in travel and tourism. They are also a good PR activity, helping staff to cement relationships and make new contacts.

5. *Competitions* – some organisations run competitions to encourage the public to buy their products and services. The prizes on offer may include holidays, short breaks or travel tickets.

6. *'Extra product'* – a customer is given additional benefits without having to pay any more. For example, a hotel may provide free newspapers for all guests, a fitness suite in a hotel may offer vouchers for a free beauty treatment to ladies who attend their aerobics classes, or an airline may provide a chauffeur-driven car from home to the airport for business travellers. 'Three weeks for the price of two', an offer commonly made by holiday companies, is also an example of 'extra product'.

7. *'Passport' or 'loyalty' schemes* – some travel and tourism organisations offer loyalty schemes to encourage people to stay with them and use their services in the future. Frequent flyer programmes operated by airlines are one of the best-known loyalty

schemes; passengers are given points for each trip made and, when they have collected a particular number, can cash them in for free flights. Similar programmes are operated by hotel companies and car-hire firms. Visitor attractions sometimes offer a 'passport' which can give free or discounted entry to the site.

8. *Point-of-sale (POS) materials* – these range from window displays, posters and merchandising units to brochure racks, hanging cards and special demonstrations, all with the aim of persuading customers to buy particular products and services.

Sales promotion can also be directed at an organisation's own staff and is also used by companies to encourage extra business from their agents. It is common for travel agencies, for example, to offer their staff bonuses and other incentives to reward high sales achievement, while tour operators will use a variety of sales promotion techniques to promote their products to the travel trade, e.g. competitions, discounted holidays, trade launches, gift vouchers, etc. Figure 22.2 shows the different types of sales promotion relationships in travel and tourism, and includes a range of the large number of techniques used.

Fig. 22.2 Types of sales promotion

The benefits of sales promotion

The essential feature of all sales promotion techniques is that they are a temporary, short-term inducement to stimulate demand. Many sales promotions are undertaken in response to the activities of competitors to ensure that an organisation retains its share of the market. The fast-moving nature of travel and tourism means that managers are constantly having to react to fluctuations in demand from customers on a daily, weekly or seasonal basis. Unlike advertising, direct marketing and public relations activities, which are essentially long-term promotional tools, sales promotion gives an organisation the flexibility needed to be able to respond quickly to such changes.

As with other forms of marketing activity, it is important to evaluate the effectiveness of any sales promotion against its objectives. It is a relatively easy matter to measure sales or usage before and after a sales promotion and calculate a percentage increase or decrease in activity. The aim of some sales promotions is to clear current stock – for example, airline seats, unsold package holidays or self-catering apartments. It is difficult to measure whether a customer who has taken advantage of a special offer may well have paid the full price at a later date. In many respects, the answer to this question is irrelevant as long as the sales promotion fulfils the original objectives.

Activity

Choose a leading travel and tourism company with which you are familiar and list the various sales promotion techniques that it uses.

Direct marketing

One of the disadvantages levelled at advertising in the printed and broadcast media is that it is not always effective in reaching its intended audience. For example, an advertisement on local radio may be missed since it is often considered as a 'background' medium; similarly, a small classified advertisement in the travel columns of a Sunday supplement may be hard to see among many hundreds of others; or a television advertisement showing a product geared specifically to the needs of men will be of little interest to women watching it. Direct marketing, however, is rarely criticised for failing to reach its target audience. In fact, some people even go as far as likening the precision of direct marketing to a 'rifle', while the imprecise nature of advertising can be thought of as a 'shotgun'. Direct marketing is the term used to describe the various techniques that an organisation can use to sell its products and services on a personalised basis direct to the consumer, without the need for an intermediary. The most common direct-marketing methods used in travel and tourism are:

- Direct mail
- Telemarketing
- Door-to-door distribution
- Direct response advertising

Telemarketing is growing in importance in travel and tourism, particularly in the business-to-business sector, where one company will provide services and facilities for another. Its use in the consumer sector of the industry is limited, but it is occasionally used for selling timeshare products.

Door-to-door distribution is popular with hotels, restaurants, attractions and leisure facilities that want to capture a local market. A certain amount of market segmentation is possible, with particular postcode areas being targeted in terms of social class, family composition, age, etc.

Direct response advertising is widely used by travel and tourism organisations that want to create a mailing list at the same time as distributing brochures and other promotional materials. Any advertisement, whether it is on the television, on local radio, in a newspaper, in a magazine or on a billboard, that asks the customer to respond in some way falls within the category of direct response. Some organisations use freephone numbers such as 0800 and 0500, reduced rate 0345 numbers or a freepost address, in order to generate more responses.

Activity

Make a chart of 10 travel and tourism organisations, some local and some national, that use direct-marketing techniques to help sell their products, facilities and services. Add to the chart the type of direct-marketing activity each uses and the reasons why you think each was chosen by the organisation.

Direct mail

Direct mail is the best-known method of direct marketing used extensively by UK travel and tourism organisations. It can be very cost-effective when compared to advertising and is, therefore, ideally suited to smaller organisations. It is very flexible in terms of timing, budgets and targeting. A direct mail campaign can be actioned very quickly and aimed at particular target markets. Its uses in travel and tourism are many and varied, including:

- A specialist tour operator that automatically sends previous enquirers a copy of the current year's brochure.
- A seaside hotel that sends all its past guests a Christmas card.
- The conference officer for a major tourist city who sends a letter and leaflet featuring conference facilities in the city to the top 100 companies in the region.
- A travel agency that sends all its previous clients a regular news information sheet with details of latest discounts and travel products.
- A local authority that sends out a leaflet with its Council Tax bills giving details of its tourist facilities and events.
- A top tourist attraction that mails details of group rates and facilities to the major coach companies in the UK every year.

One of the most important aspects of a good direct mail campaign is the mailing list, which can either be created from existing information on customers or bought in from a specialist list broker or mailing house. Lists covering all parts of the country and every conceivable interest and lifestyle category are freely available. Larger direct mail campaigns can make use of sophisticated computer-based systems such as ACORN, PIN or MOSAIC, to target by postcode areas the individuals or families most likely to want to buy a particular product or service. The use of these systems will ensure the best possible results and cost efficiency by avoiding wastage by mailing to consumers who are not in the target group.

The basic steps needed for a successful direct mail campaign are:

1. Decide on the objectives of the campaign – for example, do you want to promote a new attraction?; increase off-peak use of a sports centre?; promote your tour packages to overseas travel agents?
2. Determine the budget.
3. Agree the timescale for the campaign.
4. Create the mailing list.
5. Devise the direct mail package (see below).
6. Carry out the mailing.
7. Do a follow-up mailing (optional).
8. Evaluate the results.

A typical direct mail package will consist of:

- A personalised letter.
- An envelope, which may be overprinted to match the letterhead (see Figure 22.3).
- A 'reply device', such as a freepost address or freephone telephone number.
- An insert, which would usually be a brochure, leaflet or discount voucher.

It takes considerable skill and experience to produce an effective direct mail letter that will both inform and persuade the reader to buy or use the product or service on offer. As with all promotional techniques, the AIDA principle should apply to the design of any direct mail campaign, including the accompanying letter. This states that any promotional item should:

- Attract *attention* by using colour, bold headings, striking graphics, etc.
- Maintain *interest* by keeping any wording as brief as possible, using language and images that the reader can relate to easily.
- Creating a *desire* to want to buy the product, or at least investigate further, by perhaps offering a discount or other incentive.
- Trigger *action* on the part of the reader by clearly stating what to do next, e.g. by including a telephone number or address to contact for further information.

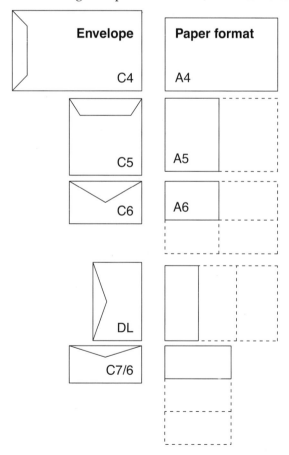

Fig. 22.3 Envelope and paper sizes for use in direct mail campaigns

Activity

Devise a direct mail package for a local tourist attraction that is aiming to increase its conference and incentive business.

Personal selling

Service industries such as travel and tourism rely heavily on the selling skills of those employed in order to achieve success. Selling is all about helping people to buy rather than selling them something they don't really want. Training in selling techniques is important for travel and tourism staff, particularly in the commercial sector. Planning prior to a sales conversation is essential, as is being able to recognise buying signals, such as nodding of the head, and signs of agreement from the customer. Closing the sale can be achieved by the taking of a deposit, credit card details or simply noting the customer's name and address. Element 22.3 looks in greater detail at the role of personal selling in relation to travel and tourism products and services.

Brochures

Brochures are one of the most common promotional materials used in travel and tourism today, aimed at informing potential buyers and, hopefully, converting their enquiries into sales. Tour operators rely on brochures to persuade customers to book with them, making the design, content and layout of a brochure of crucial importance. Some larger companies produce a range of brochures, geared exclusively to the needs of different segments of the market or different geographical areas, as shown in Figure 22.4.

Operators have to make sure that any material included in a brochure conforms to

Fig. 22.4 Brochures for different geographical regions (reproduced courtesy of Travelbag PLC)

UK and European Union regulations, including the Trades Description Act and Package Travel Directive. Price competition in many sectors of the travel and tourism industry, notably mass market tour operating, has led to the practice of producing further editions of an original brochure in the same season, to take account of variations in price and special offers. Element 22.2 looks in more detail at the importance of brochures and the role they play in selling holidays and other travel products.

Promotional techniques in action – Jorvik Viking Centre

Introduction

The Jorvik Viking Centre is independently owned by the York Archaeological Trust, a registered charity whose aim is to educate the public in archaeology through excavation, research, publication and presentation of its work. Opened in 1984 at a total cost of £2.6 million, and with visitor numbers approaching 10 million in total (see Table 22.1), Jorvik is considered to be at the forefront of 'heritage' attractions in the UK. It stands in the centre of the popular tourist city of York, on the site of an archaeological dig that took place between 1976 and 1981.

It was decided to incorporate the Jorvik Centre into the Coppergate shopping

Table 22.1 Visitor numbers for the Jorvik Viking Centre

Year	Number of visitors
1985	897,290
1986	868,445
1987	886,855
1988	865,909
1989	904,483
1990	846,225
1991	791,225
1992	785,028
1993	752,586
1994	691,514
1995	603,539

Source: Jorvik Viking Centre

development in York, housing it in a basement area as an interpretation of tenth-century life in the city. Jorvik has a 'dark ride', complete with authentic sounds and smells, life-size character figures (see Figure 22.5), plus a reconstruction of part of the excavation. There is also an exhibition of finds from the dig and a gift shop. The Jorvik Centre does not actually own the buildings or the land on which they stand. The land is owned by Land Securities, a subsidiary of Wimpey Construction, which built the whole of the Coppergate Centre. Jorvik pays a lease for the two shop units it occupies at ground and first floor level, plus a peppercorn rent for the underground exhibition area.

Fig. 22.5 One of the animated figures at Jorvik Viking Centre (reproduced courtesy of Jorvik Viking Centre)

Marketing of the Jorvik Centre

Marketing of the Centre began before it was built or even thought of, since the excavation was promoted through press and media locally, nationally and internationally. This helped to ensure that when the Centre opened in 1984, there was a 4-hour queue outside its doors! Promotional effort since the Centre opened has been targeted at the mass market, irrespective of age, sex or socio-economic grouping. Local residents, domestic and overseas tourists, conference and incentive visitors, special interest groups, clubs, societies and schools, have all been identified as target markets. Low season marketing and public relations (PR) activity are high on the list of Jorvik's promotional work. The annual Jorvik Viking Festival each February is an example of an off-peak promotional activity which attracts thousands of people, many on hotel weekend breaks. At a very quiet time of the year, hotels, guesthouses and shops have a guarantee of increased revenue, thanks to the marketing efforts at the Centre.

Some statistics of Jorvik's visitor characteristics are given in Tables 22.2 and 22.3.

Table 22.2 shows that more than half of all visitors travel in excess of 100 miles to reach the attraction, indicating that Jorvik has a national catchment. Table 22.3 demonstrates that the Centre is of greater appeal to those in professional occupations, rather than people with skilled manual jobs.

Table 22.2 Origins of visitors to Jorvik Viking Centre, 1992–93

Origin	Share (%)
UK visitors	
>100 miles	53.5
51–100 miles	26
26–50 miles	10
<25 miles + York	10.5
Overseas visitors	
USA	32
Australia	17
Other	50

Source: Jorvik Viking Centre

Table 22.3 Occupational status of visitors to Jorvik Viking Centre, 1992–93

Occupation	Share (%)
Professional	42
Retired	14.3
Skilled manual	9.4
Student	8.6
Teacher	7.8

Source: Jorvik Viking Centre

The marketing department at Jorvik employs a strategy of paid advertising and public relations activity. Their marketing campaign includes:

- Poster sites
- A colour bus
- Hot air balloon
- Mailshots
- Promotions
- Exhibitions
- The annual Jorvik Festival

The aim of the PR role is to keep the Centre in the public eye by means of 'free' publicity. This ranges from newspaper and magazine copy to television coverage at national and international level. Jorvik's high profile is thus retained to attract visitors and generate the revenue necessary to support the work of the Archaeological Trust in the city of York.

A winning formula

Jorvik has gained valuable publicity in the form of the many awards and commendations it has received since opening. It began winning accolades in its first year of operation when it captured the BTA Tourism Marketing Award for publications, followed by a special award from York City Council for outstanding contribution to tourism in the city. In 1985, it gained the Guild of Travel Writers' Award and in 1987 came the National Marketing Award from the Institute of Marketing and the International Travel Poster of the Year Award. Other awards have followed, plus regular placings in the English Tourist Board's list of most popular attractions.

The future at Jorvik

Any future changes at Jorvik will take into consideration the advances made in heritage presentation and interpretation during the decade since it opened, without compromising the academic integrity of the Centre by 'gimmickry'. The operators suggest that there may, for example, be an interactive display element incorporated into any planned refurbishment, animatronics or even virtual reality.

Jorvik has held on to its market share since opening and the challenge faced by the marketing department is to improve on this even further and increase visitor numbers to the pre-recession days of the late 1980s. As they say at the centre, 'the product is the message'.

(Information courtesy of Jorvik Viking Centre)

Case study discussion questions

1. What are the key promotional techniques used by the marketing department at Jorvik?
2. How does winning an award help boost the attraction's popularity?
3. Why do you think visitor numbers to the attraction have dropped in recent years?
4. What promotional strategy could Jorvik adopt to help stem the fall in visitor numbers?
5. Given the data on the origin of visitors to Jorvik, where should it be placing its paid advertising?

Assignment 22.1

Key promotional techniques in travel and tourism

Performance criteria satisfied: 22.1.1, 22.1.2, 22.1.3, 22.1.4

Core skills opportunities at level 3:   Communication   3.1, 3.2, 3.3, 3.4
Information technology   3.1, 3.2, 3.3
Application of number   3.1, 3.2, 3.3

Tasks

Working with a partner, you are to prepare a detailed report on the key promotional techniques used in the travel and tourism industry. Specifically, your report should:

- Describe the key promotional techniques used for marketing travel and tourism products and services.
- Describe the benefits of the key promotional techniques.
- Explain how the key promotional techniques are used in the marketing of travel and tourism products and services.
- Justify the most appropriate promotional techniques for travel and tourism organisations, in terms of relevance, cost and time.

Your report should be word processed and include relevant examples from within the travel and tourism industry, plus suitable diagrams, charts and statistics.

Element 22.2 Examine and prepare printed material for promoting travel and tourism products and services

Performance criteria
1. Describe the principal types of printed material used for promoting travel and tourism products and services.
2. Identify the cost of principal types of printed material used for promoting travel and tourism products and services.
3. Explain the role of printed brochures in promoting and selling inclusive tour holidays.
4. Describe the main sequence of events leading to the production and distribution of an inclusive tour brochure.
5. Compare the effectiveness of brochures from different inclusive tour operators.
6. Prepare a simple guide for a local tourist attraction.

Principal types of printed promotional material

All travel and tourism organisations, whether in the commercial or non-commercial sectors of the industry, rely heavily on a range of printed promotional materials to sell their products and services. The intangible nature of travel and tourism products gives promotional materials a special importance, since they must often persuade a potential purchaser to part with his or her money for a product they have never seen! Think how many times you have decided on visiting a particular resort, hotel or tourist attraction, based solely on its description in a promotional leaflet or brochure. The type of materials used varies between organisations, depending on their promotional budget, products, markets and distribution processes. Typical printed promotional items used by travel and tourism organisations include:

- Brochures
- Point-of-sale (POS) materials
- Posters
- Price lists
- Guides
- Leaflets

The particular role of brochures in travel and tourism is considered later in this element, together with aspects of brochure production and distribution (see page 308). We will now look in detail at the remaining types of printed promotional material in use in the travel and tourism industry.

Point-of-sale (POS) materials

POS materials are used to influence customers' actions and persuade them to buy a particular product or service. They are often used as part of a wider sales promotion campaign, reminding purchasers of a product they may have already seen elsewhere, e.g. in a newspaper advertisement or on a poster at a bus shelter. POS materials, as their name implies, are generally found at the point where a customer makes a purchase, e.g. in a travel agency, tourist information centre or a shop at a tourist attraction. Sometimes referred to as merchandising materials, common POS items used in the travel and tourism industry include:

- Posters
- Hanging cards
- Stickers
- Brochure display racks
- Illuminated signs
- Window displays
- TV monitors
- Pens and pencils
- Wall charts
- Calendars

All POS materials need to be carefully designed to gain maximum sales effect. Bright colours, striking graphics and famous personalities are often featured, along with the name and logo of the sponsoring organisation. As well as their immediate sales objective, well-designed POS materials can, over a period of time, help strengthen a company's image among its customers and the staff who sell it products and services.

Activity

With the full consent of the manager, investigate the range of point-of-sale materials used in a local travel agency.

Posters

Posters are a type of POS materials that have a special significance in travel and tourism. Since much of the industry is concerned with promoting destinations and attractions, effective posters can convey to prospective travellers the scenic beauty and cultural traditions of an area in a very powerful way. National tourist boards use posters as a way of creating images of their countries, distributing them to travel agencies, transport operators and tourist information centres for display. Posters can also form part of a larger advertising and promotional campaign, where they may be displayed on railway stations, by the sides of busy roads, on the London Underground and at bus shelters.

Price lists

Price lists are displayed in a range of types and sizes. The most simple will show, for example, the current season's prices for entry to a tourist attraction (see Figure 22.6). More complex lists produced by tour operators show varying prices for holidays and accommodation at different times of the year. These price grids are sometimes included in a company's main brochure, but may be printed separately as an insert to allow for price changes during the season.

Guides

In addition to the published holiday and travel guides on sale in high street news-agents, most tourist areas will produce their own guides on where to stay, what to do, where to eat, where to shop, etc., to help publicise their destinations to tourists. In the UK these are available from a variety of sources, including:

1. *National tourist boards* – the English, Scottish, Wales and Northern Ireland Tourist Boards, all produce informative guides for prospective travellers to their region.
2. *Regional tourist boards* – co-ordinate the 'where to stay' guides in their respective regions.
3. *Local authorities* – the tourism departments of county, district and city councils are active in publishing area guides, to raise awareness of their localities and to provide information on tourist amenities and facilities.

These three providers work in partnership with private sector operators of tourist accommodation and facilities when compiling their tourist guides.

Leaflets

Leaflets are a simple and inexpensive way of conveying information about travel and tourism products and services. For organisations on a tight budget, leaflets may be printed in a single colour on A4 white paper, while those with more to spend can choose from a wide variety of colours, sizes and thickness of paper. Full colour leaflets tend to give the best effect, but are more expensive than single- or two-colour printing (see Figure 22.7).

Activity

Investigate what brochures and leaflets are produced to market your local area to tourists. What image do the promotional materials you have collected portray of your locality and what products are they selling?

The role of brochures

The importance of the brochure in selling overseas package holidays (inclusive tours) cannot be overstated. It is the tour operator's main promotional and selling tool,

Spring 1996

Telephone: 01372 729560
Fax: 01372 725050

1996 OPENING TIMES & PRICES.
SUMMER NIGHTS & FRIGHT NIGHTS

CHESSINGTON WORLD OF ADVENTURES SEASON:
23rd March 1996 - 3rd November 1996 .
10am - 5/6pm (except Summer Nights & Fright Nights).

PRICES   (PRICES CORRECT AT TIME OF ISSUE.)
Adults   £16.50
Children   £13.00   (4 - 14 inclusive)
OAPS   £7.25
Special prices for groups of 15 or more.

Summer Nights
20th July- 1st September 1996.
Experience Chessington World of Adventures by day or by night as the Park remains open until 9.30pm. You can enjoy up to 11½ hours of fun and thrills or an evening of pure excitement.
Special evening entry prices between 5pm and 7pm:
Adults   £9.50
Children   £7.00
OAPs   £5.00

Fright Nights
26th & 27th October and 2nd & 3rd November 1996.
The Park remains open until 9.30pm for it's end of season ghostly extravaganza of evening entertainment with lasers, lights and special effects plus all the rides in the dark!
For further information on 1996 opening times and prices please call:

VISITOR INFORMATION LINE: 01372 727227.

An Attraction in The Tussauds Group
Reg. Office: York Court, Allsop Place,
London NW1 5LR

Chessington World of Adventures Ltd
Chessington
Surrey
KT9 2NE

Registered in England
Registration No. 408533

Fig. 22.6 Price list for a major tourist attraction *(reproduced courtesy of Chessington World of Adventures)*

Fig. 22.7 An effective full colour leaflet *(reproduced courtesy of York City Council)*

hoping to persuade clients to book with the company rather than go with one of its competitors. Given the crucial role that brochures play in marketing holidays, it is small wonder that UK-based tour operators produce more than 100 million copies every year! In addition to the general aim of persuading potential holidaymakers to make a booking, tour operators' brochures have a number of distinct functions, including:

- To accurately present products and services to the reader.
- To convey an image of the company.
- To convert an enquiry into a sale.
- To offer a means of booking a holiday.
- To explain booking and contractual conditions.
- To present the information within the bounds of current UK and European Union legislation.

Accuracy of the information contained in any tour operator's brochure is essential, since there are now strict legal sanctions for failure to comply with relevant legislation, including the EU Package Travel Directive and the Trade Descriptions Act. Tour operators that are members of the Association of British Travel Agents (ABTA) are further bound by the Association's Tour Operators' Code of Conduct, which includes detailed regulations concerning the content and presentation of brochures. The Code states that:

> Every brochure published by or in the name of any ABTA member shall contain clear, legible, comprehensive and accurate information to enable the client to exercise an informed judgement in making his choice.

Element 19.2 looked further at the importance of brochures for selling UK-based tour operators' products.

Brochure production and distribution

Most mass market overseas holiday brochures are distributed to travel agents in the August or September of the season before the one to which they relate, i.e. brochures for the 1997 summer season will go on sale in August or September of 1996. Winter sun and winter sports are scheduled to be distributed in April or May for holidays taking place in the following winter period, i.e. a February 1997 winter sun holiday will be featured in a brochure distributed in April or May 1996. The brochure production process, however, begins well in advance of these dates, with only the details of pricing being left as late as possible in order to match or beat competitors' prices, or change prices in response to other unforeseen circumstances, for example, fluctuations in currency rates. Research for a new tour programme can begin as early as two years before the final brochure is published, while detailed work on brochure preparation generally begins 12 months before the publication date.

Figure 22.8 shows the main stages in the brochure production process, which applies equally well to both mass market operators and smaller, specialist tour companies.

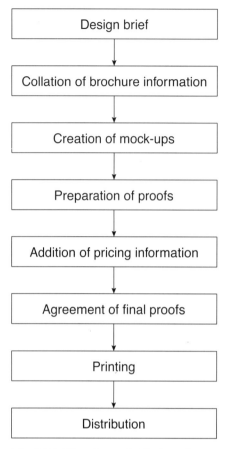

Fig. 22.8 The stages in the brochure production process

Design brief

Figure 22.8 shows us that the first stage in the process is the formulation of the design brief, which for major tour operators will involve the various product managers and relevant staff from the marketing department, together with in-house or agency designers. The written brief will focus on the brochure's content, style and extent, i.e. the number of pages, illustrations and photographs, plus details of the tour programmes, i.e. which resorts and accommodation are to be included. It will also detail what other general information needs to be included, such as booking conditions, lists of contents, airport information, etc. The brief may also include details of the total budget for the production of the brochure, although this is sometimes the subject of a separate process.

Collation of brochure information

Once the design brief has been agreed by all parties, work on collating the information to go into the brochure can begin in earnest. This will involve:

1. *Writing the brochure copy* – specialist copywriters will be responsible for the text of the brochure, mixing factual information on resorts and accommodation with language that will tempt potential holidaymakers to make a booking.
2. *Choosing photographs* – some may already be available from previous brochures or an in-house library. Other sources of photographic material are specialist, commercial libraries, airlines, tourist boards and even holidaymakers themselves! The important point about photographs is to include only good-quality material with which the target market can readily identify, and which gives a true representation of the accommodation, resorts and facilities.
3. *Adding ancillary information* – such as details of insurance, car hire, booking conditions, discounts, health, visa and passport requirements, etc.

While specialists are working on these three tasks, attention will also be paid to the design of any necessary artwork for inclusion in the brochure, plus the all-important front cover. Since the cover is what the customer will see first, it must be striking and appealing, while at the same time projecting an image that the prospective holiday-maker can immediately relate to. You wouldn't normally expect to see, for example, a picture of a group of teenagers relaxing by the side of a pool on the front of a brochure targeted at the family market. Tour operators will spend a considerable amount of time with their design agency to select the most suitable front cover image. Nowadays, many of the pictures on front covers are swamped by a mass of other sales messages, such as 'free child places', 'early booking discounts' and 'price guarantees', all designed to appeal to today's cost-conscious holidaymakers.

Creation of mock-ups

Working to the agreed brief, designers will next make a mock-up of the finished brochure, leaving out detailed information and photographs at this stage. This is presented to the product managers and marketing staff at the tour operating company for their agreement. Changes can still be made to the overall design and layout at this stage if the client is unhappy with something.

Preparation of proofs

Once the mock-up is agreed, the text is typeset and the photographs and artwork added to produce a first proof of the brochure. These are checked by staff at the tour operator, including the legal department, to ensure accuracy of the text.

Addition of pricing information

While the design process has been underway, the contracting staff at the tour company will have been finalising the prices of the holidays ready for insertion into the pricing panels left by the designers.

Agreement of final proofs

When prices have been inserted, the tour operator will agree a final set of full colour proofs before the brochure is sent for printing.

Printing

Depending on the number of copies to be produced, printing may be undertaken in the UK or overseas, where preferential rates are sometimes available. Small, specialist operators may produce a complete brochure in-house using a desktop publishing (DTP) system, which can offer greater flexibility and reduced cost. Once printing is completed, the brochures are ready to be distributed to travel agents or direct to the public.

Brochure distribution

The precise nature of brochure distribution will depend on whether the inclusive tour is being sold direct to the public or through a travel agent. Since the majority of package holidays are booked through travel agents, distributing the brochures quickly to agents is of paramount importance to the tour operator. An operator's top agents, i.e. those who have historically sold the most holidays, will receive preferential treatment in the early distribution of brochures. The tour operator will arrange bulk distribution, either through its own system or on a contract basis with a specialist company such as BP Travel Trade Services (see case study below). Agents with fewer sales will receive smaller numbers of brochures and less visits from the tour operator's sales representatives. Point-of-sale (POS) materials, such as posters, window displays and stickers, may also be sent out with brochure supplies for use by the agents in raising awareness of the launch.

Where the tour operator sells direct to its customers, in response to advertising in the consumer press and other promotional techniques, individual copies of the new brochure will be mailed direct to clients who have already made a request. It is common practice to send brochures to clients who have previously booked a holiday with the company in the hope of retaining their custom. The tour company will store the names and addresses of enquirers on a database and use this information for future mailings and for management purposes, e.g. calculating the number of enquiries that turn into firm bookings or the number of brochures distributed to generate one booking, known as the conversion ratio. Some tour operators will use the services of specialist mailing and distribution companies to distribute brochures to clients rather than carry out this function themselves, thereby allowing staff to concentrate more fully on the job of selling holidays.

Brochure distribution – BP Travel Trade Services

Introduction

Established in 1972, BP Travel Trade Services is a commercial operation that provides a range of marketing and distribution services to the travel industry in the UK. With a purpose-built 2.4 million cubic feet warehouse and distribution facility at Ashford in Kent, close to the UK end of the Channel Tunnel, BP offers travel and tourism organisations a number of specialist services, including:

1. *Bulk brochure and literature distribution* – probably the best known of BP's services, this computerised service offers clients an effective means of distributing

brochures, timetables, late availability and special offer sheets, promotions, display materials and commercial information. The service is used extensively by tour operators wishing to service the needs of travel agents.

2. *Brochurebank* – an on-line brochure-ordering system for travel agents, accessible via viewdata systems including Fastrak and Istel.
3. *Mailing services* – frequent mailings to coach operators, UK and European travel agents and numerous other mailings by post, courier or fax. Includes 'Mailbag', a twice weekly mailing to UK high street travel agencies and 'Mailbag Coach World', meeting the needs of more than 3000 coach operators.
4. *Field marketing services* – through its sister company 'The Network', BP offers audits of brochure displays in travel agencies, checking of brochure stock levels and re-ordering, briefings for travel retailers on product benefits, roadshow management, market research and 'mystery shoppers'.
5. *Database management* – a range of services related to direct marketing, including mailing list management, list enhancement, updating and manipulation, plus mailshot production.
6. *On-line services* – used extensively by travel agents, these include Holidayfinder, Flightfinder and Brochurebank.
7. *Telecommunications* – BP operates a computer integrated call centre servicing its consumer marketing operation (see below).
8. *Printing services* – in-house newsletter printing with a same day despatch option for urgent news.

Consumer marketing

In addition to its travel trade services, BP also offers a professional fulfilment service to support a company's own promotional or advertising campaign. It operates a call centre that is open seven days a week, throughout the day and evening, to answer calls from prospective travellers. Whether enquirers telephone, fax or write, BP undertakes to despatch brochures and other promotional materials promptly.

(Information courtesy of BP Travel Trade Services)

Case study discussion questions

1. What are the main benefits to a travel agency of using the services of a company such as BP Travel Trade Services?
2. What problems might a small travel company encounter when it offers its own enquiry and brochure distribution service to prospective travellers?
3. What changes in brochure distribution techniques are likely to occur up to and beyond the year 2000?
4. What role is new technology likely to play in helping holidaymakers choose between different destinations and holiday products in the future?
5. Does the location of BP Travel Trade Services give it an advantage over its competitors?

Effectiveness of brochures

Brochures from tour operators have one principal aim: to sell their products. How well they achieve this objective will depend on a number of interrelated design features, including:

- The appeal of the front cover.
- The quality of the photographs used.
- The effectiveness of the artwork.
- The quality of the paper.
- The use of colour.

In addition to these specific design factors, brochure effectiveness will also depend on a number of 'product' factors, such as:

- The price of the holidays.
- The availability of child discounts.
- The timing of flights.
- The destinations featured in the programme.
- The quality of accommodation used.
- The availability of flights from regional airports.

If you add to this such factors as the speed of brochure distribution, image of the operator, selling skills of the agents or tour operator's staff, after-sales service, promotional support and product knowledge, you can begin to see that, although the brochure is of crucial importance in the selling of holidays, other factors are involved in its overall effectiveness.

Assignment 22.2

The role of printed material in travel and tourism

Performance criteria satisfied: 22.2.1, 22.2.2, 22.2.3, 22.2.4, 22.2.5

Core skills opportunities at level 3:	Communication	3.1, 3.2, 3.3, 3.4
	Information technology	3.1, 3.2, 3.3
	Application of number	3.1, 3.2, 3.3

Situation

While on work experience with the marketing manager of your nearby regional tourist board, you are asked to help with the running of a seminar for hotel and tourist attraction members of the tourist board.

Tasks

Working with a partner, you are to research and deliver a presentation to the rest of your group on 'The role of printed material in travel and tourism'. In particular, your presentation should:

- Describe the main types of printed material used for promoting travel and tourism products and services.
- Identify the costs of the main types of printed material.
- Explain the role of brochures in promoting and selling package holidays.
- Describe the main sequence of events in the production and distribution of a package holiday brochure.
- Compare the effectiveness of brochures from different tour operators.

Your presentation should include detailed information gathered from an in-depth investigation of the full range of printed material. You should negotiate specific work tasks with the other members of your group to ensure equality of work load. You will be assessed on the content of the presentation and the quality of delivery.

Element 22.3　Examine the role of personal selling in relation to travel and tourism products and services

Performance criteria

1. Describe the importance of personal selling to the successful promotion of travel and tourism products and services.
2. Examine, using examples, the techniques used by a salesperson to sell travel and tourism products and services.
3. Identify the role of technology in successful personal selling.

Introduction

We are all involved in some form of selling activity every day of our lives. It might be a daughter trying to persuade her father to take her to the cinema or a schoolboy persuading his friend to lend him his bike. However, to many people in the UK, selling is a dirty word! There is no doubt that selling has an image problem and that, as a nation, we tend to look down on people who sell goods and services for a living, whether it is electrical goods in a shop, a telesales operator for a local newspaper or a sales representative for an engineering firm. This is rather surprising when we consider the continuing shift away from a manufacturing towards a service economy in this country and the fact that so many people derive their livelihood either directly or indirectly from selling.

Most people who work in travel and tourism are involved in some form of personal selling activity. It might be closing the sale on a two-week holiday to Florida, booking a group into an outdoor pursuits centre, working on the reception in a hotel, handling cash or answering enquiries from customers. Personal selling involves persuasive communication between two parties, the buyer and the seller. It is important to remember that the 'buyer' does not always part with cash in order to enjoy the facilities on offer. Some tourism facilities provided by local authorities will be provided free of charge – for example, museums and tourist information centres, financed from local and national sources.

In travel and tourism, it is easy to think of many situations in which selling takes place, such as:

- An overseas representative of a tour operator selling tickets for an evening excursion.
- A travel agent selling an airline ticket to a client.
- A conference organiser selling the benefits of a particular hotel to a company.
- A receptionist in an arts centre selling a course of lessons to a couple.
- A ticket agency employee selling a pair of tickets to see 'Grease'.

- A sales representative selling equipment insurance to the owner of an activity holiday centre .
- A fast-food outlet selling a family meal for four.
- Airline staff selling duty-free goods during a flight.

Even those people who are not directly employed in a sales capacity come into contact with selling as customers, often expecting the highest levels of customer service and attention.

The importance of personal selling in travel and tourism

Personal selling is an essential component of the marketing process in travel and tourism organisations. Selling is, however, much more than just part of a wider marketing activity; it should be seen as a continuous process that can help cement customer relationships, build customer loyalty and provide lasting benefits in an enhanced level of customer service.

Selling involves communication between a buyer and a seller, which is designed to persuade the customer to purchase the products or services on offer. It can be thought of as the culmination of all the marketing activities that have taken place beforehand in the organisation. It involves matching a customer's needs with the goods and services on offer; the better the match, the more lasting the relationship between the seller and the buyer.

All staff employed in travel and tourism are likely to be employed in some form of 'selling' during the course of their work, although the importance of selling will vary between different organisations. The majority of organisations in the travel and tourism industry operate in the private sector, so that selling will be geared towards meeting commercial objectives. Public and voluntary sector organisations will still be involved in selling products and services, but will be using selling to achieve different objectives, perhaps attracting under-represented local groups to a tourist attraction or campaigning for a charitable cause.

Not surprisingly, the prime objective of selling is to make a sale! This may seem a glaringly obvious statement, but there are other related aims to the selling process, including:

- Generating repeat business.
- Meeting planned increases in sales volume.
- Increasing customer satisfaction levels.
- Increasing profitability.
- Securing competitive advantage.
- Targeting specific sectors of the market.
- Raising awareness of a new facility.

Simply saying that the principal objective of selling is to make a sale, also masks the very complex nature of the sales process in travel and tourism, involving the use of a whole set of principles, processes and techniques, linked to personal, social and interpersonal skills.

Selling travel and tourism products

Selling leisure and tourism products is very different to selling other goods such as televisions, cars and dishwashers. The difference lies in the nature of the travel and tourism 'product' itself. Travel and tourism products have a number of unique characteristics, including:

1. *Intangibility* – travel and tourism is all about selling 'experiences', rather than tangible goods.
2. *Perishability* – a hotel bed or airline seat not sold today cannot be resold tomorrow.
3. *Seasonality* – much tourist activity in the UK is concentrated in the summer months.
4. *The fact that products are often consumed at the point of production* – e.g. overseas package holidays.

Travel and tourism is essentially a 'people business', where the staff are often an essential component of the experience the customer is buying. If we take the example of a coach holiday bought by an elderly couple, much of the enjoyment they experience on their holiday will be directly related to the attitude of the staff who serve them, be they waiters, coach drivers, chambermaids or staff at attractions. The same applies in travel and tourism closer to home, perhaps at a seaside café or the local swimming pool. Viewed from this perspective, you can see that the quality of a travel or tourism product is closely allied to the quality of staff delivering it.

Sales techniques used in travel and tourism organisations

Successful selling is a structured activity, not just 'something that happens'. Figure 22.9 shows the six key stages of the sales process in travel and tourism.

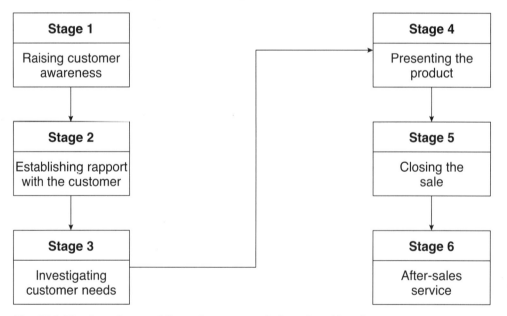

Fig. 22.9 The key stages of the sales process in travel and tourism

Raising customer awareness

Although not strictly speaking a sales technique, raising awareness of a travel and tourism product or service is an essential prerequisite to any selling activity; put simply, if customers are not aware of a product's existence, it will be extremely hard to sell it to them! Element 22.1 showed us that travel and tourism organisations use a wide range of promotional techniques to raise awareness of their facilities and products. Sometimes referred to as the 'promotional mix', these include:

- Advertising
- Public relations
- Sales promotion
- Direct marketing

If we take the example of a high street travel agency and how it makes potential clients aware of its products, it is likely to use a number of techniques, including:

- Its own advertising in local and regional media.
- Advertising carried out by the companies whose products it sells.
- Window displays and point-of-sale materials (see Figure 22.10).
- Brochure displays in the agency.
- Late availability cards.
- Newsletters mailed to existing clients.
- Attendance at holiday shows and exhibitions.
- Presentation evenings arranged in conjunction with tour operators and airlines.
- Press releases to the local media resulting in 'free publicity'.

Travel and tourism organisations operating in the public and voluntary sectors will use a similar array of techniques to attract their customers.

Activity

Carry out a small-scale survey of friends to find out how they were made aware of a recent travel and tourism product that they purchased. Present your findings as a bar chart, indicating the least and most common techniques.

Establishing rapport with the customer

Once a customer has been made aware of a product or service, the true art of selling can begin. The broad nature of the travel and tourism industry means that there will be a wide range of customers, of all ages and social backgrounds, with varying budgets. It is important that sales staff are sympathetic to the specific needs of different customers and respectful of their wishes. Being a very wide-ranging industry means also that the actual setting where the selling takes place within travel and tourism will differ from sector to sector. Selling may, for example, take place:

- *In a shop* – e.g. when buying souvenirs at a tourist attraction.
- *In a hotel* – e.g. when purchasing a ticket for an excursion or using the fitness suite.

Fig. 22.10 Window displays are used to raise awareness of products and services

- *In a restaurant* – e.g. when buying a family meal.
- *At home* – e.g. when ordering tickets for the theatre over the telephone.
- *In an agency* – e.g. when buying a holiday or travel ticket.
- *In an office* – e.g. when finalising the venue for a business conference.

Whatever the location for the sales activity, the principle of engaging the customer in conversation, or establishing rapport, still applies. In order to meet the objective of making a sale, this initial task of engaging the customer in conversation is important, since it gives the salesperson the opportunity to gain the trust of the customer and to discover his or her needs. Some customers are suspicious of any attempts to sell them products, often preferring to make their own decisions on product selection and purchase. They may consider sales staff to be 'pushy' or arrogant, but even such reluctant customers can be put in the right frame of mind to buy a particular product or service if they receive a friendly and attentive level of service.

First impressions count!

In service industries such as travel and tourism, first impressions are always important. This is particularly the case in a selling situation, when customers sometimes have to make an instant decision as to whether they can trust the person who is trying to sell them a product or service. There are a number of factors that influence customers and may ultimately make them decide to buy or go elsewhere, including:

1. *The sales environment* – is the facility clean, tidy, well maintained, well designed, the right temperature, with good air quality?
2. *The appearance of the sales staff* – are they well dressed, of pleasant appearance, knowledgeable, business-like?
3. *Attitude towards the customer* – are they welcoming, interested, attentive, willing to listen, confident, professional?

It is advisable for sales staff to avoid using the phrase 'can I help you?' as a way of striking up a sales conversation. This sort of 'closed' question simply invites the reply 'no thank you, I'm just looking'. It is far better to ask more 'open' questions, such as:

- 'How many times have you visited the attraction before?'
- 'Which particular National Park are you visiting?'
- 'Which country are you thinking of visiting?'
- 'Which company have you travelled with in the past?'

The secret of developing 'open' questions is to begin with the words 'where', 'why', 'who', 'when', 'which', 'what' and 'how'.

Sales staff must be conscious of the signals, sometimes hidden, that customers give when in a selling situation. A customer who is obviously in a hurry will not thank a sales assistant who asks complicated questions and insists on engaging in a lengthy conversation.

Having established a rapport with the customer and gained a degree of trust, the salesperson's next task is to investigate his or her needs.

Activity

Working with another member of your group, change the following 'closed' questions into 'open' questions:

1. Are you travelling to France?
2. Do you want to go on the excursion?
3. Do you want a window seat in the coach?
4. Do you want a morning flight?
5. Do you want that brochure?

Investigating customer needs

The aim of this stage of the selling process is to help the customer to state his or her needs clearly, so that the salesperson has the best chance of presenting a product or service that the customer will want to buy. Again, it is helpful to ask 'open' questions, rather than those that call for yes/no replies, to give the customer more opportunity to express a preference and to help the conversation to continue. It is important, also, not to assume that you know a customer's needs and that the process of investigating customer requirements is a two-way affair, with the salesperson acting in a supportive role.

In the case of a travel agency, the following are the types of question that will help the salesperson build up a picture of the client's needs:

- What is the size of the party travelling?
- Are there any children and, if so, what ages are they?
- When do you want to travel and for how long?
- Where do you want to go?
- Is there a particular company you prefer to travel with?
- How do you want to travel?
- How much do you expect to pay?
- Does anybody in the party have any special requirements?

Customers will not necessarily know the answers to all the questions a salesperson may be asking them, so it is important to start with easy questions to which they can give an immediate answer and go into more depth as the sales conversation continues.

Presenting the product

Having determined the customer's needs, the next stage of the sales process is to present the product to the customer. Presenting a travel and tourism product to a customer is rather more difficult than, say, showing him an electric iron or toaster in a shop. The intangible nature of the products means that sales staff are often showing the customer brochures and other publicity material to help them make a decision. This indicates the crucial importance of well-designed promotional items to effective sales in travel and tourism.

The key to success in this stage of the sales process is to concentrate on three types of statement during the product presentation, namely:

1. *Features statement* – involves highlighting the features of a particular product or service to the customer; for example, the number of rooms in a hotel or the facilities on offer at a resort complex. Often the customer's reaction is one of indifference at this stage.
2. *Advantages statement* – indicates what the product or service can do in general for the customer; for example, the fact that a departure time of 15.30 for a flight means that the client will not have to rise early to get to the airport. Again the reaction may be that the customer needs a little more specific information and persuasion.
3. *Benefits statement* – expresses specifically what the product can do for the individual customer. The information is selected on the basis of the customer's needs and is seen to be entirely relevant and easier to absorb.

Product knowledge is crucial to the success or otherwise of this part of the selling process. To enable them to speak with authority and confidence, staff must familiarise themselves with the features of particular products and take every opportunity to experience the products and facilities for themselves.

Handling objections

One aspect of the sales process that often occurs at this stage is the need to handle objections from the customer. These may be genuine – perhaps based on price or availability of services – or they may be the result of a customer being offered insufficient choice by the salesperson. Alternatively, there may be an additional need not already identified to the member of sales staff. Whatever the reason, it is important to respect the wishes of customers and perhaps investigate further in order to fully match the product to their particular requirements.

Closing the sale

With all objections having been successfully overcome, we are now at the stage of getting the customer to make a commitment, sometimes referred to as 'closing the sale'. Throughout all the sequences of the sales process, sales staff use their product knowledge and communication skills to match customer needs with identified products and services. Rapport is established and the benefits of a selection of products are highlighted. However, none of these actions commits the customer to buying the product or service, or to doing anything at all. Helping the customer to move from 'I'd like' to 'I'll buy' is what this part of the sales process is all about.

Staff should be continually looking for buying signals from the customer to trigger the process of closing the sale. Statements such as 'that sounds fine' or 'yes, I like that' clearly indicate a desire on the part of the customer to buy. When such signals are evident, the member of staff should begin to finalise the deal, remembering that clients should never be forced into making a decision that they may later regret.

Not every sales conversation will necessarily end in a sale; what is important from the organisation's point of view is to end up with the best possible outcome to the process. For large purchases, customers may wish to consider the benefits in greater detail, or discuss the sale with other people, before making a commitment to buy. In this situation, sales staff can only ensure that the customer has been given excellent customer service throughout, thus increasing the chances of an eventual positive sales outcome.

After-sales service

It is important for all organisations and staff involved in selling to remember that the process doesn't end when the customer has parted with his or her money. Just as we expect an after-sales service for consumer and household items we buy, the sellers of travel and tourism products too must offer this service to their customers. Adding a new customer's details to an existing database should be the first step in developing a long-term relationship that will hopefully benefit both the travel and tourism organisation and the customer.

Activity

Working with a partner, role play the situation of a member of the public being sold a 10-day coach tour of the Highlands of Scotland by a travel agent. Ask another member of your group to evaluate how the 'seller' performed in relation to each of the key stages of the sales process.

Technology and personal selling

Companies in the travel and tourism industry have always been at the forefront of using new technology equipment and systems to help their businesses run as effectively as possible. Using the correct equipment, even the smallest tour operator or independent travel agent, for example, can now:

- Make computerised reservations on behalf of clients.
- Investigate and confirm fares and prices.
- Access principals' databases to check availability of products and services.
- Print and issue tickets and other travel documents.
- Provide accounting and other management information.
- Access information on countries, weather, health and visa requirements.
- Fax or telex a manifest (a list of passengers) anywhere in the world.
- Accept payment by EFT (electronic funds transfer).
- Target selected customers for promotional purposes.

The VDUs and personal computers that are now so common in all travel and tourism organisations are also effective aids to the selling of products and services. The speed with which they interpret and display data means that the salesperson has immediate information on, for example, the availability of a particular holiday or flight, the price of alternative travel arrangements or the time of the next available train service. In many respects, new technology equipment often relieves the salesperson of the need to remember detailed information and gives him or her more time to devote to practising customer care skills.

The introduction of laptop and notebook computers has meant that salespeople who are on the move or working partly from home can still access data from their work base. Information such as sales volume per outlet, number of telephone enquiries and sales conversion rates are all available remotely with the help of the correct modem link.

Technology is also used in retail and catering outlets to keep a check on the availability of stock and take payment for goods, sometimes employing EPOS (electronic point-of-sale) systems.

Assignment 22.3

The role of personal selling in travel and tourism

Performance criteria satisfied: 22.3.1, 22.3.2, 22.3.3

Core skills opportunities at level 3:   Communication   3.1, 3.2, 3.3, 3.4
Information technology   3.1, 3.2, 3.3
Application of number   3.1, 3.2, 3.3

Tasks

You are to prepare a detailed report on the role of personal selling in travel and tourism. In particular, your report should:

- Describe the importance of personal selling to the successful promotion of travel and tourism products and services.
- Examine the techniques used by a salesperson to sell travel and tourism products and services.
- Identify the role of technology in successful personal selling.

Your report should be word processed and include relevant diagrams, charts and statistics.

Examine the role of advertising in promoting travel and tourism products and services

---

Performance criteria

1. Describe the benefits of advertising to the promotion of travel and tourism products and services.
2. Describe the benefits of specific advertising media in the promotion of specific travel and tourism products and services.
3. Examine the role of advertising campaigns for travel and tourism products and services.

Introduction

There are many definitions of advertising in use today, including the following from the American Marketing Association, which states that it is:

> *Any paid form of non-personal presentation of ideas, goods or services by an identified sponsor.*

All definitions stress the point that advertising involves payment, either by an individual company, a sponsor or a non-commercial body, such as a government department or local authority. Although advertising in general is very widespread in the UK, its use in travel and tourism is fairly restricted. This may seem hard to understand, particularly if we think of the number of travel advertisements on the television, in the newspapers and on commercial radio, particularly around Christmas time every year. This is the peak advertising time for most travel operators when organisations try to persuade potential holidaymakers to book early. It is only the larger travel companies that have the financial resources to be able to mount expensive nationwide television advertising campaigns. Smaller operators rely on selective advertising in the classified pages of newspapers and in specialist magazines. In an industry dominated by small operators, travel and tourism organisations have to make every promotional pound count and so devote their attention more to 'below the line' activities such as PR and sales promotion, rather than spend their limited budgets on extensive advertising campaigns.

The two main types of advertising in travel and tourism are:

1. *Consumer advertising* – when an organisation such as a tour operator or tourist attraction advertises direct to the public, e.g. Hoseasons Holidays placing an advertisement in the *Daily Mirror*, or a town museum advertising on local radio.

2. *Trade advertising* – sometimes known as business-to-business advertising, for example when a tour operator advertises its products in the *Travel Trade Gazette* or a coach company places an advertisement in *Travel GBI* newspaper.

The benefits of advertising

Advertising is considered by many people working in travel and tourism to be the most effective promotional channel, when compared with 'below the line' techniques such as direct mail, public relations and sales promotions. It can, however, also be an expensive medium, particularly when a campaign includes exposure on television and in national newspapers and magazines (see Table 22.4).

Table 22.4 Costs of full-page black and white advertisements in national newspapers

Newspaper	Cost (£)
Daily Mirror	25,900
The Daily Telegraph	36,500
Daily Mail	30,240
Financial Times	30,912
The Times	17,000
The Guardian	15,500
The People	21,750
The Observer	23,750
Sunday Mirror	20,500
The Sunday Times	47,000
News of the World	35,700

Source: BRAD

By choosing to advertise its products and services in any of the available media, a travel and tourism organisation can:

1. *Gain wide exposure to an audience* – most households in Britain have a television and radio, while sales of daily newspapers are more than 15 million.
2. *Target selected customers* – careful selection of media can help an organisation to segment its market by region, age, gender, social class, hobbies, etc.
3. *Present a creative image* – the use of colour, visual effects, graphics and sound, offers an advertiser maximum creativity and originality.
4. *React quickly to circumstances* – most advertising can be placed within a short period of time, thereby allowing organisations to capitalise on events and gain competitive advantage.
5. *Reinforce a message* – advertising can be combined with other promotional techniques to act as a reminder to viewers, readers and listeners.

Each advertising medium has its own benefits and disadvantages, as the next sections of this element demonstrate.

Advertising media

The term media is used in marketing to mean the various channels of communication an organisation can use to advertise its products or services (a single channel is known as a medium). It is important for travel and tourism organisations to seek the advice of professionals before deciding which media to choose. Smaller operators will not have the experience to gauge which medium will be the most effective for their particular products and may, therefore, be wasting their money. As well as working within budget limits, media selection will also depend on the target audience, i.e. the number and type of potential customers that the organisation is trying to reach (the coverage), as well as the number of times the advertiser wishes the message to be communicated to the audience (the frequency). All types of media will provide detailed data on their coverage and circulation, as well as detailed demographic and 'lifestyle' information on their readers/listeners/viewers. This information is usually presented in the form of a rate card.

The more an organisation knows about its existing and potential customers, the better the chance it has of selecting the right media to communicate its message. Market research, therefore, is crucial to effective media selection.

Types of advertising media

The principal media used most frequently by travel and tourism organisations are :

- Newspapers and magazines, including trade newspapers and journals
- Television, including teletext
- Commercial radio
- Cinema advertising
- Outdoor advertising
- Computers and the Internet

Activity

With reference to a travel and tourism organisation with which you are familiar, investigate the advertising media used most frequently. Explain why each particular medium was chosen and comment on its effectiveness.

Newspapers and magazines

The printed media are by far the largest group in the UK in terms of the amount spent by advertisers. The British are avid readers and buyers of newspapers and magazines, which is why they are extensively used by organisations wishing to promote their products and services. The total average daily sale of newspapers in the UK is in the region of 15 million copies, with *The Sun* and *The News of the World* being the most popular daily and Sunday newspaper respectively at the present time. Advertisers have a choice of over 9000 different magazines from which to choose. The main advantages of newspapers and magazines from the advertisers' point of view are:

- They are relatively cheap when compared with other media.
- Messages can be sent internationally, nationally, regionally or locally, depending on which publication is chosen.
- Specific segments of the market can be targeted, e.g. readers with an ABC1 social classification are more likely to read the 'quality' newspapers such as *The Times*, *The Independent* or *The Daily Telegraph*.
- Readers with specialist interests can be targeted, e.g. an organisation specialising in offering garden tours can advertise in magazines devoted entirely to the subject of gardening.
- Reply coupons can be included in an advertisement as a way of compiling a database or mailing list.
- Advertisements can normally be placed at very short notice, so giving the medium great flexibility.

As far as disadvantages are concerned, some people point to the static nature of a newspaper or magazine advertisement, poor quality printing (although new technologies have meant that excellent results are now achievable) and the poor impact some advertisements can have, particularly if they are included among many hundreds selling very similar goods and services. An example of this would be the classified advertisements in the travel sections of the 'broadsheet' Sunday newspapers, which at certain times of the year are very crowded.

Trade newspapers and journals, such as *Travel Weekly*, *Travel Agent*, *Travel Trade Gazette*, *Leisure Management* and *Caterer & Hotelkeeper*, enable travel and tourism organisations to communicate with their fellow professionals in the industry and inform them of new developments in products and services.

Television

Television is the most powerful advertising medium available, which is why it is the most expensive! Approximately 98 per cent of British households have a television set and audiences in the UK can exceed 20 million viewers for a single programme. With the developments in cable and satellite technology, world-wide audiences of hundreds of millions are easily achievable. Advertisers will pay anything up to £40,000 for a 30-second 'slot' at peak-viewing time across all ITV regions, and even more when the advertising is linked to a major feature, such as a British football team playing in the final of the European Cup competition, which will guarantee a larger than average audience. These costs only represent the 'air time' that the advertiser buys; costs of producing the advertisements themselves are extra and can sometimes be as expensive, second for second, as producing a Hollywood feature film. With costs of this magnitude, it is not surprising that many travel and tourism organisations are not able to budget for TV advertising. Only companies such as British Airways, Airtours, Thomson Holidays, Alton Towers, First Choice Holidays and Thomas Cook, have the financial resources available for national television advertising. Regional TV advertising is within the reach of some smaller travel and tourism operators, such as tourist attractions, resorts and destinations, hotel groups, leisure centres and regional airports.

When leisure and tourism organisations have the resources to be able to use TV advertising, the advantages include:

- Access to a large audience.
- High degree of creativity possible.
- Maximum impact with the use of colour and sound.
- The message is dynamic.
- The advertisement can be repeated.

In addition to cost, another disadvantage levelled at TV advertising is that it is difficult to broadcast to a particular market segment, i.e. the message will not be relevant for many of the viewers. Targeting specific segments is becoming more possible with the introduction of 'themed' satellite channels, such as MTV and SkySports, and with new developments in cable television.

Teletext

As well as being an up-to-date news and information service for viewers of ITV and Channel 4, teletext is also a fast-growing medium for advertisers. Indeed, its operators, Teletext Limited, claim that it has become the UK's leading classified holiday advertising medium, bigger than any of the leading national newspapers. Over 12.6 million homes in Britain have access to the service through their television sets, representing 57 per cent of all households. Teletext is particularly suitable for last-minute bookings and latest offers from the airlines and travel companies. There are sections dedicated to, for example, overseas tours, flights only, ski-ing, cruising, short breaks and motoring holidays. There is also a regionalised page for local airport departures and a complete section dedicated to different holidays in the UK. The use of teletext is set to grow steadily, with sales of new teletext TV sets currently at 1 million per year.

Activity

Make a list of the different travel products advertised on teletext. What are the advantages to tour operators and other travel companies of advertising on teletext?

Commercial radio

Commercial radio is an important outlet for local news and events. It is also a useful advertising medium for travel and tourism organisations that want to communicate with a local or regional audience. Travel agents will use local radio at certain times of the year to publicise their services, while private and local authority tourist attractions will advertise their facilities from time to time. Local radio is an obvious choice for such events as a local holiday show or a craft fair at a stately home. Its main advantages are:

- Production costs are low.
- It is relatively cheap when compared with other media.
- The message can be repeated many times.
- Audiences can be targeted geographically.
- It has the advantage over printed media in that voice and sound can be used.

The main disadvantage of advertising on commercial radio is that it is often seen as a 'background' medium, meaning that messages are not always conveyed to the audience effectively. Also, production quality is sometimes less than ideal.

Cinema advertising

The recent introduction of 'multi-screen' cinemas and multiplex facilities, linked with the general improvements in levels of quality and customer service, has meant that there has been something of a revival in cinema-going since the mid-1980s. This renewed interest has led advertisers to look again at the cinema as a means of conveying messages to the general public. Cinema advertising has all the advantages of commercial radio, namely the ability to promote local facilities and services, plus the impact and movement associated with the 'big screen', but it does have the disadvantage of high production costs. Cinema-goers are predominantly in the younger age groups, making it a particularly suitable medium for advertising products and services to a sector of the population which, in general terms, has a high disposable income and is motivated to buy travel and tourism products.

Outdoor advertising

Outdoor advertising includes a much wider variety of media than just posters and billboards; flashing signs, tube trains, delivery vans, representatives' cars, taxis, advertisements on buses, sports ground advertising, hot air balloons and fascia signs are all part of outdoor advertising in travel and tourism. Outdoor advertising is often part of a much wider advertising campaign involving many different media, acting as a reminder of a message that may already have been shown on television or included in a newspaper advertisement. Some local authorities advertise their tourist facilities at poster sites in their locality and may co-ordinate this activity with a mailing of leaflets to local residents or advertising on local buses. The London Underground is a particularly popular medium for travel and tourism organisations, which use clever and evocative images to appeal to a 'captive' audience of commuters. The Highlands and Islands Development Board (now Highlands and Islands Enterprise) has run a very successful campaign on the tube for a number of years, extolling the virtues of clean air and breathtaking scenery (two features that the Underground is not noted for!).

While production costs are high for outdoor advertising, overall costs per site are lower than comparable coverage using television advertising.

Computers and the Internet

Sometimes called the information superhighway, or simply 'the net', the Internet is a non-centralised network of computer databases, which offers users a wide range of global services, including financial data, newspapers, country information and travel services. There are currently in excess of 30 million subscribers to Internet services world wide. Organisations are beginning to recognise the selling power of the Internet, with airlines at the forefront of Internet advertising in the travel and tourism sector. Companies, including Virgin and Cathay Pacific, already offer Internet services, while British Midland has taken the service one step further, being the first airline in the world to provide a booking service with payment on the Internet. Known as CyberSeat, the British Midland service went on-line in December 1995.

There is little doubt that the growth in ownership of personal computers world wide, coupled with the proliferation of Internet access services such as the World Wide Web, will have implications for the way in which goods and services are bought and sold in the future. The rise in popularity of selling travel and tourism products and services on teletext (see page 332) is perhaps an indication that travel and tourism organisations need to take the threat, and opportunity, offered by the Internet very seriously, when contemplating their future advertising strategies.

Activity

Choose one national and one local travel and tourism company and list the different advertising media each chooses to promote its products and services.

Advertising campaigns

The term 'advertising campaign' is used to describe a planned and costed programme of design, placement and monitoring of advertising, to meet specific and clearly defined objectives. The scope of a campaign is sometimes very small, using only a single advertising medium for a short period of time, e.g. a travel agent placing two display advertisements in a local newspaper on consecutive Fridays to advertise an evening cruising promotion. Some campaigns can have budgets running into many millions of pounds, using a variety of media and running over periods of many months, e.g. a major mass market tour operator's main summer sun advertising campaign, with TV, national newspaper, poster, local radio and travel trade advertising.

Smaller travel and tourism companies that advertise on a limited scale may choose to run their own campaign and deal direct with their selected media. Medium-sized and large-scale organisations, however, will invariably use the services of an advertising agency to help develop and carry out their campaigns.

Planning an advertising campaign

Whatever the scope and scale of an organisation's advertising, and whether or not an agency is used, campaigns should all follow similar steps in their planning and execution, as shown in Figure 22.11.

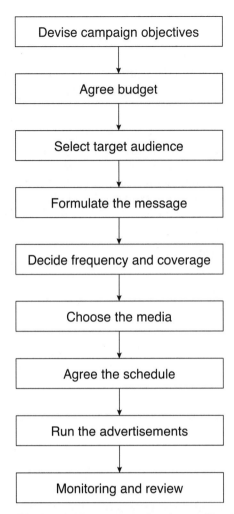

Fig. 22.11 *Key steps towards an effective advertising campaign*

Campaign objectives

Figure 22.11 shows us that any advertising campaign must start with a clear statement of its aims and objectives. This will give the advertising agency or travel and tourism organisation a benchmark against which to measure success or failure. Specific objectives of advertising campaigns in travel and tourism will vary between organisations, but may include:

- Creating awareness of an organisation.
- Increasing sales of a product or service.
- Informing customers about a new product or service.
- Promoting the benefits of one product over another.
- Offering a product or service to a new market sector.
- Filling unused accommodation.
- Publicising an event.

- Stimulating enquiries from the trade.
- Launching a new image (see case study on London's image on page 337).
- Maintaining customer and brand loyalty.
- Announcing a range of special offers and discounts.
- Increasing market share.

Budget

The budget available for an advertising campaign will sometimes determine the type of media that can be chosen. On a limited budget, the more expensive media, such as advertising on television and in national newspapers, is likely to be ruled out. Comparative costs of advertising in different media can be a helpful tool when budgeting, although figures such as the cost per thousand (CPT) should not be considered in isolation. CPT is calculated as follows:

Cost of TV advertisement $= £30,000$

Audience $= 15$ million

$$\text{Cost per thousand viewers} = \frac{£30,000}{15 \text{ million}} \times 1000 = £2$$

The CPT in this example is therefore £2.

It is important to remember that any budget set for an advertising campaign must include the costs associated with producing the advertisements as well as the costs of placing the advertisements themselves. The production of a colour advertisement in a magazine, for example, may include design, model making, copy writing, artwork and photographic costs. Once a budget is established, it will be the job of the account executive in the advertising agency to make sure that it is not exceeded.

Target audience

All advertisers must have a clear idea of their intended target audience, since this will influence the type of media chosen and the way in which the message is conveyed. Market research may be needed to find out the characteristics of the audience, e.g. age, interests, social status, occupation, leisure pursuits, etc.

The message

An advertising agency can help to determine the right message for a particular campaign, as well as to suggest the particular style and tone to be adopted. No two messages are the same and the skill of the creative teams in the agency is to work with the clients in developing a style with which they are happy, within the available budget. Storyboards and mock-ups will be used at this stage to give the client an impression of the finished product.

Frequency and coverage

The frequency with which an advertisement is shown and the minimum number of the target audience that will see it (the coverage) are very important considerations in any advertising campaign. Both will be determined to a large extent by the available budget. There is a minimum threshold of frequency below which an advertisement is unlikely to have a major impact on its audience. Advertisers talk of the OTS, which stands for opportunities to see. If a campaign target is 20 OTS, the advertisement will need to be repeated on more than 20 occasions.

Choice of media

Once the campaign's message is set and details of the target audience are known, the task of selecting the most appropriate media can begin. It is unlikely that a single medium will convey the message to all of the proposed target group, making a mixture of different media the most likely. The media planners in the advertising agency can advise on an appropriate combination to gain maximum exposure to the target audience.

Scheduling

Scheduling the timing of placing the advertisements will be influenced by budgets and frequency, with the media buyers being responsible for booking space in publications and airtime on television and radio.

Running the advertisements

If all has gone according to plan, the advertisements should appear in the correct media at the correct time, and the responses should come flooding in!

Monitoring and review

The agency will track progress just in case there has been a hiccup in the process and may be asked to record responses to the advertisements and any sales conversion rates. Further advertising campaigns may be altered on the basis of the review process.

Activity

Study a selection of travel and tourism advertisements from television, newspapers and magazines, and make a note of what you consider were the objectives of each campaign. Discuss, with other members of your group, whether you consider the objectives were met successfully.

Advertising campaigns in action – London's new identity

Introduction

A new identity for London, created to spearhead an £8 million tourism marketing campaign for the capital, was launched by the National Heritage Secretary, Virginia Bottomley, on 30 January 1996. The new single brand identity, together with the new marketing drive, aim to increase the revenue from overseas visitors to London. Co-ordinated by the London Tourist Board (LTB), the campaign concentrates on promoting the capital's strengths both as a destination to visitors and a global investment centre.

The new identity

The London Tourist Board commissioned research from the British Market Research Bureau across the three key inbound international markets to London, namely South East Asia, Europe and the USA. The research provided a range of perceptions of London, but the most significant point to emerge was the lack of awareness of the more modern aspects of the capital. In short, London was perceived to be something of a living museum. In developing the new identity, there was a need to retain the more traditional elements of London's heritage, while at the same time emphasising its vibrancy, diversity and friendliness. Consultation and research with the tourism industry were undertaken at all stages of the design process and the final design was approved by the Focus London team.

The new identity represented by the London marque is a registered trademark and will become the internationally recognised symbol for London (see Figure 22.12).

Fig. 22.12 London's new identity

The new logo will provide a unifying focus for the co-ordinated marketing of the capital. The new London marque, with its dancing figures and vibrant colours of blue, yellow and red, coupled with classical typography and allusions to heritage, was developed to represent the true character, spirit and experience of London. It was designed by the London-based design consultancy Beresfords, specialists in creating brand identities.

The need for a new identity

The number of visitors to London, while increasing on a year-by-year basis, has not increased in line with the growth of tourism in the rest of the world. London is losing market share and, over the last 10 years, spending by visitors to London has been growing at less than half the world average. The comparative average growth rates in visitor spending are:

- World average   +12%
- Britain   + 8.8%
- London   + 5.6%

A large number of organisations spend considerable time, money and resources on promoting London both as a leisure and business destination, but in the past there has been insufficient co-ordination. London has never had a single unifying marketing strategy and visual symbol all of its own; the new image hopes to redress the balance and act as a catalyst for growth in London's visitor numbers.

Defining the London product

A key feature of the £8 million marketing campaign was the need to identify particular aspects of the experience of a visit to London and to promote these benefits in future promotions concerning the capital. As a result of market research, the following five themes will feature in all future promotions of London:

1. *Heritage and pageantry* – although London is identified as a city rich in heritage and pageantry, customers felt that heritage needs to be presented in a more contemporary and personal way.
2. *Friendly and safe* – relative to other cities, Londoners are seen to be friendly and welcoming and the city is seen to be safe.
3. *Diversity* – some of the more contemporary aspects of the capital, such as fashion, restaurants and music, need to be further highlighted.
4. *Accessibility* – through its extensive transport links, London's accessibility needs to be promoted to prospective visitors.
5. *Arts, culture and entertainment* – London is a world centre for creativity in the visual and performing arts, fashion, literature and nightlife.

Campaign partners

The new identity was developed by the Focus London group under the leadership of the LTB. Focus London includes the Department of National Heritage, the British Tourist Authority (BTA), London First and representatives of the tourist industry, including hotels, restaurants, entertainment and tour operators. Over 70 London-based companies, including British Airways, the Port of London Authority and British Airports Authority, have pledged to use the new identity in future promotions and over 2000 requests have been received from travel agents and tour operators for guidance on using the new logo.

Funding of the campaign

The Department of National Heritage and the BTA have each contributed £2 million to the overall campaign costs of £8 million, the remainder being financed from the private sector.

(Information courtesy of the London Tourist Board)

Case study discussion questions

1. What are the aims of the new £8 million marketing campaign for London?
2. How is the campaign being funded?
3. Why was there a need to develop a new image for the capital?
4. How could any tangible benefits of the campaign be measured?
5. Which organisations are set to benefit from the new image and the associated marketing campaign?

Assignment 22.4

The role of advertising in travel and tourism

Performance criteria satisfied: 22.4.1, 22.4.2, 22.4.3

Core skills opportunities at level 3:   Communication   3.1, 3.2, 3.3, 3.4
Information technology   3.1, 3.2, 3.3
Application of number   3.1, 3.2, 3.3

Situation

While on work experience with Francesca Browning, the senior partner in a Belfast-based advertising agency, you are asked to help her prepare for a speech she is due to make to a group of Northern Ireland travel agents.

Tasks

You are asked to prepare the draft of the speech for Francesca on the subject 'The role of advertising in promoting travel and tourism products and services'. Your draft should:

● Describe the benefits of advertising to the promotion of travel and tourism products and services.
● Describe the benefits of specific advertising media.
● Examine the role of advertising campaigns for travel and tourism products and services.

Your draft speech should highlight examples of particular advertising campaigns relating to the travel and tourism industry.

Index